CONTENTS

——————————— *Continued overleaf* ———————————

Continued from previous page

LIB
LOAN
320.941 SDU
DE No: 548855
29/01/14

NOTES ON CONTRIBUTORS

Rosalind Gill is a Lecturer in Sociology at Goldsmiths College, University of London. She is author of *Gender and the Media: Representations, Audiences and Cultural Politics*, Polity Press 1997.

Phil Cohen is Director of the Centre for New Ethnicities Research at the University of East London, and author of *Rethinking the Youth Question* (forthcoming in 1997).

Cynthia Cockburn is a researcher and writer based at City University, London, where she is a research professor in the Centre for Research in Gender, Ethnicity and Social Change.

Susan Wicks is author of *The Clever Daughter* (1996) and *The Key* (1997).

Linda Chase is author of *These Goodbyes*.

Mario Petrucci is author of *Shrapnel and Sheets*.

Amanda Dalton is director of the Arvon Foundation's centre for creative writing, and author of *Room of Leaves*.

Frances Angela has worked in mental health and as a photographer.

Duncan Green is a researcher\writer at the Latin America Bureau and author of the LAB's *Silent Revolution: The Rise of Market Economics in Latin America*.

Jayne Ifekwunigwe teaches at the department of sociology at the University of East London, and is author of *Scattered Be-Longings: The Cultural Paradoxes of 'Race', Nation, Gender and Generation in the English-African Diaspora* (forthcoming in 1997).

Brian Goodwin is an Honorary Professor of Biology at the Open University. He is author of *How the Leopard Changed Its Spots* (1994) and co-author, with Gerry Webster, of *Form and Transformation* (1996).

James Curran is Professor of Communications in the Department of Media and Communications at Goldsmiths College, and the author or editor of eleven books about the mass media.

Sarah Benton is a previous News Editor and Political Editor of the *New Statesman*.

Esther Leslie has written on Walter Benjamin, and is now exploring connections between the modernist avant-garde and animation. She teaches in the Department of Cultural Studies at the University of East London.

Continued overleaf

Angela McRobbie is a Reader in Sociology at Loughborough University.

David Hesmondhalgh's PhD thesis, awarded in 1996, compares the production politics of post-punk and dance music. He now teaches in the Department of Media and Communications at Goldsmiths College.

Jonathan Burston is writing his thesis on 'The megamusical: new forms and relations in global cultural production' in the Department of Media and Communications at Goldsmiths College.

Kevin Robins works at the Centre for Urban and Regional Development Studies, University of Newcastle Upon Tyne. He is the author of *Into The Image: culture and politics in the field of vision*, Routledge, 1996.

Tony Dowmunt is a director of APT Film and Television and teaches documentary in the Department of Media and Communications at Goldsmiths College. Most recently he has edited *Channels of Resistance: global television and local empowerment*, BFI/Channel 4.

Tim O'Sullivan is Reader in Media Education and Cultural Studies in the Department of English, Media and Cultural Studies at De Montfort University, Leicester.

Correction: In the previous issue Maureen Mackintosh should have been listed as the author of the article 'Accountable Insiders? Reforming the Pension Funds'. Contributors to the article 'Complexity, Contradictions, Creativity: Transitions and the Voluntary Sector' included Sue Conning, who worked for the Family Welfare Association; Colleen Williams, who used to be a policy officer for the voluntary sector in a local authority; and Vera Gathy and Zsuzsa Szeman who work at the Institute for Social Conflict Research, Hungarian Academy of Science.

Soundings is a member of INK, a loose association of independent and alternative publications which co-operate on distribution and publicity matters. INK launched officially in November 1996 with a joint subscription offer, a website, and the publication of a pilot list of newsagents who stock at least two INK titles and carry the INK logo. If you know of any newsagents who regularly stock *Soundings* please drop us a line.

Questions which remain

It is too late now to regret what has not been done over the last four years or so. We are reconciled, reluctantly and yet again, to the fact that even if Labour wins the next election this country will not have the kinds of politics we would like to see. This is partly because what we'd like to see is a minority persuasion (though why that is so and whose interests are served by keeping things that way is a subject worthy of some thought). But it is also because it is now too late. We are up against an election - maybe one will be called before this issue of *Soundings* lands on your mat. And, above all, we do not want four more years of Conservative government.

A historic opportunity has been let slip. But we are now where we are, and must hope and work for a Labour victory.

And yet...

Yet the political process of the formation of Tony Blair's version of Labour will not end with the election. In the cold light of having to govern the country, old, unresolved questions will return to haunt us. And new issues will arise, and problems will be posed, which will set new challenges to Blair's definition, may even urge it in some ways to become more radical.

Above all, there will be the questions posed by neo-liberalism itself. The last twenty years of right-wing government have been long and forceful enough to reveal the sterility and the contradictions in their own approach. We know now, through painful experience rather than intellectual argument, that market relations alone are inadequate to run an economy, never mind a society. We know that forms of calculation other than monetary ones must be used in many areas of social interaction. We know that there *has* to be such a thing as society, even if it is not self-evidently there but has to be created. Moreover, the 'we' here is a broad one. These things are, at least latently, part of popular understanding. They are not confined to a coterie of political commentators.

Tony Blair is wont to say that this present Tory government has 'run out of steam'. This is the most inept of propositions. For one thing, if that were true we would be only too glad - the last thing we want is to goad it into reinvigoration, implementing yet more ideas from some right-wing think-tank. But the real point is quite different: this government has not run out of steam; more importantly, it has run into the buffers of its own contradictions.

A huge element of politics is about moulding the questions people ask, providing the commonsense for the stock replies. Margaret Thatcher did this. And her reformulations were immensely successful. For a while. Their inadequacies are now becoming increasingly clear. There are questions now, in the air and on the streets, which demand formulation and address. Questions posed precisely by some of the dislocations produced by the last twenty years. Questions posable now which would not have had any resonance even only five years ago. It is in this sense that this moment provides a historic opportunity.

No such thing as society?

What then is New Labour's political assessment of the present conjuncture? To judge by recent statements and policies, it believes that, since nothing whatever has changed since the early days of the Thatcher revolution, Labour's project must be strictly tailored to those severe and confining limits. Thus matters like the levels of taxation and public spending are regarded as permanently fixed, mired in the concrete of the crippling horizons of the 1980s. There is nothing Labour can do but to reproduce the neo-liberal vision, and adapt in every particular to the Thatcherite terrain. In effect, the Thatcherite definition of political and economic reality, which John Major inherited and tinkered around with but largely retained, is now the definition of political and economic reality *tout court*. Hence the cryptic but resonant obeisance which, from time to time, Tony Blair has made to his great predecessor. We will forebear to point out how long ago it is that sources politically not a million miles from this journal first pointed out that, unless the left could match, in vision, depth of rethinking and imaginative reach, the hegemonic scope of the Thatcher revolution, it would find itself driven to operate on the terrain which Thatcherism had redefined, as surely as the trapped animal - wriggle as it may - is held in the noose of an ever-tightening net. Such now are the conditions of existence of New Labour's illusory 'freedom of manoeuvre'.

But if everything is exactly as it was, why does Labour have a chance to win office which it manifestly lacked in the 1980s? Yes, the Tories have massively blundered, are corrupted by their long tenure of office, are deeply divided, constitute a spent and empty force. But if that is all, then Labour's chances depend on the very slender thread of 'we're tired of this lot: let's give the other lot a shot'. That is the sort of feeble support which vanishes with three or four weeks of hard campaigning. For all our sakes, the calculation had better be somewhat more robust. What Labour must be calculating - for it is what we all believe - is that there has been a significant shift in the popular political mood; and that this is a shift - not of very extensive proportions, perhaps, for ordinary voters, but politically significant nonetheless - against the worst excesses of the neo-liberal revolution: and specifically against its rampant individualism, its profound selfishness, against 'the only thing that matters is to look after Number One'; against the philosophy that 'there is no such thing as society, there is only the individual and his (sic) family'; in rejection of the belief that market forces are the only criterion of social value and should be 'free' of all limit and regulation, to drive blindly and ruthlessly through society, destroying the social fabric and the bonds of reciprocity between people - and the devil take the hindmost.

Curiously, there is also an echo of this in what Dick Morris (Bill Clinton's right-hand man) argued when he was analysing why Bob Dole's promise of across-the-board tax cuts fell flat on its face in the recent presidential election: 'Through the sexual revolution of the sixties, the "me" decade of the seventies, the yuppie adventures in hedonism, and into the selfish, money-hungry eighties, we tested life [sic - we think he means the 'free market society'] to its limits. But people's personal well-being was impaired more by the dysfunction of society as a whole than by a lack of money for themselves ... we realised that the 1990s were a "we" decade ... the poll showed us how wrong a tax cut that appealed to self-interest would be'.[1] And this is America we're talking about.

This assessment might be wrong, but if so, New Labour owes it to us to tell us

---

1. Cited in the *Guardian*, 14.1.97.

where it thinks the voters who are supposed to be floating towards Labour, and whom its strategy is principally designed to mobilise, have come from. But if it is right, then a certain logic follows, even within the narrow electoral terms which New Labour has set itself. It must follow that, in order to win their support, New Labour must address their concerns; and those concerns have to do, precisely, with the social fabric, with strengthening the bonds of social reciprocity, and with strategies designed to address 'the whole' society - rather than just what each individual 'and his family' can take home in a personal pay-packet.

Somewhere, deep in his bones, Tony Blair knows this too. When he invoked the people who 'want to do well ... to get on ... to succeed', he added, 'but you can only do so within a society which is compassionate, with a sense of decency and obligation to others'. Quite so. The question is how to imagine this; how such a societal form is to be created; what structures of supports will be needed. What is required is a different philosophy.

The concept of stakeholding seemed for a moment to hold out the potential for a move in the right direction, at least on some primarily economic fronts. It was potentially developable into a coherent and progressive framework (see *Soundings* 2, editorial). Yet after a brief flurry of attention the concept seems to have been lost. The suspicion must be that it was indeed potentially too radical. Could it be taken up again?

In our last issue, Maureen Mackintosh edited the theme on 'the Public Good'. In her editorial she analysed the nature of social settlements, and in the articles which followed ideas were presented for new kinds of social settlement. The authors not only addressed the individual/social issue, but also pointed to the necessity of coming to grips with the fact that both society itself, and the way in which we think about it, have changed and continue to change. Here were addressed both the need for social cohesion and the imperative to confront social division: the necessity for the solidarities of universal provision *as well* as the imagination fully to address the fact of difference.[2] Ways forward do exist. (It might also be noted, *en passant*, that this kind of original thinking completely ignores the immobilising confrontations between 'traditionalist' and 'moderniser' which frame so much of

---

2. Maureen Mackintosh, Introduction to Public Good theme, *Soundings* 4, Autumn 1996, pp104-8. Gail Lewis in 'Welfare settlements and racialising practices' in the same issue (pp109-119) explores these possibiities in the context of one of the deepest divisions, that of racism.

what currently passes for debate.)

Instead of such original thinking, however, we have been treated to communitarianism, opportunistic moralising and the occasional resort to tabloid Christianity. The inadequacy of these forays is painful to behold. Jack Straw worries about getting children off the streets by late evening, while leaving completely unaddressed the wider moral bankruptcy of the world in which we now live. By such means questions of ethics are reduced to individual behaviour, and the individuals singled out for opprobrium are the usual collection of targets: single mothers, working-class lads, beggars, unruly schoolchildren, the 'underclass', and various 'rabble elements'. Nothing is said of the wider context. As Kate Soper recently pointed out, 'Our schools have remained havens of morality by comparison with the finance markets and the boardrooms of the arms exporters'.[3]

A rhetorical flourish on Labour's part, and a dollop of Christian moralising, will not strike a different balance from the one pioneered by Thatcherism - between individual success and social co-operation, between market forces and social regulation. Yet, precisely on this delicate cutting-edge, New Labour has consistently and regularly failed. It has consistently defined 'modernisation' as requiring us to make a choice *between* these alternatives - and has itself chosen the Thatcherite path (There is no alternative), instead of finding new forms with which to capture the popular imagination, for a new balance between them, a new deal, a new kind of social settlement. Following the most tumultuous seventeen years of political upheaval and change, this is a dramatic - and devastating - historic failure of political imagination.

Not feeling so good

One of the recent 'mysteries' of politics has been: if the economy is in such good shape (and at the turn of the year six ministers were paraded to give us this good news) then why is there no, or so little, 'feelgood' factor? It is a question which in itself bears witness to the emptiness of current political calculation. The aphorism 'it's the economy, stupid' may have a lot going for it, but economics and especially economic indicators are not all there is to life, or even to politics. Just take the same question, but pose it, not as from the Chancellor of the Exchequer puzzled at our lack of *joie de vivre* and gratitude, but as from the daily lives within which

3.   Kate Soper, 'The moral high ground', *Red Pepper*, no 31, December 1996, p5.

we experience that economy: if the economy is in such good shape, why am I having to wait so long for my hospital appointment? why are there no books in my children's school? why are we treating old people so badly? On this last, there have been cuts in meals on wheels, cuts in home helps (and in what they are allowed to do - as a friend commented, the 'social' has been taken out of social services), there are now payments for services once provided free, there are shortages of hospital beds, and a lack of money for nursing-home care. The generation now in its eighties (that generation which so often lost parents in the first world war, which survived the grim years of the depression, fought the second world war and established the welfare state) ... that generation is now, when it really needs it, unable to rely on the secure provision for which it fought and which it built. In a society where this is so, how *could* there be a feelgood factor? If there were it would be obscene.

The first and most obvious answer is that the 'feelgood' factor (more generally, the quality of life) cannot be measured by macro-economic statistics alone. To start with, there are different *modes* of growth, each with their own effects. We have for twenty years been treated to the neo-liberal mode, of which the best-known effect is the production of inequality.

New Labour, as far as one can tell, has accepted the broad framework of neo-liberalism. Essentially Hugo Young is right in his assessment that, in the recent definitive statements by Labour on taxation and the acceptance for two years of Tory spending targets, a historic moment has been defined. These statements consolidate much of what has been emerging over the past 18 months, but they give the character and prospects of Labour in office a definitive and - until we hit the shoals and rainstorms of 'government' - irreversible stamp. The implications of all this are worth teasing out. First, 'it defined what the left alternative to right-wing politics...is'. This is the whimper with which the historic response from the left to 17 years of the Thatcherite neo-liberal revolution terminates. This is the farthest point to which the assembled intellectual and political resources of New Labour can take us. An alternative to the right does exist, Hugo Young assures us; but 'its aspirations are narrower than any the Labour Party has ever had before'. Second, it abandons any serious concern with equality. This too has been in the pipeline for some time. But it is worth remarking on just because Tony Blair is fond of saying that, despite all the changes, New Labour is still committed to the principles of the Party's tradition. However, we do not make the argument here from the perspective of 'tradition'. The point is that this abandonment of any commitment to equality follows a period in which the grossest inequalities between the well-off and the rest have reappeared and in which there has been a grotesque feathering-of-nests by those in a position to determine their own salaries, perks and share options. That, indeed, was Labour's own analysis. And the decision to remain within Tory spending targets, and to refrain from increased income tax for the rich, is its considered response. New Labour's view is either that the inequalities engendered by neo-liberalism are no longer socially significant, or that they do not impair the vision of 'the good society', or that governments cannot do anything about them. Much of what is currently going on looks like the third option - educating the electorate towards diminishing expectations. This, in turn, provides a useful gloss on what is now meant by 'social justice' (the code phrase which has replaced 'equality' in New Speak) - and puts flesh on the observation by Blair that the purpose of Labour in government is to help those who 'have ambition and aspiration, want to do well ... want to get on ... want to succeed'. Even in the context of 'compassion', this still really means success to the successful, to those who fail, failure. Here, a word from Outer Space seems in order: as John Redwood commented, if Tory tax levels and spending targets are right (and, we may add, the share-out of goodies is 'fair' and 'just') what possible argument is there for a change of government?

It may, of course, be possible that everything that New Labour wants to do in health, education ('Education, education, education'), transport, etc, (and has spent its entire time in opposition criticising the Tories for *not* doing) can be funded out of the windfall tax plus savings here and there, without any substantial rise in either public spending or in taxation. On the other hand, pigs might fly. We do not know any seriously-informed person who believes it and we don't believe the 'ordinary folk out there' are deceived by it either. A more plausible response is that New Labour is treating the electorate as if they could be 'spin doctored' like everybody else - not an approach congenial to winning an electorate's hearts and minds, especially once the election is over and the problems identified remain unresolved. Just to stay, for a moment, with education and 'the vision thing': 'we've got to see... that other countries are educating more of their children to a higher standard ... We are bad at educating the whole of the population' (Blair, *Sunday Independent*, 19 January 1997). Do Tony Blair or David Blunkett really believe that this is being achieved among our 'Tiger' competitors in South-East Asia by holding spending on education 'steady'? Or that Chris Woodhead, who has made himself the chief apologist for and instrument of Tory education 'reform', and whose continuity in office Labour has just confirmed, really is the best and the only person to see a radical shift from the present drift to selection through to a successful completion?

Of course, moving people from the dole queue to jobs will gradually reduce the swollen social security budget but, apart from 'training', New Labour has no substantive economic strategy to create jobs and seems no longer to believe that it is government's task to have one. Welfare-to-workfare *is* something New Labour fervently espouses - what in the American context Dick Morris describes as 'triangulation' - 'a combination of the intentions of the Great Society and the Tough Love concept of discipline and responsibility'. One doubts whether, even after 'zero tolerance' and the New-Speak version of The Leader as Good Samaritan ('No, I don't give money to beggars, actually'), the electorate actually is aware of where all New Labour's brightest and best ideas are coming from. But little by little it is becoming possible to understand what New Labour's 'triangulation' project is really about.

Moreover, the presence or absence of the feelgood factor involves far more issues than these. New Labour is clearly aware, for instance, of the employment conditions on which the present form of growth has been so widely built. It speaks frequently of the casualisation masquerading as flexibility; it supports the limit of 48 hours on the working week: it will sign up to the Social Chapter. All this is eminently positive. But there are bigger issues here, about the nature of the work-culture in which we are embroiled. The hours worked in this country, by full-time workers, are longer than elsewhere in Europe. Much of the growth of the 1980s depended, especially in professional sectors, on a macho workaholism which reinforced the already highly gendered way we organise paid employment. Surviving in some sectors of the labour market meant having either an unpaid (usually female) partner or a low-paid (usually female) domestic help. In turn this reinforced, even could be used to legitimate, men's historic under-performance in the home. And it promoted the growth of a divided culture - of the resources-rich but time-scarce folk versus those with no money but time on their hands. The question of economic policy is, or should be, not just about how much growth, but about what form of growth and on what terms.

All this is just to touch the surface of why we're not feeling so good. The point is that a party which had its finger on the pulse, a party which dared to ask big questions, could not only address these issues but (thinking more instrumentally) use them to re-align political debate on to terms more in tune with its own priorities.

Changing the terms

Tony Blair has spoken a number of times of his admiration for Margaret Thatcher. A part of the left declared itself horrified by such a 'confession'. But this reaction was surely both dishonest and disingenuous. How often during the 1980s did we not say that we wished that we too had someone with her degree of commitment, her strategic sense of purpose, perhaps above all, her sense of whose side she was on? So to feign horror at Blair's general proposition now rings hollow. Rather, the proposition should be more sharply interrogated: *what*, precisely, has Tony Blair learned from her? And what has he *not* learned?

One thing, for sure, is that he has not learned how useful adversaries can be. We have commented already in *Soundings* on how New Labour's politics has tried to become so all-inclusive (at least towards the middle-ground and the right) that no-one will suffer as a result of them (except, of course, by exclusion from attention altogether) (and the parentheses here are of devastating importance).

But a further thing which Tony Blair has failed to learn from Margaret Thatcher goes right to the heart of the approach to politics of New Labour. It is that political subjects, political constituencies, have to be created. Quite contrary to the passive approach of the minute statistical interrogation of opinion polls (where, in James Naughtie's recent words 'voters are statistics embroidered with human attributes, and not much else'), the creative aspect of being a politician is to tap into those incipient discontents and desires, perhaps as yet barely expressed, possibly even not yet consciously recognised, but which always exist to be drawn upon within a changing society. Political creativity consists of giving voice to these things, of bringing them into the open and moulding them into a politics. Now is the time to tap into the discontents wrought by neo-liberalism.

Tony Blair and New Labour are, famously, very nervous about 'Middle England'. It is this section of the population which they feel they must attract, in terms of votes, if they are to succeed at the election. They are correct. In a society in which Galbraith's 'culture of contentment' covers such a large part of the population it would be dishonest to argue that one could succeed on the basis of the poor and the excluded alone.

But Mrs Thatcher, too, needed to win over Middle England. One of the vital keys to her victory was the group of skilled working-class people in the West Midlands - Middle England geographically, upwardly mobile economically, trade-unionists then ripe for conversion to unbridled individualism, a group well-used to voicing their demands and at that time experiencing discontent with the welfare-state-as-was, and with perceived local authority ineptitude. They were not an identifiable force, but she made them into one. They were not born Thatcherite subjects. They could easily have stayed with Labour. But she touched chords which converted them to her own convictions. Mrs Thatcher did not just appeal to this section of Middle England - she created it. She moulded it, along with other sections of the population, in a particular political direction.

Tony Blair must create (or should have created) his own Middle England too. Admittedly, his task is a more difficult one than hers. His Middle-England-potential, of the home counties and of suburbia, is perhaps more settled in its ways, more wary of change: more conservative with a little 'c'. And yet it is evident that there are desires and discontents here too, understandings that all is not well in Conservative Britain. Some aspects of this have already been referred to: the lack of a feel good factor when economic indicators are apparently so rosy; the fact that we have lost a sense of what might be 'the social'. Other desires and discontents Labour is making some, though as we have argued rather feeble, attempts to address: the desire for security in old age, a gnawing fear about the decline of the NHS. (Yet surely some more passionate, imaginative, campaigning - drawing out those feelings and relating them to the nitty-gritty of actual policy proposals - would have enabled the policy proposals themselves to be more radical?...)

But there are other issues too where - had we started four years ago - at least some elements of Middle England could have been mobilised as a potentially radical force. Environmentalism is one such. New Labour is certainly making efforts in this direction, but it is piecemeal and passionless. Could not a clearer commitment, the communication of a sense of purpose, around this issue not only have touched chords in Middle England but also have connected up elements of that group with the concerns of a multitude of other sections of the community? It is this *creation* of political constituencies, pulling people in by appealing to aspects of their identities which draw them together on particular issues - though they may be way apart on others - which surely should be the stuff of politics. Indeed, it will happen willy-nilly, as a result of 'the media' or the pontificating of political pundits, so Labour needs to seize the process into its own hands. The point is that on this and perhaps a range of other issues a different, more radical, Middle England could potentially have been created. Not the recording of opinion surveys and focus groups but the touching of nerves and the turning of those sensitivities into political positions...and political support for a more progressive government than the one we seem likely to get.

Internationalism is another such area of potential. There are few things more horrifying about the current pre-electoral debate than its pathetic insularity. This goes beyond the explicit chauvinisms lurking in any discussion of Europe, or even of BSE (see *Soundings* 3, editorial). It is more the fact that debate over the EU is virtually the only context in which international issues are addressed at all. What is never even formulated as a question is what might be a progressive approach towards the UK's position in the wider world.

There are many elements to this, potential policy-areas to weave together into a coherent position. Perhaps most prominent among them is globalisation. We have already carried debate on the degree and nature of this phenomenon and we shall be taking the argument further in future issues.[4] The character and form of globalisation are - must be - the subject of real argument.

Tony Blair, however, accepts a simple version of globalisation fully as a fact of life. He does so, presumably, in part because it enables him to hold up helpless hands in the face of demands he doesn't want to deliver on. ('Couldn't possibly do that ... we're living in a world of globalisation you know.') He may also believe it: that the whole global economy is now in thrall to a few transnational corporations and the apparently uncontrollable (does nobody control them?) flows of virtual money between the financial centres of the world. But to accept this version of globalisation at face value is to refuse to face a whole range of issues.

Perhaps most importantly, it denies the fact that governments too play their part in determining in what measure, and how, the world economy will become globalised. Mrs Thatcher abolished exchange controls; western governments

4. Paul Hirst and Grahame Thompson, 'Globalisation: ten frequently asked questions and some surprising answers', *Soundings* 4, pp47-66.

enthusiastically (with a few quibbles over sub-clauses) signed up to the Uruguay round of GATT. There was virtually no political debate in this country about either. And Tony Blair, from what one can tell from his pronouncements on the subject, is also totally in favour of 'free trade'. So the globalisation which so unfortunately ties his hands on a number of potential policy issues is, it seems, something of which he is fervently in favour.

Furthermore,globalisation is not only an emerging material fact (whatever its precise shape and nature); it is also a discourse. It is a pivotal element in a powerful political discourse, one which is normative, and which has its institutions and its professionals (the IMF, the World Bank, the WTO, Western governments); this discourse is produced in the North, and it has effects. In the North (the First World), it is, as we have seen, the basis for decisions precisely to implement it, and, having done these things, it is an excuse for inaction. In the South it has enabled the widespread imposition of structural adjustment (with all its disastrous effects on the already-poor, and on women in particular), and the enforcement of export orientation over production for local consumption.[5] Globalisation, in this guise, is not so much a description of how the world is, as an image in which the world is being made.

Surely any party which considers itself even mildly progressive should be posing the question 'what kind of globalisation might we be working towards to produce a more egalitarian world economic order'? At the moment such a question has no likelihood of being raised by Labour; and yet, during the neo-liberal 1980s international as well as intranational income inequality increased. And globalisation is just one aspect of international questions. What of the arms trade, and our policy on aid? This too is a range of issues on which a more radical politics might connect with the growing feelings of unease which exist in Middle England.

We have touched on just four themes: the question of what is society?; the quality of life; environmentalism; internationalism. These are just examples of the kind of big questions which could be broached now; some of them will have to be addressed at some point, but so far New Labour has failed to do so.

It may be too late for New Labour to raise such questions now, before the

---

5. See the article by Duncan Green in this issue.

election. They conjure up debates which will take time to mature; they will not lead immediately to rapid rises in electoral popularity. But they are on the agenda, and they each touch deep understandings,if not always acknowledged, of what is wrong with society today. And each could be a focus for the reformulation of political debate on to more progressive ground. It is a shame 'twere not done earlier. But politics will continue after the election. It is time we began staking out the ground.

DM & SH

SPECIAL ISSUE
After the election:
Setting the Agenda in
post-Conservative Britain
September 1997, 128pp
FREE to Subscribers

Colluding in the backlash? Feminism and the construction of 'orthodoxy'

Rosalind Gill

Rosalind Gill argues that to talk of feminism as an orthodoxy is to play into the hands of those who call us 'femi-nazis' or 'political correctness thought police'.

The 'feminist fatwa'

Earlier this year, Ros Coward wrote an article for *The Guardian* which enraged other feminists.[1] She argued that feminism was responsible for putting a 'gag' on debates about fatherhood, with the suggestion that even raising it as an issue would be treated as 'an act of treason'. Coward went on to assert that 'there's scarcely a leading feminist who has not added her own thoughts about the redundancy of fathers', and added that mere mention of fatherhood at a feminist gathering would be sufficient to have one branded as 'suffering from nostalgia for the patriarchal authoritarian family'. My aim here is not to get involved in an argument about

---

1. Ros Coward, 'Make the father figure', *The Guardian*, 12 April 1996.

fatherhood; instead, I wish to draw attention to the *rhetoric* of Ros Coward's argument, and to explore some of the political implications of her characterisation of feminism as a rigid orthodoxy which permits no dissent.

Beatrix Campbell picked up on this in her reply to Ros Coward.[2] She described as bizarre the spectre conjured by Coward of a 'feminist fatwa', and argued: 'There is no party line, therefore no taboo and no treason'. I agree completely with Campbell. However, what struck me was not how *strange* Coward's construction of feminism was, but how *familiar* it has become. Increasingly, feminists seem to be taking part in a sport which was once the sole province of right wing misogynists: the construction of feminism as a set of narrowly defined and rigorously policed beliefs - a dogma or an orthodoxy. This is not just happening in one domain - I come across it in newspaper articles, in feminist journals and in academic writing; more and more, feminists seem to be queueing up to attack the prevailing 'feminist orthodoxy'. Sometimes the 'orthodoxy' they want to challenge concerns the apparent neglect of an important feminist issue - for example, motherhood or beauty oppression.[3] On other occasions the challenge is to supposedly 'orthodox' ways of thinking about gender issues - classic examples here being sexual violence and pornography. Interestingly, there seems to be no consensus among these feminists about the *nature* or *content* of 'feminist orthodoxy'; for example, protagonists in different camps of the pornography debate routinely claim to challenge it, while, in discussions about the status of mothering in feminist theory, some claim that feminism has been preoccupied with it, while others claim that it has been virtually ignored. What unites these writers, then, is not any agreement about the nature of 'feminist orthodoxy', but a clear sense that *there is an orthodoxy*.

Am I alone in feeling disturbed by this? Let me state my position straight away: as far as I am concerned, feminism is not, and has never been, an orthodoxy. Indeed, feminists have disagreed about almost everything of importance to us - including the reasons for, the nature of, and the ways to challenge women's oppression. Feminism has always been fluid and dynamic, never static and unitary. But to suggest that *now*, in the 1990s, feminism is an orthodoxy seems the height of folly. Never has it been more open, and more contested than today, as differences between women - relating to 'race' and ethnicity, class, sexuality

---

2. Beatrix Campbell, 'Good riddance to the patriarch', *The Guardian*, 15 April 1996.
3. For example, Maureen Freely's *What About Us? An Open Letter to the Mothers Feminism Forgot*, Bloomsbury 1995; & Naomi Wolf's *The Beauty Myth*, Chatto & Windus, 1992.

and ability are at last taken seriously and debated, and as ideas from poststructuralism and postmodernism challenge the very idea of a unified gendered subject around which feminists can mobilise. It seems to me that now, perhaps more than ever before, feminism is a space of permanent contestation, of strategic alliances, and of a politics of articulation. In fact, it is highly questionable whether it is even possible to speak of feminism any more as if it had a clearly identifiable referent; better to talk of diverse and heterogeneous feminisms.

> 'We condemn each other - and all in the name of "rescuing" feminism from hostilities'

To suggest that feminism is an orthodoxy, then, is, in my opinion, to misrepresent us.[4] More worrryingly, it is to play into the hands of our critics. Not only does it give them ammunition to use against us, but it actually uses *their discourse*. It suggests implicitly that critics of feminism are right about it, that it *is* a rigid dogma, a 'line' to which strict adherence is required. It conjures up distinctions between authentic and inauthentic feminists, between the fully paid-up, card-carrying members of the orthodoxy, and the renegades. It thus cedes almost all our ground to those who would call us 'political correctness thought police' or 'femi-nazis'. What the suggestion of a 'feminist orthodoxy' does is to re-present decades of diverse thought, argument and practice as a single, unitary, systematically policed position. Above all, to speak of 'feminist orthodoxy' is to deny what feminism needs most - *a positive discourse of difference*: a discourse, or discourses, that would allow us to think about differences between us not in terms of problems to overcome or transcend, but as inevitable and welcome features of any movement aimed at radical social transformation.

Suppressing debate

So what is going on when feminists claim to challenge feminist orthodoxy? As a rhetorical strategy, the claim to attack orthodoxy is deeply embedded in Western individualism. It affords the writer an almost 'heroic', romantic status; she is cast as brave critic, as one who courageously speaks out against received wisdoms, often

---

4   It is clearly problematic to speak of 'us' as if 'we' constitute a self-evident and uncontested group. I use it here inclusively, to signal not the homogeneity of those who identify as feminists, but their diversity.

at some personal cost, not least that of being cast out of the movement. The subject position it offers the person making the assertion, then, is a positive one - the truth-speaking individual, not cowed by the orthodoxy. What it offers feminisms, however, is less positive. It flattens out all the differences between us, represses the dynamism, excitement and genuine debate within our movement, and presents us as our attackers see us.

Sometimes the claim is made in a serious context and with the aim of advancing feminist debate.[5] Lynne Segal's most recent book, *Straight Sex*, for example, seeks to challenge what she describes as the current orthodoxy that heterosexuality is the basis of men's domination of women.[6] The book makes several important criticisms of particular writers' positions. But the attribution of a feminist orthodoxy troubles me. It transforms the writings of a handful of women, who were struggling to make sense of women's oppression, in particular historical and cultural locations, into a rigid dogma. It is important to be clear that I am not suggesting that we should not argue with each other; on the contrary, I am suggesting that we *should* - and *we do*. But the notion of feminist orthodoxy denies this. It re-presents differences between feminists as a binary divide - between the orthodox and the rest. Not only does it buy into the discourse of feminism's attackers, but the corollary of the argument seems to be that there is also a small group of women who 'control' the content of feminist knowledge, and who suppress dissident voices.

Interestingly, this leaves open the possibility of the construction of an identity as 'victim of feminist orthodoxy'. Feminist newspaper columnists seem, with increasing regularity, to take on this role, recasting for their readers the questioning they have received from feminist friends, over issues such as shaving one's legs or buying designer clothes, into a kind of full-scale victimisation by the orthodox feminist police. Such writers are then able to present themselves to the world as brave and defiant challengers of feminism's narrow and restrictive beliefs. Ros Coward uses this kind of rhetoric in her article about fatherhood, suggesting that not only have fathers lost out as a result of feminism's stifling of debate, but that

---

5. The examples I have chosen were selected merely because they were to hand, but they seem to me to be part of a much broader trend. My wish is not to single people out for criticism; nor to debate the substance of their arguments. I am interested simply in the political effects of claiming that feminism is an orthodoxy.
6. Lynne Segal, *Straight Sex: The Politics Of Pleasure*, Virago 1994.
7. Maureen Freely, 'Keeping Mum', *Everywoman*, November 1995.

ultimately we are all victims of it.

A similar example can be found in Maureen Freely's writing about motherhood. Her entire argument - that motherhood should be taken seriously - seems to be premised on a caricature of feminism as a small cabal of cold, childless women, whose energies are primarily invested in being hostile to mothers. Take this introduction to a recent article:

> Talk about taboo. Talk about unpopular subjects. There is no faster way to get up mainstream feminists' noses. And if you don't believe me, try yourself. Try standing up in front of a group of child-free feminists - they can even be any age, they can even be friends - and say, actually, there is something to be said in favour of mothers... Here's a few of the slurs you can expect if you persist: fifties throwback, maternal revivalist, elitist, ethnocentrist. And worst of all, essentialist.[7]

Freely suggests that women who are mothers have been so victimised by feminism, that even speaking of motherhood requires gross 'daring', and one risks becoming a 'martyr'. I find this portrait unrecognisable (and I am a mother). Perhaps it is the adversarial nature of contemporary academic and journalistic life - the pressure to make one's own name by attacking other people's ideas - which leads Freely to argue that 'orthodox feminists' claim 'anyone who becomes a mother is colluding with patriarchy'. What it achieves for her is the status of a heroine who will not be silenced, will not be constrained by (what she identifies as) the 'feminist canon', and who is prepared to sacrifice herself for the future of all other mothers. But she is attacking a straw target. Her attacks on feminism do great injustice to the many feminists who have written and argued about motherhood, campaigned for better maternity leave and for workplace nurseries, and struggled for decades to secure real choices, to combat isolation and to improve the quality of life for mothers and women without children alike. Perhaps more worryingly, her portrait of feminism gives more ammunition to those who wish to eradicate our ideas altogether.

Colluding in the backlash

Closely allied to the tendency of feminists to identify a feminist orthodoxy is another disturbing trend. This is the tendency *not to challenge* reactionary and oppressive accounts of our history or our movement. Over the last five years or so I have noticed a growing reluctance on the part of a wide variety of feminists to challenge lies and misrepresentations about feminism. Negative statements about feminism of the 'feminists are...x' or 'feminism is...y' variety, which would previously have attracted criticism or complaint, are increasingly allowed to stand in public discourse. Even more worryingly, some feminists are actually beginning themselves to endorse these reactionary portraits of feminism. Where once we would have cried out to challenge the stock caricatures - ugly, man-hating, bra-burning, etc - increasingly, some feminists are reproducing them, if only to relativise them historically - 'feminists *were* like that, but *we* are different' - or socially - '*some* feminists are like that, but *we* are different.'

This trend is not limited to feminism, but has become a feature of much political discourse of the left. Whilst writing this article I came across a typical example of it, relating more broadly to affirmative action policies. In this example, an ostensibly positive stance on anti-discriminatory practices is prefaced by a statement which would make the most right-wing populist ideologue proud:

> The overstaffed race units with inflated budgets have long since closed down. 'Red Ken' and 'Barmy Bernie' vanished aeons ago. Baa baa black sheep, black bin liners and 'black coffee, please' are no longer outlawed. And the thought-police who once dominated the corridors of power in Britain's town halls are living in comfortable retirement.' [8]

Where once we would have expected a 'quality' broadsheet journalist to challenge these racist and politically-motivated lies about metropolitan councils, now we have them uncritically reproduced - even as the article goes on to offer a more considered assessment of anti-discriminatory policies. This is not an isolated example. And it does not come from the *Daily Express* but *The Guardian*. Increasingly - or so it seems to me - we are failing to challenge pernicious statements about progressive movements generally - particularly feminism - and we are even recycling them ourselves.

I say 'we' deliberately, because I do not think it is helpful to assume that those of us who are implicated here are 'not real feminists'. Better that we try to understand the social and cultural conditions that make 'feminist bashing' so

---

8. Sally Weale, *The Guardian*, 20 June 1995.

difficult to resist - in order that we can find new ways of challenging it. The primary reason must be the hostile climate in which Western feminists currently find themselves. The backlash against feminism and other progressive movements has been devastating. Despite - or, perhaps, because of - the huge gains made by feminism, it is becoming more rather than less difficult to identify as a feminist - outside certain relatively safe environments.

A gainst this background it is not difficult to appreciate why we reproduce, or fail to challenge, oppressive accounts of feminism. Mostly it is well-intentioned; sometimes an act of damage limitation; at other times an attempt to distance 'our' feminism from negative perceptions of feminism more broadly: a dynamic is set up within the argument which distances 'them' (extreme, mistaken, excessive, etc) from 'us' (moderate, responsible, realistic, etc); on other occasions still, sheer weariness comes into play. Generally, it is done for strategic or tactical purposes - it salvages some semblance of a positive identity for the speaker, whilst also seeming to 'rescue' contemporary feminism (or some strand of it) from complete dismissal. 'If we don't contradict their caricature of us in the 1970s', we may think, 'then maybe we can win them round to seeing just how different and important our struggle is today'. Or 'If we just go along with their view of lesbian feminists, then we can persuade them that our feminism is much less threatening'. So runs the perverse logic - perhaps. Divisiveness has set in. We condemn each other - and all in the name of 'rescuing' feminism from hostilities. It is easy to understand. It is also entirely mistaken. There is a high price to be exacted from reproducing ideological accounts of our movement.

I can see part of the price being paid when I talk to my eighteen and nineteen year old students. For them, what I regard as lies, misrepresenations and hostile caricatures, represent the consensus, or indeed, the *truth*, about what feminism is - or has been. I have still not got used to the certainty with which they will routinely pronounce that feminists in the 1960s, 1970s (and now even the 1980s) were all man-hating extremists who went 'too far'. Small wonder, then, that so few of them regard themselves as feminists - and even less surprising when they may have heard the same statements endorsed by feminists.

The highest price, however, is paid by us directly. It is as if we have internalised the backlash. We have allowed hostile commentators to set the agenda, and to define the 'legitimate' face of feminism. This can only lead to the fragmentation of our movement. Going along with ideological accounts of feminism may seem to make sense in the short term and in terms of *realpolitik*, but in the longer term it will lead to our destruction.

Towards positive discourses about differences

The trend to treat feminism as an orthodoxy, and the trend to collude with - or even actively to reproduce - ideological accounts of feminism are intimately related. What is happening in both cases is that feminists are drawing on and reproducing the discourse of those who are hostile to feminism. In both cases, feminism is reified. Feminism - or particular strands of it - is treated as something which has ossified, is rigid, closed and irrelevant. Moreover, in both cases, violence is done to the diversity of opinion within feminism. In the first case, differences are handled by the construction of a binary divide - between 'orthodox feminists' (an entirely flexible discursive category), and the rest of us. In the second case, differences between us are handled by discursively distancing ourselves from other feminists - largely, it seems, for misguided reasons of political expediency. In both cases, differences are treated as problems. This is a measure of both the force and pervasiveness of the backlash against feminism, and - more disturbingly - a contribution to it. What we desperately need are positive discourses for talking about differences between feminists, as well as between women more generally. As long as we characterise feminism as an orthodoxy, and recycle hostile myths about our sisters, then this will elude us.

I am very grateful to Manjit Bola, Karen Henwood, Ann Phoenix, Caroline Ramazonoglu and Bruna Seu for their helpful comments on, and discussions of, the ideas raised in this article.

Beyond the Community Romance

Phil Cohen

History will call it the Decent Society, a new social order for the Age of Achievement for Britain. We will respect family life, develop it and encourage it in any way we can because strong families are the foundation of strong communities.

Tony Blair, Speech to Labour Party Conference 1996

There is much in this culture that dramatises wrongdoings and failures of character; personal doings become public and fights often arise when such business is discussed. Life is filled with expressions of pleasure and happiness, yet there are also constantly observable tensions and hostility. People here as everywhere do not live up to the ideals of community. But they accept that this is life's way. They see that rivalries and dissensions - between the young and the old, men and women, the friendly and the selfish (bashful) - are deeply embedded in life. These oppositions are not viewed as destructive of community, even when ideals are departed from dramatically; such contrarieties, like everything else in life, must be both ameliorated and celebrated.

Roger Abrahams, 'The Man-of-Words in the West Indies'

Are we that name ?

Community, like citizenship, has become a buzzword in the race to give old words apparently new meanings, and to revive the exhausted political vocabulary of democracy in the West. In Britain 'community' is evoked by One Nation Tories, New Labourists and Liberal Democrats with about equal enthusiasm, each claiming the notion as their own exclusive ideological invention and inheritance. Even Mrs

29

Thatcher, that sociological agnostic, used the term to conjure up an image of the nation as a kind of big happy family threatened by black sheep within and without.

Of course community means one thing to right-wing libertarians and quite another to left-wing communitarians; when fascists talk about community they have a vision of a corporate society in which anarchist communes will certainly have no place. One group's sense of community can become another's living hell. There is probably no word in our political vocabulary which spans the whole ideological spectrum from extreme individualism to ultra collectivism with such ease, and whose rhetoric embraces so many conflicting reality principles.

'We are much more sceptical - or is it paranoid - about what might be lurking within the welcoming embrace of those who claim to represent The Spirit of Community'

Not surprisingly then, the term has become a byword for conceptual confusion and political duplicity. This is partly, I think, because during the 1980s its use seemed to have been appropriated by the New Right beyond any possible retrieve. Thatcherism's imagined community was an all too effective device to rationalise a concerted attack on those actual working-class communities, like the miners, which were the very paradigm of 'organic' solidarity. In the sphere of social policy, community care became a euphemism for mentally ill people wandering the streets, and community policing another name for do-it-yourself racial harassment. More recently we had the example of the Commissioner of Metropolitan Police reviving the early 1980s moral panic around black muggers, in the name of improving 'community relations'.

In the political discourse of the post-Thatcher era, portmanteau words, words that can be made to mean almost all things to all people, have grown in popularity as hooks to catch the floating (or sinking?) voter. The rhetoric of community has become a means for the main political parties to occupy the centrist stage at a time when more substantive ideologies and programmes have lost their hold over the imaginations of an overwhelmingly cynical electorate.

In part this move has been imposed by a large shift in public sympathies away from a discredited political culture and community centred on archaic, undemocratic state institutions; this has been accompanied by a movement towards a new kind of community and cultural politics, which spotlights the social injustices suffered by minority groups, and celebrates their achievements in struggle. So much for the good news. The bad news is that these movements are not always or necessarily progressive. They are just as often animated by right wing populism, religious fundamentalism, or ethnic nationalism. Louis Farrakhan's Nation of Islam is as heavily into community politics as, in a different context and for different reasons, are the Liberal Democrats.

There are still those who think that the politics of community is a good thing in and of itself, whatever its ideological complexion. There are still some followers of the famous Saul Alinsky principle, that if a community goes racist, it is the duty of the community activist, if not to go with it, then at least to stay with it, and not abandon the people to their own worst prejudices. But in the 1990s, in the era of ethnic cleansing, it is hard to hold on to the kind of long term optimism which underwrites this kind of populism. We are much more sceptical - or is it paranoid - about what might be lurking within the welcoming embrace of those who claim to represent The Spirit of Community. Open up the idea to inspection and you are likely to find a can of worms.

On what might still, just, be called the left, the term tends to arouse two equally extreme responses; on the one hand it is uncritically espoused as an ideal associated with sharing and caring for others, realised in particular institutions and practices of popular self government and grass roots organisation - community is the moral basis of democratic socialism. On the other, harder left, we tend to find a sneering repudiation of what is seen to be little more than a smokescreen for the maintenance of particular forms of social inequality, exclusion and injustice.

In this context the language game being played by Tony Blair takes on especial significance. It seems to involve sublimating the 'class instinct' associated with the old political community of labour within a highly moralised framework of community politics, as a means of exposing the brutalism of the hard left. Community is central to Blair's vision of one nation labourism precisely because it rewrites the particularisms which have made the party increasingly unelectable, into the terms of a universalising rhetoric of civic responsibility. But before we can judge what that move might actually entail, or deliver as a political project, we perhaps need to consider what it might potentially articulate.

The fall of the public man ?

I think we have to start by recognising that, on the whole, and with a few notable exceptions, the current reach for community does express a genuine determination to reassert the primacy of the public realm, over and against the pervasive privatisation of political, economic and cultural life which has taken place over the last fifteen years under the aegis of the New Right. But we have to ask what kind of public realm we are talking about - or, if you like, whose public realm. Because, of course, historically, this has been the privileged domain of a certain type of Public Man, belonging to a certain class, educated into a belief that private advantages entail public responsibilities, and primed to undertake the enlightened reform of society as part of a civilising mission to those less fortunate than themselves. If Liberalism and One Nation Toryism draw heavily on this public sensibility, so too in a different way does Labourism. The Labour ideal of public service certainly draws on a wider social base than the others, but it was essentially modelled on the same paternalistic, and indeed patriarchal principles.

Recently, Will Hutton and others have argued that the cumulative impact of individualistic consumerism has all but destroyed this culture of the Public Man: it has thrown up a new kind of professional middle class who have opted out of their traditional involvements in public life; at the same time, the material conditions no longer exist which made it possible for significant numbers of people from outside the administrative elite to have the time, energy and motivation to be 'public spirited' in this way. The insecurity and demoralisation engendered by the Thatcher years have taken their toll; and meanwhile a younger generation has grown up to reject decisively this whole model of public life.In place of long term personal commitments to voluntary service on public bodies, we have the instant gratifications of the National Lottery ; the only parties young people are interested in are raves.

It seems to me that the Fall of the Public Man has been a bit overdone. Even if more middle-class people are sending their children to private schools, opting out of public pensions schemes or the national health service, voting for regressive taxation, and generally looking after their own; and even if there is a dramatic decline in the kind of direct working-class politics which hitherto sustained a more generous vision; there is still a sufficiently committed minority to keep much of public life going along the old familiar lines.

It has in any case frequently been argued that if the old Public Culture is in terminal decline that may be no bad thing; it may open up opportunities for groups who have hitherto been excluded or marginalised by its masculinism,its middle-class values, or its whiteness. There does indeed seem to be some evidence that significant numbers of women and members of ethnic minorities have in the last decade moved out of their defensive emplacements in community organisations, to occupy positions of power and influence in the mainstream of public life hitherto reserved for the Public Man; their presence has undoubtedly helped to change the ethos of public service. Just as importantly, the emergence of what are loosely called new social movements has helped to sustain an alternative public realm, in which young people often play a decisive role in setting new agendas of debate over major areas of social policy, in relation to health, housing, education, and the environment.

The question, then, seems to be whether the appeal to Community is an appropriate strategy for reorganising the public realm so that it becomes more plural, more dynamic and more open to new social forces, or whether it is simply a rhetorical device for rehabilitating the Public Man in a more genial guise. This is a crucial test for Blairism. Is the vision of a rejuvenated culture of citizenship based upon opening up new spaces of political representation for those who have been hitherto excluded from the official body politic, or is it just a glib phrase bandied about by the new prefects to curry favour with the electorate of middle england?

In judging which way the communitarian wind is blowing, it may be as well to remember the double standard which is conventionally applied to the term's use. 'The community', without further qualification, is invariably taken to imply 'the "indigenous", those people whose history has sedimented into a cultural geography of common custom, sentiment and belief, and who thereby possess certain normative entitlements. Its indeterminacy, its universalism, contains in fact a very particular determination. Whether 'the' community refers to neighbourhood or nation, and especially with the elision of the two in a nationalism of the neighbourhood, the discursive effect is either to completely assimilate immigrants and minorities of every kind, or to deprive them of membership in the polity altogether. To identify these 'special cases' it then becomes necessary to interject a specialised descriptor - the black community, the bangladeshi community, the gay community, the deaf community, and so on. What is supposed to make populations so particularised into communities is precisely their common experience of not belonging to 'the' community, by virtue of their deviation from its norms. The attempt to counter this effect by using 'community relations' as a euphemism for 'race relations' only underlines the strategy of exclusion which is practised in its name. But is this the effect of a certain ideological deployment (and not others), or is it something intrinsic to the term itself?

Community as soap opera

My argument is that the popularity of community as an item of public speech derives from the fact that it provides a space of representation in which social contradictions and conflicts of every kind can be publicly played out, yet within a framework promising to contain them. The discourse does not resolve contradictions; it dramatises them within a narrative which renders them into inevitable but essentially manageable tensions.

Perhaps the most powerful model for this process is provided by soap opera. *Brookside, East Enders, Coronation Street, Neighbours*, or *The Archers* do not simply construct clearly delineated forms of face to face community, in a sociological sense; in these programmes, issues of political difference or cultural diversity, social division and deviance - which in other circumstances might tear societies apart - serve to bind them ever more closely together. Vital matters of class, gender and race are exploited to create situations of interpersonal conflict which are grist to the soap opera's mill - they become functional elements in sustaining its dramatic unities of time and place.

The way this is done follows almost classical lines. Suspense is created by the carefully controlled irruption of the unpredictable, and audience interest is held by the way these elements are negotiated through the deployment of familiar conventions and traditional routines. The addictive quality of the story does not depend on the unravelling of a plot, but on the spinning out of many separate narrative threads into a never ending yarn. The fact that the audience knows there is never going to be a final big denouement, only lots of little outcomes, excites its desire to know what happens next. And just as the story is pledged to continue, from episode to episode, week in, year out, so too the community is guaranteed to survive crisis after crisis because that is the name of the game.

These overriding principles of containment and continuity permit all manner of social disjunctures to be explored. The type of public agendas which are taken up vary considerably according to the sociological *mise en scene*. You would not expect *East Enders* to deal with the same issues as *Dallas*! Yet the devices of internal tension management are very similar. Structures of social contradiction are translated into emotionally loaded patterns of interpersonal conflict which are then worked through within the framework of an established characterology. For this purpose Soap Communities must be neither too homogeneous nor too polarised. If things become too samey and predictable the story ceases to be worth telling; if things fall apart to the point where no-one is speaking to anyone any more, then there is no longer any story to tell.

'Audiences are drawn together across all the social divisions you might care to name'

Soaps thus offer a vision of a civil-ised society which has devised customary ways of people rubbing along together, co-operating where possible to tackle common problems, and otherwise agreeing to differ. In the language of moral philosophy, they offer a liberal,humanistic model of community as a kind of conversation between largely reasonable individuals, who eschew extremisms in order to inhabit a mutually tolerable world. Soaps also, of course, create communities around themselves, loyal audiences for whom what happens in Coronation Street or Ambridge is as real and sometimes more important than what happens where they actually live or work.

Soaps offer vicarious participation in social worlds which may lie well outside the direct purview of the audience. That is part of their attraction.It may be a case of voyeurism, of wanting to know what life is like on the other side of the class or race tracks. But soaps also represent imagined communities of aspiration and belonging for groups who in real social terms are excluded from them. *The Archers* has a strong following amongst black and Asian listeners for just this reason. The result is that viewing communities may be pulled in from a much broader cross-section of society than the one represented in the programme itself. Audiences are drawn together across all the social divisions you might care to name, and united in a common and often passionate debate about the pro and cons of particular characters, and turns of event. The drama creates an audience in its own Rortian image.

There are a number of distinctive features of soaps which deserve more comment than they usually get from academic commentators. They are nothing if not imagined communities,yet they are by definition organised around immediate face to face encounter. They are relayed around the world yet they celebrate the power of local concern. They are structured around the classical dramatic unities of time and place, but compressed into fragmentary, self referential episodes. In that sense they transgress the usual distinctions between traditional, modern, and post-modern forms. Or rather recast them. For the 'traditional' community built around primary groups of family, friends, workmates and neighbours, which is supposedly being destroyed by the forces of modernity, is here being reconstructed as the crucible of a new 'post-modern' social imaginary.

In Britain the soap community is still largely modelled on an idealised and essentially insular vision of the nation writ small. Its historical norm is the village,and its latter day urban reconstructions. This locale may be tied to a sentimental image of working-class culture, with its close-knit solidarities and open doors; a similar model of insular cosiness may be just as easily be applied to expatriate colonies of 'the english abroad', or to evocations of country life ; more recently the focus has shifted to small, relatively closed, occupational communities - schools,hospitals, prisons,oil rigs,police,fire and ambulance stations;here divisions of labour can be held within a liberal humanitarian frame while larger issues of social justice are wrought dramatically through the life and death of characters whose individual conflicts are decided case by case.

All these *mise en scenes* have in common the fact of privileging local situated knowledge possessed exclusively by 'insiders', and the implicit (and sometimes explicit) relegation of 'outsiders' to a position of ignorance or unwelcome interference.Outsiders are almost never used in the function of a '*deus ex machina*' to resolve contradictions in the plot. They are either foils or 'fall guys' who enable the inside story to be better told. At one level this is simply a calculating device to encourage brand loyalty and reward regular viewers - who are thereby allowed to entertain a privileged 'inside' relation to the unfolding story line. But at another, more unconscious level,it serves as a trope for a national culture whose meanings are immediately given only to 'insiders' and which remain opaque to those who are not born and bred in this 'native land'.

One reason why soaps are so reassuring is that their sense of imagined community presumes a spontaneous process of recognition, something which does not have to be worked at, but automatically places people and events within a consensual framework where meaning is always and already guaranteed. In multi-ethnic societies, where only the most socially insulated manage to avoid the experience of finding themselves strangers in a not so promised land, that sense of easy familiarity, based on mutual toleration and respect, seems eminently desirable. Even, and especially, when they introduce 'ethnic' characters, soaps celebrate a principle of fictive kinship based upon an effortless process of negotiating difference. This wishful multiculturalism enables racism to be portrayed as an interpersonal encounter between voices of bigotry and reason; bigots can be made to see the error of their ways, victims set themselves up as soft targets of humanitarian concern, and the protagonists of common sense and fair play triumph.

This imaginary village is not just the nation writ small; it is also a family writ large, with its public feuds, rivalries, alliances, partings,makings ups all patterned on the intimate domestic scene. We can see this in the way conflicts are resolved. Erstwhile villains are routinely rehabilitated in the fashion of 'black sheep' being welcomed back into the family/community fold. Where the psycho-drama of guilt and reparation is not on the cards, there is only one alternative - death. Sentence is duly passed on all those characters who transgress the narrative norms - either because they have become too predictable, or have fulfilled their role in counterpointing the main characterology; they are killed, or otherwise written out of the script, in order that both story and community can maintain their moral equilibrium and go on. If life outside the 'family' and its extended kinships is just not possible, death confirms the immortality of the script.

This is not, clearly, a version of the community of nation or neighbourhood as 'one big happy family'. It certainly does not entail a vision of civil society in which all conflicts have been mediated, or resolved through adherence to some higher principle of unity. It is not about any religious sense of convocation guaranteed and shared by those of common faith. Nor does it offer any secular, ideological equivalent of spiritual harmony. The soap's signature tune may be more popular than the national, anthem but it is not a hymn to some Greater Good, or God. Nor is it about what anthropologists call *communitas*, a ritual celebration of egalitarianism consequent upon the temporary overturning of hierarchy in some common metaphysics of presence. In contrast to these mystical unisons, soaps portray a decidedly profane and contrapuntal reality, in which everyday conflicts engendered by difference and domination are exploited as devices to make life interestingly manageable, and hence worth narrating.

This rendering of conflicts which might otherwise undermine national unity into family disputes which implicitly uphold a kind of constitutional settlement is, I would argue, the key to the soap's success as a model of political community in the West. It is also perhaps why they travel so well to the so called 'third world'. For here, wrapped up in the carapace of consumerism, we have a package of 'traditional values' tempered by a democratic and secular vision of modernity; taken together this seems to offer an attractive alternative to the autocratic structures of caste, clan and priestly clientage which continue to preside over both state and civil society in so many of the so called sunrise economies.

Closer to home, it is perhaps worth emphasising that the community ideal portrayed in soaps is not merely a collective representation of 'the good society'; it moves significant numbers of people to action. Soaps do not merely reflect social aspirations, they construct them. We will never know how much *Brookside* did to articulate demand for home ownership amongst the aspirant working class. But there are certainly a a lot of housing estates built in the early 1980s boom which are the spitting image. What effect do *The Archers* have in stimulating middle-class

> 'Communities praised for their "close knit family values" are routinely pathologised as soon as they stand up for their rights'

flight from the city and the creation of ex-urban commuter villages? Again it is hard to say, but we do know that there are quite a few people who are disillusioned because actual village life does not live up to expectations fostered in part from media sources.

Meanwhile, on the other side of the tracks, *East Enders* and *Coronation Street* provide complementary images of an insular working class, living in an urban village of its own making, a model which is still implicitly evoked in many rhetorics of struggle against the interventions of both capital and state. According to this myth, Community is something which the working class used to have in the good old bad old days of factories and slums, but have now lost, as a result of gentrification, deindustrialisation, and urban renewal; at the same time, community is something the middle class never used to have, but have discovered in their quest for the good life beyond the rat race.

Community has thus become a special kind of cultural capital, and is increasingly the subject of a politics of envy fuelled by divisions of race as well as class. For migrants, refugees and exiles of every kind, the creation of community is both a condition for maintaining actual networks of diasporic communication with links to a real and/or notional homeland, *and* a site of roots resistance to various forms of racism encountered in countries of settlement. But these efforts become quickly misrepresented through a double standard imposed by the host society. A line is drawn between model minorities who are held to have reinvented traditional values of caring and sharing, and those pariah groups whose 'anarchic and alien' ways of life pose a threat to the social fabric. Thus Asians are supposedly thriving because their sense of community is based on private, individualistic, or 'confucian' family values; whereas Afro Caribbean structures of communal feeling are widely regarded as dysfunctional because they are public, collective and 'in your face'. Perhaps it is no coincidence that communities which are praised for their 'close knit family values' are routinely pathologised as soon as they stand up for their political rights.

It is partly because of this double standard that the debate around 'community safety' has been so easily hijacked by the New Right into a moral panic about 'black muggers'. The importance of tackling problems of street crime, racial violence, and harassment in public places became subsumed under the moral imperative of drawing a dividing line between the respectable law-abiding Asian and Jewish communities on one side and the yardies, rastas, and others who are held to characterise the 'black presence'.

This example should perhaps alert us to the fact that we are always dealing with invented traditions. The imagination of community, as a binding together of civil society through direct presence in some golden age of unmediated exchange, represents the symbolic retrieval of a situation which never existed in the first place. Moreover, as the discussion of soap opera indicated, the mythopoetics of what I am going to call the community romance, is often accomplished by means of social technologies which have in any case made face to face communication a far less decisive influence on social outcomes.

The debate on community safety also illustrates a general and perhaps equally obvious point - that the reach for Community is provoked by a sense of its absence. Increasingly, its rhetoric provides a home from home for those who feel displaced, alienated or lost in a world where the signposts of class, nation, family, religion or race have become, for various reasons, hard to read. Community is a magical device for conjuring something apparently solidary out of the thin air of modern times, a mechanism of re-enchantment for those who have become disillusioned with the sleazy manoeuvres and cheesy slogans of contemporary politics. But, by the same token, it can also offer a persuasive flight from engagement with divisions and inequalities which have become not just more complicated, but more deeply entrenched.

This relation between political idealism and denial is central to the distinctiveness of community as a structure of contemporary feeling. Perhaps, by exploring this deeper, more unconscious, level of ambivalence we can begin to understand why so many people still cling to the term, and what there might be in the nature of this clinging that points to both its positive and negative possibilities.

Between matrilocal and patriglobal :
some varieties of Community Romance

I have suggested that, underlying the liberal humanist model of community, as the hidden limit and condition of its discursive tolerances, are the conjoint figures of family and nation. These subsist as a kind of silent undertow, twisting altruistic gestures of caring and sharing into more restrictive, and often racialised, definitions of political and cultural belonging. In its mythopoeic linkage of continuity and containment, the rhetoric of 'community' can become a fatal link between the sanctuary, the ghetto and the concentration camp. Yet what is it that makes that linkage possible?

If we think about the stereotypes of spontaneous community which continue to haunt the liberal imagination of the good public life - children playing in the street, the flirtatious conviviality of youth, women gossiping across backyard fences, old men sitting in town squares - it is clear how overdetermined these paradigms are by deeply entrenched patriarchal assumptions about the organisation of civil society.

If, for example, the community romance has largely been conceived as a matrilocal affair, it is because so many women have been confined to the home for so long while bringing up children. It is women who run neighbourhood committees, organise around issues to do with education, health care and the environment - and thereby define local cultures of citizenship, around claims to entitlement over amenity and resource.

It is not surprising then, that narratives of community romance, of which the soap opera is only the most developed example, have been modelled on the customary forms and pre-occupations of women's talk: the intense detailing of everyday incident celebrated in gossip, the conjuring of foreign adventure out of domestic accident, absence, or abandonment in fairy tales. The public men, who often feature, and sometimes front, these 'women's activities', to give them a 'wider' legitimacy, have become increasingly redundant. But their tenancy of what might be called the patriglobal realm has hardly withered away. It is still the public men who get to do most of the jet-set travelling, who are in charge of global movements of capital, run global cities and surf the internet. Even more than their predecessors who travelled the globe to administer the old colonial empires, the business elites of today are transnational citizens, for whom the barriers experienced by immigrant labour simply do not exist. As for the more exotic side of the story, the sex tourists who visit the child brothels of the third world are only following in the footsteps of the wild colonial rovers whose exploits made the Empire into an adventure story for eminently Victorian naughty boys.

Of course there have been notable exceptions to this rule: women explorers, travel writers, anthropologists and missionaries; public men who stayed at home and busied themselves with local tasks of self improvement. But these figures, in their extraordinariness, only serve to highlight the fact that the malestream trend goes the other way.

The picture is even more clear-cut if we shift our vantage point from the bourgeois public realm to that of the working class. Again with a few notable exceptions, it has, until quite recently been the young men of the West who got to travel, as casual and migrant labourers, seafarers, apprentices, journeymen and artisans, and who thereby carried back tales of far countries, foreign habits, and exotic pleasures not to be had nearer home. For the rest matrilocalism seems to have ruled OK. (At least according to the famous study of Wilmott and Young, *Family and Kinship in East London*, which highlighted the practice as central to the maintenance of working-class community life. Daughters left home only to get married and have children and then lived as close to their family of origin as they could. The mother/daughter tie was strengthened rather than loosened by marriage and meant that children grew up within a strongly bounded maternal speech community, where mother's, not father's word was law.)

Doubts have subsequently been cast on the warm rosy glow which Wilmott and Young's description sheds over this aspect of working-class life. Matrilocalism was just as likely to be a recipe for implosive family conflict, the stifling of ambition, or the suffocating equivocation of 'secrets and lies' as shown in Mike Leigh's recent film. Either way, a kinship system which pivoted on the maintenance of the mother/daughter tie created certain centrifugal pressures. It tended to not only give women the upper hand in family matters, but also pushed their legislative role outwards into wider and more public spheres - as moral regulators of what goes on in the street, the neighbourhood, and the estate. They became agents of public propriety, responsible for defining and defending community traditions and values; it was from this vantage point that they were addressed and sometimes mobilised by improving discourses which urged them to act as civilising influences over their children and menfolk; and from here too that they echoed or turned a blind ear to the siren calls of popular racism, urging them to clean up the neighbourhood and keep it safe from foreign intrusion.

Working-class children thus grew up within a universe in which fathers, and men in general, played only a peripheral role, albeit one which enhanced their mystique as exclusive inhabitants of the promised land of manual labour associated with masculinity and its apprenticeships. To be able to make that journey, boys had first to free themselves from their mother's apron strings; or rather they had to venture beyond mother's lap, and its immediate extensions in street and neighbourhood policed by the maternal eye, in order to set out on an adventure to colonise other more exciting and dangerous playgrounds and turn them into safe dens. And so were created those exclusively masculine territories on the frontiers of matrilocal world, those little homes from home, where boys and grown men played at king of the castle and chased off dirty wee rascals, made themselves feel big and powerful as a group by constructing exclusive spaces of social combination while cutting other rival groups down to size. It was from this position that gangs were formed, and the most disadvantaged and powerless imagined themselves as a some kind of local ruling class; you belonged in this microcommunity only in so far as you successfully staked your claim that the area belonged to you, and not some other rival group.

But what was this territory over which exclusive rights and prerogatives were claimed, if not an analogue of the maternal body? Because masculine prides of place remained tied to this unconscious premise, their assertion entailed an aggressive repudiation of everything to do with women's work and the feminine world. The fetishism of 'hardness', the cultivation of a body whose fighting fitness was the price of admittance to male physical fraternity, only barely concealed this achilles heel. The stake might have been symbolic ownership and control over public space or amenity, a pub or club, the right to hang out in a particular bit of street or park, but what was unconsciously being defended and attacked was always the mother's body. The lad struggled to become a Hard Man, but the hard man remained a mummy's boy through and through. The tattoos showing death and glory on one arm and Mum in hearts on the other were one sign of this contradiction. The figure of the skinhead, the bald bother boy, dressed to kill as a new born baby, was another.

M atrilocalism may have propelled a minority of lads into substantial adventures beyond the long emotional arm of its law, but most remained home boys, immobilised between its all too familiar frontlines and the backyards of the patriglobal world; billy liars dreaming of 'getting away', making the big break, but only getting to travel with their mates, in the safety of numbers, on a holiday trip abroad or to support their local football team. In this way, restricted opportunity structures, governed by class, were naturalised and doubled over in a gendered form of white ethnicity which was thrown up by the defensive assertion of male autonomies associated with laddish culture.

For working-class boys, then, community has been where the tug-of-war between infantile masculinism and disavowed feminisation has been played, or rather fought, out; for girls, in contrast, it has provided an arena where the struggle to avoid chronic little motherhood has fed into the active drive to extend the scope of matrilocal power beyond the safe confines of the maternal role, into erstwhile male territory. Yet whether patterned on aggressive macho disavowal or feminist assertion, the template of labour's body politic remained maternal.

T he institutions of apprenticeship and the family wage, and the whole sexual division of labour which underpinned this culture, have of course collapsed, along with the occupational structures and production processes which mandated them. At the same time, the growth of single-parent households has tended to strengthen matrilocalism, which has assumed an ever larger importance in defining the boundaries of both real and imagined community. Thus, at a stroke, the boy's dependency on the maternal is increased, whilst the customary wage and labour forms which have hitherto enabled him to distance or dissociate himself from his feminine positioning *vis a vis* male elders have weakened. The feminisation of labour makes the customary moral economy of boyz2men communities largely redundant as a transition to work, but that does not mean that they simply wither away. A minority of young working-class men may respond by actively embracing their feminine side; normally this move is confined to a transitional phase of sexual experimentation and takes place within the protective frame of youth cultures which encourage some degree of gender bending. For the majority, the decline of manual labourism has served to reinforce psychic investment in ritual displays of physical hardness, from hard drinking, punishing athleticism, and aggressive dancing, to violent language, and domestic brawls. These 'labours' of masculinity are central to laddish culture, and because they are so radically disconnected from any possible sublimation in more socially productive techniques of the body, they take on ever more florid and dysfunctional forms.

In this context it is perhaps worth noting that certain types of manual work, or worker, have today taken on a hyper-inflationary value, not so much because of skill or wage level, but because they require or permit the public display of masculine communitas otherwise outlawed or made redundant. The building worker, the trucker, the rigger, the cowboy, the steel erector, the miner, the fisherman, even the garage mechanic, these heroic hard men doing dirty or dangerous jobs, are celebrated, often with strongly homo-erotic overtones - in Country and Western music, in buddy movies, in soft porn magazines and comics, in corporate advertising, and, not least, in TV soaps. This idealisation has little to do with the realities of the jobs; it is not an invitation to learn the intricacies of these particular 'rough trades'. It has everything to do with the performance of masculinity as a sexualised masquerade of working-class community. These figures are celebrated for being ruggedly individualistic, *and* for restoring a lost sense of physical fraternity to work processes 'undermined' by the feminisation of labour; and they speak not just to the old manual working classes but to the nation as a whole. They have indeed been invented as the standard bearers of a new white race - which is only the old lost white race of colonial frontiersmen cast in a new guise.

As the current crisis of family and nation gathers momentum, alongside the collapse of customary practices linking growing up male, working and class, imagined communities of race have provided one magical solution to these problems. Unemployed masculinities are put back to work in the construction of exclusionary territories of belonging, based on a sense of being 'born and bred' to certain privileged entitlements, now mobilised to retrieve lost prides of place. Home boys rule OK where and when ever the working class goes 'nativist'.

It is no coincidence that this new brand of popular white supremacism couples the figure of the horny young single male migrant with the rampantly reproductive 'black mamma', to create a scenario of demographic 'swamping'. This construct speaks to a pervasive anxiety about racial emasculation, which no amount of muscle-flexing or manual labour seems to assuage.

Significantly, this scenario ignores the feminisation of immigrant labour itself. Some feminists have welcomed the increased geographical mobility of working women as a progressive development, in so far as it promises to liberate them from customary ties of family/home/nation, and create the conditions for a new global consciousness of gendered oppression. But if women have increasingly begun to travel long distances across continents and seas, in search of work or asylum, or both, it has usually been only to reinforce their matrilocal position. Whether as au pair girls or domestic servants, as home workers or child carers, they have been made to carry a double burden of representation; externally they are rendered invisible and internally they are made to define the boundaries of the 'home nation', to preserve principles of

'Community is preserved as a heart in a heartless world only by freezing out whole populations from its warm embrace'

continuity and containment in the culture of immigrant communities, against the threat of their dispersal.

Diasporic cultures, in fact, generate a particularly intense form of the community romance, linked to the mother's body. Narratives which centre on the theme of return to a 'promised land' organise feelings of separation and loss arising from the experience of migration, in a way which invests them with a special redemptive message. In these stories, the original suffering attendant on forced eviction from the first home/land is followed by a phase of exile which prolongs and deepens the wounds of abandonment, but is nevertheless assuaged by new principles of hope: next year in Jerusalem, Mecca or Addis Abbaba. If these declaratives are to be more than hollow promises, they have to be encoded in a historical narrative which invests them with a real performative effect. Their utterance must be both a reiteration of ancient entitlements, and a rehearsal for the 'end of the story' which is the triumphant return to reclaim the lost object.

In some diaspora stories, the theme of return may be taken literally, in the form of a programme to materialise the imagined motherland in real institutions, a real territory, and usually in a state. If it ever becomes actually possible to return, the imagined community of dispersal is rapidly transformed into a real concentration of power which sets about the ugly business of purging the new body politic of all its alien elements. Even where the journey is purely symbolic and involves a return to cultural roots, a somewhat similar process of 'ethnic cleansing' can sometimes be observed at work, removing all 'anxiety of influence' in order to pursue an authenticity of communitarian forms. Invented traditions conveyed through the 'mother tongue' are thus naturalised by association with mother's milk, and the maternal lap becomes the privileged place where the sense of community becomes fatally elided with the transmission of a national heritage cast in a patriglobal mould.

Thus, part of the difficulty of breaking from the problematic of the maternal body and its disavowal in the imagination of community thus stems from the large psychic pay-offs which derive from clinging on to it, especially in conditions of social upheaval and rapid change. The appeal of the community romance certainly does not derive from the ethic of altruism so often associated with it; that is a secondary gain. Rather it offers a pattern of symbolic identification with lost objects in a way which evokes deep rooted feelings of abandonment, exile and loss and connects them with the desire to return home. The story line, the myths of origin and destiny which tell the tale, move continually between Cenotaph and Jubilee, nostalgia and triumphalism, echoing the pattern of our earliest relationships to the maternal breast. This in turn tends to emphasise processes of splitting in the construction of social ideology. The community becomes an ideal internal (lost/found) object', always and already threatened by destructive external forces, projected onto the Other: immigrants, foreigners, ethnics, gays, Trotskyites, etc, who are threatening 'our' vision, our way of life. By a terrible irony, community is preserved as a heart in a heartless world, only by freezing out whole populations from its warm embrace.

One final example, perhaps somewhat closer to the bone for many *Soundings* readers, may help to clinch the point. In the discourse of postwar labourism we frequently find references to a golden age of community life, a time when doors were always open, friends, family and neighbours were always on hand to help, street parties and outings were the order of the day, and people stuck together through thick and thin. But then came the war, or high rise flats, or the recession, or immigrants, or foreign ideas like Thatcherism, or even post-modernism, and nothing was quite the same any more; kids run wild, families break apart, dog eats dog, drugs, crime and violence are rampant.

The nostalgia for a return to labour's 'true' origins can be given various political articulations. The hard left version of the story suggests that if only we could get rid of the puny and pusillanimous figures who have usurped or betrayed the great Ideals, and replace them with real leaders who walk in the footsteps of the giants or giant killers of yesteryear then perhaps it might be possible to recover the true road to socialism, and emerge finally victorious with everything that had seemed lost for ever now once more restored.

Tony Blair's political philosophy appears, at first glance, to break decisively with this whole nostalgia trip. The direction of the story line reverses from past tense to future. Modernity becomes the process whereby Labour gives birth to itself as a morally regenerative force in the 'stakeholder society'. In fact Blairism conserves certain of the key elements of the 'golden age of community' myth, but gives them a new political twist by shifting their centre of gravity from the discourse of labour to that of nation.In the triumphalism of this happy ending, melancholic yearning for Labour's lost patrimony is transformed into a feeling of jubilation in a born again sense of national community as Labour wins the next election. The members of this community naturally comprise all those who share the common vision and identify with the forces of modernity/rebirth. En route the categories of those who are excluded has been enlarged (we might even say democratised). They now include capitalists without a conscience, aristocrats who abuse their privileges,and all those members of the middle class whose claims on the polity are not matched by their investment in it. They join the traditional cast of juvenile delinquents, feckless parents, and other denizens of the underclass in the rogues gallery of antisocial types. The rationalisation,or rather moralisation, of that Great Divide is the special 'magic' worked by the rhetoric of 'New Labour, New Britain'.

For all its opposition to the dogmatisms and closures associated with 'Old Labour', Blairism seems hopelessly enmeshed in an equally profound regression from a sense of political community which actively articulates difference to one based on bonding with a unitary and quasi-organic body politic. The big change,I've suggested, is that this is no longer modelled on the actual labour movement (that most fractious and fragmented of beasts), but on a vision of the Party as speaking up for Middle England, conceived afresh as a normative community of reason, decency and fair play.It is as if Blairism wants to arrive at the happy equilibrium promised by the Rortian plot, while writing the family quarrels (which alone make the story worth telling) out of the script. If politics is ever to become a matter of popular concern beyond the present soap opera of sexual scandal and sleaze it seems unlikely that the Blair formula will do the trick. Despite, or rather because of, the focus groups and the sound-byte thinking, it is recipe for switching off.

It may also lead to more people switching to alternative channels. Blairism produces a certain fall-out effect amongst those have been excluded or marginalised by the mainstream political process. The liminal quest for Communitas in these groups in any case leads away from the stakeholder society, either towards the assertion of immanent and absolute difference as with separatist organisations, or identification with some source of transcendental power in the case of sects and cults.

What has been called the 'neotribalism' of contemporary youth culture also belongs within this frame, characterised as it is by a unique metaphysics of presence. A thousand young people standing in a field high on Ecstasy may not be what the communitarians have in mind, but rave culture has created a form of togetherness which is safe, non violent and seems to require little or no demonisation of the Other. I say 'seems' because The Other has in fact been transubstantiated into a pharmacological version of the maternal body, and en route taken on a globalising rather than a localising function. Ecstasy creates a womb-like sense of oneness which relies on a collective but extremely dissociated state of mind; it supplies instant oceanic gratification but precludes any real human contact or relationship. Whereas traditional Carnivals are site specific communities constructed around social rituals of masquerade, Raves represent a masquerade of communitas bound to immediate physical sensation, the same for everyone everywhere tuned in to that particular musical/drug-induced brain wavelength. This may be, as its enthusiasts claim, an instinctive democracy of the body at play, but what implications does it have for the workings of more mundane instances of civil governance ?

Virtual communities ? Not in my back yard!

It is frequently suggested that the process of globalisation is making the 'old' sense of community redundant, by creating more fluid and open networks of affiliation, or else that community politics has emerged as a defensive and largely reactionary assertion of local autonomies in the face of the new spatial economy of population and information flows. These are really two sides of the same argument. I want, finally, to argue that the current transformations of 'community' remain mysterious, and their outcome undecidable, as long as they are understood in this fashion.

Those who insist on a distinctive 'post-modernist' state of culture, economy and society, invariably invoke a notion of community no longer based on shared geography or history, where social interaction is not dependant on face-to-face presence, or shaped by identities derived from family, nation and the mother's body. Membership in civil society has become thoroughly deterritorialised; it no longer requires even the most notional anchorage to locality, but is organised around common interests or affiliations, abstracted from shared loyalties to family, workmates or neighbours. In the post-modern model, people can be simultaneously members of many different communities without experiencing any sense of conflict, because nothing has to be given up to join and any number can play. Whereas the 'old community' entailed a trade-off between rights and obligations, security and autonomy, the new community is essentially a communications network which people can enter and leave at will, provided they have the right credentials to begin with.

'There is a pervasive feeling that to travel hopefully is no longer better than to arrive'

The internet is commonly cited as the paradigm of post-modern community, an interface between faceless, disembodied individuals, each bulletin board or home page a virtual encounter group where no-one need ever meet, but where the most intimate kinds of information can be made public and exchanged without sacrificing anonymity. In the language of technohype, the experience of surfing the internet is conveyed in almost mystical terms as a kind of oceanic feeling of communion with kindred spirits across the globe. The culture of the home computer is set up to replace ecstatic religion as a site of instant communitas.

I n principle, the new informatics would seem to render the matrilocal/patriglobal distinction redundant. Housewives can travel the world without having to leave their kitchens; home boys can rule cyberspace from their bedrooms, even if they are afraid to cross the street. It has even been suggested that the close interface between technology and the body is creating the conditions for a permanent mutation which blurs or fuses the boundaries of both to create a new community of hybrid beings (which Donna Haraway presciently labelled cyborgs), whose life-styles cut across all manner of dichotomous social roles.

Urban folk tales tell a rather different story however; they feature spotty adolescents who turn into computer nerds because they cannot handle real relationships, and take out their frustration in perverse, masturbatory forms of 'computer sex'. Whatever the actual facts of the case, perhaps these stories point to the symbolic truth that we are not dealing here with a simulation of face to face community, but with the dissimulation of existing mechanisms of power through their impersonation of human interactivity as a technology of magical action at a distance.

Internet mythology entertains the phantasy of a perfect meeting of minds, realised through an entirely transparent but all powerful medium which penetrates every nook and cranny of the modern world; it is a model of community as a kind of global mindfuck which, far from dissolving gender divisions, institutionalises the phallic knowledge/power games of the public man; the patriglobal now entirely subsumes the matrilocal, as a template of communication, irrespective of whose hands are on the keyboard.

Enthusiasts for the cyborg revolution and the politics of 'new times' are undaunted by such critiques. They claim that the traditional political cartographies of left and right have been definitively surpassed by more fluid and dynamic social movements. According to this line, the language of barricades and front lines, mobilisations and 'they shall not pass' belongs to the old era, another kind of urban space, where large crowds were not just a collective pose for the mass media, but were direct agents of the historical process.

Nevertheless, in a world supposedly dominated by globalisation, where forms of political protest rooted in stable communities of local interest have supposedly been rendered obsolete, the most obdurate struggles continue to break out in and around the front doors and back yards of whatever is called home. Yet, just as surely, what is often at stake here are identities which transcend their immediate anchorage and become indices of membership in communities whose affiliations stretch across fixed national boundaries and act at a distance from one side of the world to the other.

The phenomenon of Not In My Back Yardism, which animates so much contemporary community politics, is a confused response to this new local/global dialectic. At one level it expresses a pervasive feeling that to travel hopefully is no longer better than to arrive. The goal of life is to achieve some kind of domestic security in an increasingly chaotic and dangerous world. The first priority is to prevent the intrusion of any outside force which would disturb that sense of internal order. NIMBYism is, characteristically, the ideology of the little man or woman whose interests are threatened by the bulldozers of corporate capitalism and the state. As such its political articulation is ambiguous. It may become associated with the libertarian philosophies of the New Right, but it may also, and especially in Britain, link to certain invented traditions of the 'freeborn Englishman' still current within certain versions of home grown socialism. More usually it is a contradictory amalgam of different tendencies.

But are there any alternative channels which might give expression to a rather more encouraging vision of what 'new Labour, new Britain' might entail? In the second of these articles, which will be published in a future issue of *Soundings*, I will look at some of the arguments which have been put forward in support of a youthful and dynamic counterculture centred on post-fordist or post-modern forms of labour and leisure. How far do they point beyond the present identity politics, towards a sense of political identity in which differences can be validated without investing any of them with an absolute power to determine claims over amenity or resource? Is it possible that amongst all the critical babble about 'post-modernity' we might discover, heavily coded and covered in media hype, the obscure figures of a definitively new, but still recognisably working-class community struggling to be born?

Wrong and wrong again

Women for peace in Israel

A Photo-Narrative by Cynthia Cockburn

In the cattle yard at kibbutz Megiddo is a ruined stone building. At one time it was used as the carpentry workshop. If the Jewish kibbutzniks notice it at all, it reminds them of the early days of the kibbutz. Escaped from the European Holocaust, constructing shelter, clearing the stones from the newly-settled land from dawn till dusk.

For the Palestinians looking down on the kibbutz today from the hill villages of Musmus and Musheirifa it's a reminder of something else. Before 1948 an Arab village stood where today the Jews' dairy cows are milked. This building was its mosque.

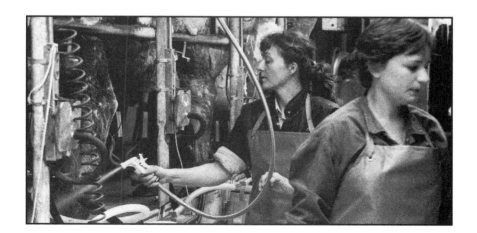

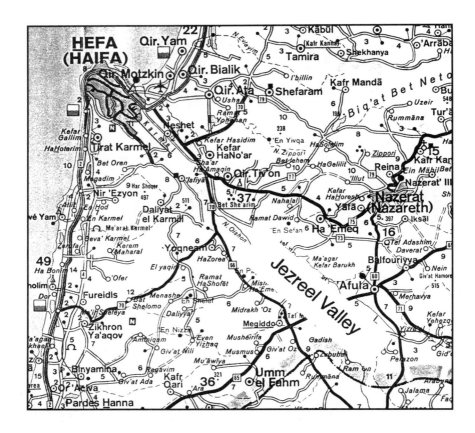

What they remember is how the homecoming of the Israeli diaspora created a Palestinian one, scattering 750,000 to refugee camps and exile. Conflictual meanings, contrasted trajectories - but consonant memories of being wronged.

The difference is, the Jews today control the state. And the rather few Palestinian Arabs who hung on in there, now a fifth of the Israeli population, feel themselves second class citizens. Judaism is the established religion, Jews worldwide have their right of return to the land of Palestine. Arabs don't.

Kibbutz Megiddo is on the edge of the Jezreel Valley, to the south of Galilee. Round here are many kibbutzim, spread confidently across the fertile land.

On the kibbutz you live simply, without cash. You eat in a dining hall with several hundred others, use collective transport, own little personal property, enjoy verdant gardens, work at whatever task arises: in the laundry, the kitchens, the factory, the dairy.

Your children start in the creche, progress to the kibbutz school, go on to the armed forces. You aren't religious, are probably socialist. You live surrounded by Jews, mostly Zionists like you. The few Arabs you see are hired manual labourers.

On Kibbutz Megiddo jobs include laundry and jewellery manufacture.

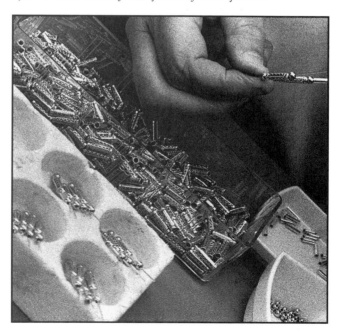

But this is also the part of Israel with the highest concentration of remaining Arabs. They aren't agriculturalists any more. They're confined to ever denser villages and small towns, building upwards.

In Musmus, or Nazareth, or Umm El Fahm, or Ar-Ara you live in a flat in your family home, and the family is everything. You invest your earnings in house, car, jewellery, clothes. You struggle and compete. You probably worship in church or mosque. And may well be a communist.

For Arab women the range of occupations is narrow, and there's a glass ceiling. Right: sewing (for a Jewish entrepreneur) swimsuits she'd never wear.

Your children play in a pot-holed street where the sanitation is poor. They go to an under-resourced school, learn in Arabic, rarely meet a Jewish child. Your young are not called to the army. (Could you trust an Arab to fight Arabs?) Anyway, this is one right you perhaps feel better off without.

One region, two lifestyles, two languages, two cultures, no mixity. *Bat Shalom* (Daughter of Peace, Issue of Peace) is a women's group, a bridge between Israeli Jewish and Israeli Arab worlds.

The women meet because they want to know each other. For that, a Jew risks being called 'whore of Arafat'. And the Palestinian? Her cousins in the Occupied Territories (or Lebanon) may see her as a collaborator.

Together they organize events and workshops. And they demonstrate for peace, for the creation of a Palestinian state. With placards in Hebrew and Arabic they stand on the junctions of major roads, way out there in the countryside, and receive, with equal passivity, the supportive honks and hate-filled jeers of passing motorists.

On the day after Hamas bombed a Jerusalem bus, on the very afternoon of the Dizengoff Centre suicide bomb, the women were together on the roadside signalling: don't let this de-rail the peace process.

But behind and beneath the area
of agreement is an area of silence:
uncharted differences.

Together one day, in a
hired bus, the women of
Bat Shalom visited the
ghost villages of Biram
and Iqrit where the
Palestinians, displaced
almost half a century
ago, are still stubbornly
squatting a church.

The women listened as the villagers put their case: 'the courts supported our claim to this place, the government won't honour it'. They listened to the spokesman of the kibbutz that now farms this land. 'But I was born here. We planted these orange trees.'

The women argued the wrongs and wrongs. It hurt. There was no-one who didn't feel history quake beneath her feet.

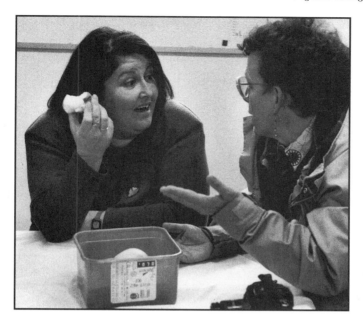

A Janus-faced dilemma trailed the bus home: too many differences hidden beneath the table make for a fake alliance; too many placed on the table make an alliance impossible. What do you need to hear me say before we can work together? Are there things you would prefer I didn't ask to know?

This essay derives from a research project on gender and cross-communal relations in conflict zones, on which I am working in the Centre for Research in Gender, Ethnicity and Social Change, City University, London. It is the last of a series of three photo-narratives in Soundings, *earlier issues representing women's projects in N.Ireland and Bosnia. I would like to thank the Lipman Trust, the Scurrah Wainwright Charity and Womankind Worldwide for grants towards materials, and to record a specially warm thank you to the women of Bat Shalom living in and around the Jezreel valley in Israel for including me in their activites and sharing their thoughts with me.*

The Institute of International Visual Arts

is an independent contemporary visual arts organisation which promotes the work of artists, academics and curators from a plurality of cultures and cultural perspectives. The Institute has four areas of activity: **exhibitions, publications, research and education and training** enabling it to work collaboratively with a range of institutions such as **galleries, publishers and universities, as well as individual artists, writers and curators.**

For further information on the Institute or to receive a copy of the *agenda* programme leaflet and our publications list, please contact us.

Funded by
THE
ARTS
COUNCIL
OF ENGLAND

LONDON
ARTS BOARD

Registered Charity no. 1031721

inIVA

Institute of International Visual Arts
Kirkman House, 12/14 Whitfield Street
London W1P 5RD, United Kingdom
+44 171 636 1930 Voice
1931 Fax
email
institute@iniva.org

Five Poems

True North

My early morning sleep is a map
spread under migrating geese. Through dreams
I hear them, their torn skeins pulled taut
as the horizon recedes, as the hills flatten
to wing-flap and heart-beat, their raucous
repetitious honk in startled blue
like someone gasping for breath. Through eyelids,
the drawn white of curtains,
I sense sunlight vibrating, this March morning
cool and traversable, the sudden mirrors
of lakes. And I imagine them
changed by this overwintering, ragged,
their struck reflections leaving
pink vapour-trails of blood, that last shadow
on the V floundering, struggling
to keep up, the yards of clear air
unbridgeable. Harsher and more intimate
than sleep, their voices come to me
from the south: imagined half-life;
migration. Forgive me.
A wing dips to evening, the deep black
bones of waiting trees. I see us
teased out over creaking pines,
ragged, reforming
in a perfect arrow-head; I hear us
as we fly north to try the ripe ice
of Canada, flapping, honking like crazy.

Susan Wicks

Would Madam?

Would Madam consider the Atlantic Ocean?

Something a bit smaller is what I have in mind.
A Great Lake or the Dead Sea,
or the Ganges between us would do
to keep us from taking out the garbage together.
I don't want yours and you don't want mine.

The Atlantic, then Madam,
would be ideal for inaccessibility.
It's practically raft-proof and therefore
unlikely to foster domestic connections
from one side of it to the other.

Yes, but something quite a bit smaller
might be better, after all.
What if I need to see across it
to check the current or the depth?
Perhaps something shallower,
something moving a little slower.

Am I to take it then, Madam,
the Atlantic won't do?
Of its kind, it's surely the best.
What else can I possibly show you?

I'd like something with a plug
in case I want to pull it.
And a bit less salt.

Linda Chase

Bird

(The Abruzzi, February 15, 1944)

The pot-hole of his gut -
mauve, still smoking
under white rods of ribs

and the raven jerking eels from him
working the corner with his beak
round and into his groin.

Couldn't aim for shaking.
Until someone from behind:
amico, che fa? -

and the bird snapped up its head
haughty as Mussolini, shook it,
let loose the worms of nerve

came straight at me
beak for eye, eye
of yellow poison, and I

hardly heard the cartridge burst
or felt the butt jerk at my shoulder -
there was just the unanswered

question, the air
rank with offal
a black fall

of feathers

Mario Petrucci

Cut Off

She gathered up our photographs of you
and one by one cut away the high
trees above your head, sliced through
chair legs and discarded all the sky.

You're intact, assembled in a frame
beside her bed. You in thin air.
You somewhere. She can't even name
the town or room you're in. She couldn't care

less but I've spent ages searching the bin
for scraps of garden and the old settee,
to put them back around you, to leave you in
a place you know with half a chance to see

the light on in the yard, the kitchen door
still open for you, wider than before.

Amanda Dalton

The Rent Man

Old Jepson scuffled door-to-door
every Friday tea signing rent-books
in worn down shoes and clothes that could
have stood up on their own.
He left his thumb-prints in the margins,
doubling back the covers.

His perk was the greenhouse against
grandma's wall. She grumbled it made
her alcoves damp and encouraged vermin.
He padlocked its double doors
worried by the spite of children.

She said his house was 'black
as the ace-of-spades'.
He spread the table with hoarded
newspapers that soaked up cold tea
and the sour drips from milk-bottles.
'You could grow things on that lino,' she said.

Yet she sat there on a Saturday morning,
'a little tipple' in their tea,
heads bent over the sports-page,
picking horses for their weekly flutter.

I'd fancied they might get married.
She would have scorned the idea,
'the dirty divel' that he was -
a heathen to boot.

Frances Angela

Latin America and Free Trade

Duncan Green

Duncan Green *examines the impact of free trade
ideology on Latin America, exploring the human
cost of the region's 'Silent Revolution' since the
onset of the debt crisis in 1982.*

It hits you from hundreds of yards away, the rich sweet smell of fermenting wood floating through the crisp air of a Chilean night. The scent emanates from several huge mounds of wood chip, silhouetted against the dockside floodlights. Dwarfing the wooden houses and shops of the southern port of Puerto Montt, the mounds steam gently as they await loading onto the Japanese ship which rides at anchor in the bay. Each pile contains the remnants of a different species of Chilean tree, hauled from the country's dwindling native forest.

Along the southern coast, the wire-mesh tanks of innumerable salmon farms dot the picturesque fjords and inlets. On the beaches, the black strings of *pelillo* seaweed lie drying, before being sent to Japan for processing into food preservative. In the ports, the fishmeal factories grind mackerel into animal fodder. All these products will be shipped overseas as part of the Chilean export boom, a vast enterprise which has turned the country into the fastest-growing economy in Latin America and the flagship of the region's shiny new neoliberal model of development.

The phenomenon is being repeated across the region. On the runway at Guatemala City airport, a forklift truck loads boxes of leaves into a cargo plane. Within hours the lush tropical foliage will arrive in Miami, for use in the next day's flower arrangements throughout Florida. In Colombia thousands of women toil, drenched in pesticides and fertilisers, among extraordinary swathes of colour.

They are growing carnations for sale by the florists of Europe. Other, less palatable entrepreneurs have also got in on the act; one drug kingpin of Colombia's Cali cartel was convicted after 22 tons of cocaine was found hidden in consignments of frozen broccoli bound for the US.

These burgeoning 'non-traditional exports' are part of Latin America's new thrust for export-led growth, cashing in on improved transport and packing technologies to diversify the kind of primary products which have traditionally dominated Latin American exports. The other side of the export drive is an attempt to increase the exports of manufactured goods, usually low-tech products such as shoes or textiles, or the output of assembly plants, such as the *maquiladoras* strung along the US-Mexican border, where imported components are assembled by cheap Latin American labour.

The export drive lies at the heart of an ideological U-turn which has swept across Latin America, a 'Silent Revolution' which has seen market forces enthroned as the saviours of the region's economy, and the state reviled as inherently corrupt and inefficient. The revolution took off in August 1982, when Mexico slid into a debt crisis, swiftly followed by the rest of Latin America. The search for debt relief pushed the region into the arms of the IMF, which used its new-found influence to pressure governments into introducing radical market-led solutions, sometimes jokingly referred to as *Thatcherismo*.

The debt crisis marked the end of a 50-year experiment in 'import substitution', during which governments concentrated on building up local industries and supplying their domestic markets, and largely turned their backs on world trade. As in Eastern Europe and other parts of the South, state ownership failed to produce competitive industries, and by the 1970s, import substitution was fast running out of steam. Governments staved off collapse by running up huge debts, but when the crash finally came, the debt burden merely made the ensuing 'adjustment' all the more painful.

The Silent Revolution has entailed huge social costs in the shape of escalating poverty and inequality, while bringing meagre macro-economic rewards. Its supporters still promise that take-off is just around the corner but doubts are growing across the region. In trade terms, the trip to market seems to have trapped the region in a backwater of world trade as a producer of cheap raw materials for the powerful industrialised nations.

Statistics and ideological debate, as always, only tell half the story. Orchards fill the Aconcagua valley north-east of Santiago de Chile. Parallel rows of peach trees stretch off to infinity, playing tricks with the eye. The monotony is punctuated by the occasional fat-trunked palm tree or weeping willow, shining with new leaf on a cold and dusty spring day.

Carlos Vidal is a union leader, president of the local *temporeros*, the temporary farm labourers who plant, pick and pack the peaches, kiwi fruit and grapes for the tables of Europe, Asia and North America. A shock of black curls streaked with grey fringe his round, gap-toothed face. A freezing wind off the nearby Andes blows across the vineyards as Carlos tells his story.

On this land there were 48 families who got land under [former President] Allende. We grew vegetables, maize and beans together, as an *asentamiento* [farming cooperative]. There were a few fruit farms then, but we planned them. After the coup the land was divided up between 38 families - the others had to leave. Then it started to get difficult, we got the land but nothing else - the military auctioned off the machinery.

Then the *empresarios* started to arrive, especially an Argentine guy called Melitón Moreno. The bank started taking people's land - foreclosing on loans - and Moreno bought it up. Three *compañeros* committed suicide here because they lost their farms. Melitón got bank loans and bought yet more land and machinery. He planted nothing but fruit - grapes at first, then others.

My father was a leader of the *asentamiento*. The first year after the coup we were hungry, lunch was a sad time. We began to sell everything in the house, then we looked for a *patrón* to sell us seeds and plough our land for us, and we paid him with part of the harvest. Next year we got a bank loan and managed to pay it off, but the following year they sold us bad seed. We lost all the maize and the whole thing collapsed. We had to sell the land and Melitón Moreno bought it.

Of the 38 families, most are now *temporeros*. We all sold our land but kept our houses and a small garden to grow food. Trouble is, even the gardens are no good, the water's full of pesticides from the fruit. This area used to be famous for water melons and now they don't grow properly any more. They chuck fertiliser and pesticide everywhere, it doesn't matter that the earth is dead because the fruit trees live artificially. No-one grows potatoes or maize any more - it's cheaper to buy the imported ones from Argentina.

Life is hard for the *temporeros*, most of them women. 'They work you like a slave here, squeeze you dry then throw you out', says Roxana, a smartly dressed 30-year-old. She can only find work during the harvest and packing seasons, seven months in the year. The few permanent jobs all go to men, she complains. Roxana's house is a wooden hut with a tin roof, a few sticks of furniture, no heating and no glass in the windows. The family bakes in summer and freezes in winter. Cold poverty is not as blatant or exotic as the tropical poverty of Haiti or Nicaragua, but the runny-nosed children are pale and bronchitic and the cold cuts to the bone.

Carlos' allegations about pesticides have been confirmed by a series of horrific birth defects. In the regional hospital at Rancagua, investigations showed that every one of 90 babies born with a range of neural tube defects in the first nine months of 1993 was the child of a *temporera* working on the fruit farms. The Rancagua figure is three times the national average. Pesticide poisoning is a feature of non-traditional agriculture throughout the region. Women in the Colombian flower industry report miscarriages, premature births and respiratory and neurological problems, while in Ecuador 62 per cent of workers in one survey said they had suffered health disorders from exposure to pesticides at work.

The ownership of farms producing non-traditional exports varies widely. In Chile or Colombia, many are in the hands of wealthy local growers, while foreign ownership is widespread in Costa Rica. Of the 14 largest flower growers there, only two are Costa Rican. The degree of foreign control also varies according to the crop; Del Monte in Costa Rica and Dole in Honduras produce the majority of pineapples and bananas respectively, and control virtually all the transport and marketing (often the most lucrative parts of the production chain).

Ownership tends to be in the hands of rich farmers, whether local or foreign. Peasant farmers rarely have the access to technology or capital required; flower plantations, for example, require a capital investment of $80,000 per acre and few banks are prepared to lend such sums to poor farmers. When small farmers do manage to scramble aboard the export bandwagon, they run serious risks. Costa Rica's countryside is littered with failures like that of Norberto Fernández, a small farmer in the north. Norberto received a loan in 1990 to switch from growing corn for the domestic market to red peppers for export. He says that a non-traditional promoter passed through his village 'promising riches, a new car, a better house, education for my children,' if he switched crops. When his crop of red peppers came in, Norberto was told they did not meet export quality control standards. He had to sell his 30 cows to repay the loans.

There are other drawbacks to the non-traditional craze. As more and more developing countries leap aboard the bandwagon, the increased competition floods the market. As one author asked 'how many macadamia nuts or mangoes can North Americans be expected to eat, even at lower prices?' In the Aconcagua valley, growers are hacking down hectares of kiwi fruit trees because of a world glut. Chile's apple growers suffered a different kind of setback in 1993 when they triggered off a bout of first world protectionism by competing with EU producers - the EU responded to a bumper apple crop at home by virtually closing its doors to Chilean apples.

> 'The neoliberal response to falling prices resembles a hamster on a treadmill, churning out ever greater quantities of raw materials'

This is little more than a new twist to Latin America's historical travails with the terms of trade. The silent revolution has done little to reduce the region's traditional reliance on the commodity trade; two thirds of Latin America's exports still stem from agriculture or mining. With each passing year the region has had to export more and more raw materials to import the same amount of manufactured goods. One study showed that some $75bn out of the $179bn of debt accumulated by Latin America between 1980 and 1988, or 42 per cent of the total, was accounted for by the deteriorating terms of trade. The neoliberal response to falling prices resembles a hamster on a treadmill, churning out ever greater quantities of raw materials to compensate. Consumers in the northern countries reap the benefits of cheaper broccoli, fresh strawberries at Christmas or exotic tropical leaves for their winter flower arrangements, but in developmental terms, it is a strategy with no future.

One of Thatcherismo's other favourites - privatisation - helped pushed Latin America along the commodity trail, as foreign companies scooped up controlling interests in newly opened up mining sectors and rapidly boosted mineral exports.

In Chile, government economists acknowledge these limitations, and argue for a new kind of industrialisation, based on natural resources and destined for export rather than import-substitution. Chile should export wine, not grapes, and furniture instead of wood chip. By processing natural resources before selling them, Chile would capture more of the final selling price of the finished product, made up of the price of the original commodity, plus the 'value added' in turning it into something fit for a supermarket shelf. In the longer term, it should try and mimic

Finland, which successfully found a niche in the world market when it developed timber processing and paper machinery on the foundations of its forestry sector.

To date, however, the Chilean government has failed to shake off its neoliberal inferiority complex, believing that the state can only harm the economy by stepping in to protect and nurture this process. There has been sharp growth in a few areas (wine exports have grown at over 50 per cent a year for the last five years), but without a concerted government industrial policy, the leap to a broader resource-based industrialisation will never happen, even in a country as uniquely endowed with natural riches as Chile.

Cheap labour

A step across the 2000-mile US-Mexican border takes US companies into a corporate paradise of cheap labour, compliant unions, and lax environmental, health and safety regulations. Hundreds of factories have moved there from the US since the border strip was turned into a long snaking free trade zone in 1965. Since 1994 that border strip has effectively been extended to the whole of Mexico by the North American Free Trade Agreement (NAFTA).

The Border Industrialisation Program allowed export-oriented assembly plants to set up within 12.5 miles of the border. The plants paid no duties on imported parts, which they then assembled into the finished product, packaged and sold back to the US. The result by 1994 was a chain of 2,056 factories employing around 580,000 people, and a massive boost in 'Mexican' manufactured exports. In terms of the net value added (i.e. the difference in value between the imported parts and the exported final product), *maquila* exports rose from $454m in 1975 to an estimated $7bn in 1994. The 1982 debt crisis was a watershed for the *maquila* industry. When Mexico was forced to devalue the peso in 1982, the dollar value of wages fell from $1.69 an hour in 1982 to just 60 cents by 1986. This was one third of Taiwanese wage levels, and foreign investment flooded in. The 40 per cent devaluation of the Mexican peso in early 1995 brought another boom for the *maquiladoras*, which promptly increased their exports by 20 per cent in 1995.

The arguments over who wins and loses from the *maquiladoras* are heated, and central to the debate over the North American Free Trade Agreement and the rapid spread of free trade zones (also known as export processing zones) throughout Central America and the Caribbean. 'New duty-free trading zones are emerging from North America to the Southern Cone, creating opportunities for both established and emerging transnational corporations to lower production costs', gushes a brochure from the Economist Intelligence Unit, advertising its *Seizing Free Trade Opportunities in the Americas* publication, a snip at just £210 ($300) a copy. Jobs in the zones, which usually resemble industrial parks, include everything from making clothes and assembling TVs and computers to data input; doing the electronic drudgery for US supermarket chains and credit card companies. In return for setting up there, companies are allowed to import goods for final assembly and then re-export them free of taxes or restrictions on profit repatriation. The only value that accrues to the host country is that of the jobs generated in the zone and the usually low level of 'linkage' with the local economy in the form of local materials or services.

For their employees and local people in the border zone, the experience of the *maquiladoras* and other free trade zones offers pointers to what can be expected under NAFTA. Local residents have complained at the pollution created by *maquiladoras*, which are often run by 'dirty industries' fleeing the US to avoid its expensive environmental protection legislation. Individual workers complain at the low wages, ailments stemming from overwork and poor health and safety standards, minimal job security and frequent industrial injuries. But protests over such abuses have been largely ineffective, since most trade unions are in the pocket of the Mexican government, which is determined to avoid rocking the *maquiladora* boat by enforcing environmental legislation or antagonising employers. In any case, most unemployed Mexicans would jump at a job in a *maquiladora*, where conditions, although bad by first world standards, are often better than those in nationally-owned factories.

In the US, the *maquiladoras* have been used by US business to depress wages and cut costs, either by relocating to Mexico, or threatening to do so during negotiations with US employees. In the mid-1980s, General Motors' Packard Electric Division gave its employees in Cleveland Ohio a taste of things to come, when it threatened to move their jobs to Mexico unless they accepted a 62 per cent pay cut for all future employees. Since GM already had tens of thousands of workers in Mexico, it was no idle threat. Negotiations eventually reduced the cut to 43 per cent. In Centralia, Ontario, Fleck Manufacturing's employees refused to be bullied by similar threats and went on strike; hours later the plant shut down and moved to Ciudad Juárez, Mexico.

Wages in free trade zones elsewhere in the region are even lower. In Nicaragua's

Las Mercedes Industrial Free Zone, Korean and US textile companies were paying 58 cents an hour in 1993, including vacations and social security. In the Dominican Republic, hourly wages in 1990 were a mere 35 cents.

Latin American trade since 1982

Since the onset of the debt crisis in 1982, new primary products and *maquiladora*-produced manufactured goods have led the drive for the neoliberal goal of export-led growth, yet results to date have been patchy. The regional ratio of exports to GDP, often used as a guide to the importance of trade to an economy, rose from 14 per cent to 22 per cent between 1980-92, but this was partly because GDP performed so badly. Exports which had shot up seven-fold in value between 1970 and 1980 rose by just 32 per cent from 1980-93, although rebounding world commodity prices greatly improved the picture in 1994 and 95. Yet over the same period, world trade almost doubled, and Asian exports quadrupled. Latin America has continued to slide down the global pecking order as its share of world trade slipped further from 5.7 per cent to 4.0 per cent. Export-led growth is barely getting off the ground.

In the early years of the debt crisis, the IMF's standard recipe of severe devaluation and import controls in Mexico and Brazil (hardly part of the neoliberal panacea, but sins to which the IMF turned a blind eye) not only made Latin American goods more competitive on the world market, but also made imports from abroad prohibitively expensive. The result was a slump in imports and a large trade surplus, used to pay off vast sums in debt service rather than in productive investment.

From the late 1980s, under pressure from the international financial institutions, Latin America began to liberalise imports at a breakneck rate, despite the lack of any reciprocal opening from US or European governments. In all the major economies, maximum import tariffs which had typically exceeded 100 per cent were reduced to 35 per cent or less.

Neoliberals argue that liberalising imports improves economic efficiency and benefits everyone. Local factories can import the best available machinery and other inputs to improve their productivity, while consumers can shop around, rather than be forced to buy shoddy home-produced goods. Competition from abroad will force local factories either to close, or to improve their products until they become competitive with other countries' goods, paving the way for increased manufactured exports.

In practice, import liberalisation unleashed a brief consumer boom, as Latin Americans flocked to snap up imported goods at bargain prices, with a drastic impact on the region's trade balance. In the early 1990s, Mexico and Argentina ran up huge trade deficits as import bills rocketed - in Argentina imports quintupled between 1990 and 1994. Then it all came crashing down as foreign investors pulled the plug on the Mexican economy, prompting a region-wide stampede branded as the 'tequila effect'. Without foreign capital to plug the trade gap, Mexico and Argentina in particular were forced to clamp down on imports by triggering a recession, in Mexico's case coupled with a massive devaluation.

As in many other areas, the neoliberal revolution has increased inequality between countries, as the largest economies have strengthened their position and the weaker ones have fallen behind. Between 1982 and 1992 the largest economies, Brazil, Mexico and Argentina (a distant third), increased their share of Latin America's exports from 49 per cent to 61 per cent, with a similar rise in their share of imports. All countries increased their exports of low-tech manufactured goods such as furniture or footwear, but only the largest economies moved into high-tech exports such as cars, steel or electronics.

Agreeing to trade

Everybody's doing it. Since the late 1980s, Latin America's economists have been spending a large slice of their waking hours negotiating a bewildering variety of bilateral, trilateral and multilateral regional trade agreements (RTAs) with each other. By mid-1994, Latin America could boast 22 bilateral accords and several sub-regional pacts. However, the best known (and most controversial) is the only RTA between first and third worlds. The North American Free Trade Agreement, between the US, Canada and Mexico, came into force in 1994 despite fierce opposition within the US from an unlikely opposition movement including Ross Perot, the US trade union establishment and grassroots environmentalists.

RTAs enshrine comparative advantage at the heart of the economic relationship between nations. If each country sticks to what it does best, goes the argument, and imports everything else it needs, everyone will be better off. In the case of NAFTA, Mexican and US exporters and investors will obtain guaranteed access to each other's economies; Mexican consumers can enjoy the benefits of cheap food imports, the latest computer technology, and even experience the joy of an invasion of US fast food chains. According to the comparative advantage school of thought, the best option would be a free trade world, but an RTA can be a step towards it.

When signing RTAs, governments typically agree to phase out, or drastically reduce, tariff barriers between RTA members and eliminate non-tariff barriers such as import quotas. Over time, RTAs may lead to deeper forms of integration such as a customs union, which charges a common external tariff on imports from outside the RTA, a common market which allows free movement of labour and capital between members, or even a monetary union as agreed by the European Union in the Maastricht Treaty.

Within Latin America, the upsurge in RTAs has involved reviving and strengthening moribund agreements from the previous round of free trade areas in the 1960s and 1970s, such as the Andean Pact (originally made up of Bolivia, Chile, Colombia, Ecuador, Peru and Venezuela). This first generation of agreements sprang up in the 1960s in response to the difficulties experienced under import substitution, principally the limited size of domestic markets for locally-produced goods. The aim was to nurture import substitution's 'fledgling industries' by providing a large captive market for their goods (in essence an extension of import substitution's protectionism to a wider geographical area).

The early RTAs floundered and eventually collapsed at the onset of the debt crisis. Such organisations never solved import substitution's basic problem of the shortage of hard currency; Peru needed dollars, not Bolivian pesos, to buy manufactured goods and to pay its debt service. In addition, within each RTA the stronger economies tended to swamp the weak; El Salvador's industry boomed as it exported to the more backward Honduran and Nicaraguan economies, which ran up large and unpaid debts.

So why have Latin Americans turned again to RTAs as part of the solution to their troubles? Supporters of the new RTAs argue that they share a fundamentally different purpose from their forebears. The new generation of agreements aims to reap the benefits of an expanded domestic market *in order* to increase exports to the world outside. Where once they were merely a defensive laager of uncompetitive nations, RTAs are now portrayed as an 'export platform' from which to sell goods to outside markets, principally the US. Optimists also see them as a stepping stone to ever broader integration, as the different areas join up to form a single hemispheric or preferably world free trade area, such as that envisaged by the World

Trade Organisation. Tariff reductions within the RTAs are merely complementary to (and slightly greater than) the general tariff reductions taking place under structural adjustment.

In the face of recession and rising protectionism from the industrialised economies against Latin America's manufactured exports, and low commodity prices for their primary exports, RTAs within the region have several advantages. The outside world's main interest in trading with Latin America is to gain access to its raw materials, but when Latin American countries trade with each other, there is usually a much higher proportion of manufactured goods involved. In 1992, 56 per cent of intra-regional trade was in manufactured goods, compared to barely a

'RTAs are now portrayed as an "export platform" from which to sell goods to outside markets'

third of its trade with the outside world. RTAs can therefore help stimulate the industrialisation process.

In addition to reviving existing, but moribund, RTAs, numerous new ones have been created, notably the giant of Latin American integration, Mercosur (*El Mercado Común del Sur*), bringing together two big fish - Brazil and Argentina - and two minnows - Uruguay and Paraguay. Established by the Treaty of Asunción in March 1991, Mercosur introduced a common market between all four members by 1996.

Thanks to a combination of RTAs and the recovering regional economy, intra-regional trade more than doubled between 1987 and 1992, to reach $24.5bn, representing 15 per cent of the region's total trade. As a proportion of total trade, however, the recovery only restored intra-regional trade to the levels that Latin America had enjoyed on the eve of the debt crisis. By 1994 the figure was up to 19 per cent and rising.

NAFTA

On New Year's day 1994, NAFTA came in with a bang. Unfortunately for the Mexican government's public relations team, it was the sound of gunfire in the southern state of Chiapas, as 2000 fighters of the previously unknown Zapatista National Liberation Army rose in rebellion against the oldest one-party state in the world. The uprising was an extraordinary hybrid of ancient and modern. Exhausted Indian fighters speaking little Spanish slumped next to their barricades in San Cristobal de las Casas while a few yards away, tourists queued up to take cash out of the automatic teller machine. The largely indigenous rebels were protesting age-old grievances such as the discrimination against Mexico's large Indian minority, but the trigger for the uprising was the silent revolution: the government's reversal of their constitutional right to communal land, and NAFTA, which they described as a 'death certificate for the indigenous peoples'.

NAFTA is a very different entity from the proliferating Latin American RTAs. It is the first ever RTA between a first and third world economy and, in the words of one writer, 'a crucible in which advanced technology, subsistence farming, global finance capital, massive underemployment and contrasting legal and political systems are mixed for the first time'. Whereas Latin American RTAs are, at least to some degree, a marriage between equals, the disparities within NAFTA are stark. The US economy is over 20 times larger than Mexico's and the technological gulf is even wider.

NAFTA gradually eliminates almost all trade and investment restrictions between the US, Canada and Mexico over 15 years. Side agreements, concluded in August 1993, require the enforcement of some environmental and labour laws, under penalty of fines or sanctions. At its heart lies the growing incompatibility between nation states and the workings of international companies. In many ways NAFTA is a misnomer, since the bulk of the text concerns investment rather than trade, and in almost every case, it concerns Mexico, rather than the US or Canada. NAFTA opens up formerly protected areas such as mining and (partially) petroleum, it binds Mexico into strict new patent rules for pharmaceuticals and computer software and prevents Mexico from trying to delay or obstruct the repatriation of profits by transnational companies. In short, Mexican law will have to treat US and Canadian businesses exactly like Mexican companies. Mexico's 2000-mile border with the US ceases to exist for investors, though not for Mexico's would-be migrant workers, who if anything will find it harder than ever to get across.

In addition to its growing role as a cheap labour 'export platform' from which transnational corporations can export their products back to the US, Mexico also constituted an attractively large and willing market for US companies. By 1993, the average Mexican already spent $450 a year buying US products, four times more than Japanese consumers. Unfortunately for Washington, the Mexican crash of 1995 wiped out their market, as domestic recession hit demand for imports, turning Mexico's huge trade deficit rapidly into surplus. US exporters watched as their markets withered away.

NAFTA was the brainchild of Mexico's President Carlos Salinas de Gortari, who promptly became a darling of the US and international financial establishment, before going into an equally swift decline after leaving office. By mid-1996 his brother was under house arrest on suspicion of laundering drug money and Salinas was nowhere to be seen, but was rumoured to be keeping his head down somewhere in the US.

Although Salinas and his predecessor Miguel de la Madrid had pushed through a free market/ free trade transformation of the Mexican economy since the debt crisis hit in 1982, there was as yet nothing to stop future presidents reversing the process. Now, NAFTA will 'lock in' Mexico to an agreement with the US by making it much more costly to revert to statist or protectionist models. It also locks in the US at a time of rising protectionist sentiment in Washington, thereby ensuring that Mexico will be inside the fold should the US ever return to its isolationist past. With each year that passes under NAFTA, the three economies will become more integrated, and the economic and political price of prising them loose will rise ever higher.

Salinas hoped that locking in neoliberal reforms via NAFTA would make Mexico a far safer prospect for foreign investors deciding where to locate their factories and banks, or whether to make loans or buy shares in Mexican companies. But his hopes proved short-lived when the Achilles heel of Mexico's adjustment programme - its huge trade deficit, plugged with short term foreign investment - finally proved its undoing. As the Mexican economy went into free fall in 1995, two million Mexicans lost their jobs, and foreign investors saw local demand disappear in the recession. Their loss proved the *maquiladoras'* gain, since Mexico's devaluation once again sent the dollar value of Mexican wages crashing. The factories created 150,000 new jobs during 1995, taking total employment up to 700,000, but barely denting the two million jobs lost in the recession over the year.

The rest of Latin America has watched the coming of NAFTA with anxiety. Although the US has always stressed its intention that the agreement should be but the first step on the road to creating a free trade area 'from Alaska to Tierra del Fuego', the initial impact on other countries in the region was negative. Governments in Central America and the Caribbean are particularly vulnerable. Within months of NAFTA coming into effect, they had seen textile factories, which formed a crucial part of their drive for non-traditional exports in the 1980s, relocating to Mexico.

Those hoping to extend NAFTA to the rest of the region received a boost in December 1994, when President Clinton went to Miami to host the 'Summit of the Americas' with every Latin American head of state bar Fidel Castro. Despite earlier fears that rising protectionism within the US might prevent any further agreements, the summit agreed to establish a 'Free Trade Area of the Americas' by the year 2006. In a separate announcement, the NAFTA members also announced the beginning of talks with Chile over its accession to the agreement. Clinton predicted that at current trends, the hemispheric RTA would by then 'be the world's largest market - more than 850 million consumers buying $13 trillion of goods and services'.

Despite the statements made in Miami, however, the 2005 deadline for the completion of negotiations is not binding, and the fate of the Free Trade Area of the Americas is bound to be hostage to political developments in the intervening years. Already the Mexican crash has prompted growing doubts about the merits of NAFTA, and protectionism is once again on the rise within the US Congress.

Winners and losers under NAFTA

Politicians and pressure groups have conducted the heated debate over NAFTA in terms of which countries will win or lose from the deal, but in fact all three countries contain both winners and losers. Assessments of NAFTA are more about positions in the economic pecking order than about nationality. Opponents have dubbed the agreement a corporate bill of rights which seeks to maximise business profits by setting worker against worker.

Chief among the beneficiaries are the US corporations who can cut costs by relocating to Mexico, or move in to supply the Mexican market . US consumers will also benefit from cheaper agricultural imports from Mexico. In Mexico the *maquiladoras* will generate jobs and the larger Mexican companies will be able to take advantage of guaranteed access to the US market. Mexican consumers will be able to buy cheap US grain for their tortillas.

The greatest losers in terms of numbers are the Mexican peasantry, two million of whom will find their home-grown maize undercut by US agribusiness. Smaller producers elsewhere in the economy are also likely to be wiped out by cheap US imports. North of the border, unions will face an acceleration in the southwards flight of jobs.

Conclusion

Any shift of the magnitude of Latin America's silent revolution is bound to create winners and losers. In macroeconomic terms, the region has seen meagre gains in the form of renewed, if sluggish growth. But this has been bought at the cost of enormous increases in poverty and inequality in a region that was already the most unequal in the world. In the longer term, seduction by the siren calls of comparative advantage has led Latin America away from the road to admittedly flawed industrialisation, and back into a position in the world economy based on exporting its raw materials and cheap labour. It is a position it has occupied since the Spanish Conquest, and which history suggests is unlikely to lead the region towards the golden future of prosperity and equality promised by the apostles of the market .

Notes from a journey to South Africa

David Goldblatt

West London, 12.10.95, 9.15 am

'Mr and Mrs Mthembu (residents of KwaMashu township, Northern Durban, factory and domestic worker respectively) invite you to the marriage of their daughter Phumzile Mthembu (COSATU arts worker turned trauma counsellor) and Alex Slater (English public schoolboy, political journalist, DJ and committed herbhead). 11.00am sharp, Paradise Valley Nature Reserve, Durban, Natal.' David Goldblatt (London Jew of long lost South African descent) to attend as best man. People ask me what it will involve. I have no idea. I read some history and buy a suit.

Southern Natal, 31.12.95. 11.00 am

In a heavily loaded station wagon we pull onto the coastal drag of the N2. After three days on the road from Cape Town, the final stretch to Durban. We skirt past Port Shepstone. On Christmas day a few k from here 800 IFP militia paid a call on Shoshashobane squatter camp. They burnt the place down. Twenty dead, hundreds wounded, thousands homeless. On the four-lane motorway, caught in the swarm of traffic, there is no sense that you are in a war zone. But we are. Three quarters of South Africa's murders happen here. Welcome to Kwazulu-Natal, the new province Buthelezi would like to run like the old Bantustan. The heat of the day is rising exponentially but no amount of sun can burn off the dense moisture of the

Indian Ocean. Behind the windscreen we start to swelter, watching the landscape change at an ever faster rate. Seaside towns, Margate and Scottburgh, with their strips of beach, hotel, buggies and *booikies*. Surf culture is in the air, on the road and riding the waves. Every town, every strip of commercial development, is paralleled on the other side of the road by its township. The vegetation is lush and deliberately placed, but it is pierced by breeze blocks, polythene sheets and wide dirt roads, by lines of hitchers and fruit sellers, and boys hunched on the hard shoulder poised to race across when the traffic drops. There are no crossings. South Africa's horrific road accident statistics are reported daily on the radio.

The road widens to six lanes and the Durban industrial corridor gathers pace alongside. I am in sociological overdrive. Late industrialisation in tooth and claw. The landscapes of the bricked-up and torn down West Midlands, the lunar greenfield Nissan boxes of Tyneside, dissolve. Factories, warehouses, factories, goods yards, factories, generators - the whole infrastructure of manufacturing hugs the road lined by pylons, cables and wirenetted fencing. Awesome and empty. Today is a holiday, but there is no mistaking the crucible in which a working-class is forged. And then on the hillock, the apartheid twist. Looking down on the corrugated metal rooftops, smoke stacks and ventilators - hostels. Red brick, unadorned, flat roofed on bare ground. Four storeys high, twelve tiny windows to a floor, seven in a row. Fenced round and wired up tightly. Thin figures on the slopes in their shadow on the iron flights of stairs, smoking and talking. I find myself using unfamiliar, almost biblical langauge.

Umgeni Road, Northern Durban, 31.12.95, 1.30 pm

800,000 people on one of Durban's poorest, hilliest plots of land, and no road signs. The only white people that used to come here were the army and they had their own maps. KwaMashu finally has road signs. We take the slip road, go on pot-hole alert, and merge with the stream of black taxis and beaten corporation buses. KwaMashu went ballistic in 1985. ANC street committees and Inkatha militia in the few hostels on its outskirts fought each other and the army for control of the streets. These days it is predominantly ANC, which may help to explain why the KwaZulu Natal provincial government has been so slow to spend any money here. But it means a certain kind of peace. Plain old criminal violence rather than political violence. Tootsicomrades - youthful freedom fighters turned gangster. The

89

phones have been out for over two weeks now - someone stealing cables for copper scrap - so we don't know what the mood is. More likely than not it will be OK, but Natal is volatile enough for it to be otherwise. The road begins to twist across the low but steep hills of Newlands East. An Indian township, untidy and cramped low brick bungalows, patches of affluence, Hindi temples, the odd swimming pool. Then, across the ridge, Newlands West with its waves of the characteristic state-ordained housing for coloured people, three storey, beige plaster. We mount another hill, a burst of unruly vegetation alongside, and there below and around is KwaMashu. The industrial districts of Phoenix and Inanda lie on the horizon. Outcrops of newly arrived squatter camps are erupting on its edges, filled by war refugees as much as economic migrants. 100,000 tin-roof, matchbox African order dwellings, seven to ten people to each, plenty with plenty more. Alex sort of remembers the way. We look for C section - the new maps have given the old sections names but it turns out that no one is using them. We're somewhere in the D thousands when we should be in the C twelve hundreds, then we're in E section. We panic a little. The kids we ask for directions are more confused or more frightened then we are. Finally a landmark catholic church. C1299, the Mthembu's. We are met with cheers and embraces, quizzical neighbours, and a detailed debriefing on our trip. Boiled chicken, steam bread, tea.

KwaMashu, 02-05. 01.96

Family have been arriving all week. We endlessly ferry mothers, brothers, sisters, cousins, nephews and nieces from Durban airport to all points KwaMashu. Too many trips, not enough cars, not enough people who know the way and can navigate KwaMashu's roads. The policy is that a car full of white people is not always politic - depending on time of day, route and context. We constantly tread the line between security and paranoia, liberal optimism and local experience. We 'make a plan' as all South Africans seem to say whenever faced by difficulty, inconvenience or intractable problems. The faith in inspired improvisation is infectious. C1299 is heaving with friends and neighbours, invited and uninvited. The temperature is in the thirties, but on some days the cloud is so dense we hardly see the sun. We all swelter together. Mrs Mthembu organises and orchestrates from behind the sewing machine, takes measurements, holds sittings, sips at her brandy. Every room is taken and she retires after and wakes before me all week. I never establish whether she manages to sleep and, if she does, where.

Alex, Phumzile and I frantically live by our lists and phone cards, notes and memos. The social and economic geography of Durban ensures that everything is much more difficult than it should be. Phumzile's brothers and sisters are sent off on errands, shift rooms, book buses, soothe nerves, move beds, adjust and accommodate. Car hire in downtown, caterers in Umgeni, the search for barrelled beer and crates of industrial frozen chicken. Wood to heat the grey smoky Zulu beer brewing at the side of the house involves an iffy trip to B section, said by some to be PAC territory. The goat arrives, the ox arrives with Mr Mtombela - the Mthembu's leathery negotiator. Its thinness is remarked upon, but this is an urban ox from Inanda or Phoenix. It would have been better to go to northern Natal, but there is war going on there. Mr Mthembu and I discuss its merits, how to kill the goat, the significance of the ox's horns, the blessing of the ancestors and the virtues of menthol cigarettes. Money is missing from bank accounts. What happened to the transfer, searching for banks and forms and documents - we'll make a plan. How will we get the food to the wedding? Have we enough caterers? No, definitely not, the last plan did not quite work out. Mpu tries to round up volunteers to work through the night. Networks are mobilised, friends called upon, favours called in, new obligations established and options investigated. Relatives ring who have not received invitations, things to be smoothed out, differences to be negotiated. Notorious local freeloaders and professional wedding guests are identified and repelled.

Will there be speeches after lunch? Will the families exchange traditional gifts before or after? Will there be music then or later? People pause over the idea of a Quaker wedding service - no priest, short vows, silence. Then it clicks - if the spirit takes you, address the meeting. No Zulu speaker is phased by the idea of speeches, performance and an audience. Conversation is mainly in Zulu. Alex picks up the basics and we get selected highlights that always seem insufficient accounts of the dialogue, the gestures, the positions being outlined and the ground being staked. In the front garden, in the back yard amongst the chickens and the washing, in the crowded bedrooms, around the sitting room table, along the wall by the shower, we gather, meet, disperse, debate, assess. This is wedding by committee, but multiple overlapping committees, no one person knows everything that is happening, more than one plan is being made all the time. Conversation, huddle and conclave are the points of co-ordination. Talk is the medium of social solidarity. In a quiet moment Thanxolo, Alex and I pick over the differences on a point of translation. Thanxolo, for whom Zulu is his mother tongue, shakes his head in disbelief, 'My Zulu is not good. I do not always understand it. It is so deep, so deep.' Last minute shifts: food to come in a taxi from D section. I run through the plan with Shiekle the MC, chorister, bank-clerk and neighbourhood lynchpin. Duncan the juggling engineer from Zimbabwe arrives, late as always.

Johannesburg Airport, 10.01.96, 3.00 pm

Frankie drives me across the North Johannesburg suburbs. Slipways become freeways become loops, twist through a clover leaf and turn to dual carriageway. We take the scenic route, Frankie gives me a running commentary on the sites: malls, shopping centres, new superfortress block housing developments, the Holiday Inn. When the architectural features slip out of sight and all that is left is the residential prairie, we move on to comparative property prices. Fairways is somewhere in this horizontal grid. We drive up to their block. Two gates, security guard, underground car-park. Every flat is burglar barred, every flat has two doors, one discreetly signed - service. We discuss the problems of carrying such a large and complex bundle of keys.

The flat is white, white, white. Carpets, sofa, walls, linens - except of course for Nancy, the domestic worker from Alexandra. Sheila, my cousin, ran a boutique down the road for years. Frankie was in textiles. Now they're here in paradise, retired, comfortable and paranoid. This seems to be the deal. They hover between bitterness and resignation, though even Sheila has been charmed by the good looks and smooth talk of Cyril Ramaphosa, the ANC's general secretary. We spend the afternoon trading family history, trying to keep clear of politics, eating scones and chocolate cake. But why and how Alex and Phumzile got married, and how I could live with Africans for a week, are charged questions. Frankie asks me in authentic disbelief, 'When did you acquire such a...such an Africanist point of view?'. We find common ground on the subjects of of death and dying, illness, hospitals and funerals. My mum's, Frankie's, Sheila's parents. Excitedly, we retrace my grandfather's movements. School in Ladysmith, runs away to Mozambique after the First World War. Joins the British army in India, goes Awol two years later. Sheila hasn't done this with anyone for some time. I realise that the family here has fragmented. The clan I was expecting has long since been frayed by geography, labour market and family feud. We tie some skeins together. The trail gets confused after this. Time in Hong Kong or Shanghai - my Grandfather could always count to ten in what he said was Chinese - time in the merchant navy. Then, in 1931, he turns up on the door of Sheila's family, Ealing West London and works in their cinema business. Meets my grandmother, never leaves, never writes, never follows Sheila back to Jo'burg. I am left with the questions: Who would I have been had he done so? Would I have done the right thing here? Frankie has been digging through the old photo boxes too. Waving an old theatre programme 'Des O'Connor, I saw him at the Palladium in 1959. When you could really go somewhere on the Rand. Fantastic'.

Grant, my younger cousin, comes and saves me - we go out for a night on the dual carriageways and burger bars of Randburg. Stop off at his amazingly authentic English pub on a long strip of car dealerships - horse brasses, shelves of books and pewter junk. Pissed Scotsman and England losing at cricket are familiar, outdoor pool tables are not. We end up on Fountain Hill, topped by an old concrete water tower. A lone peak in the surburban flat lands. White teenage hippies smoke, snog and chatter, invisible drunk Afrikaaners crack open another can. Grant translates - they are arguing about women. We all stare out on the daisy chains and fairylights of the autosprawl below. KwaMashu grass turns them kaleidoscopic, blue and green.

Johannesburg, 11.01.96 11.00am

Frankie, Sheila and I drive to Brixton on the northern edge of downtown, behind the characteristically ugly public sector architecture of SABC's HQ and television studios. An old wooden hall marks the entrance to this Jewish cemetery, long full up. The gilt on the star of David above the double doors is pretty thin, but the floors and the gilded wall boards of benefactors are newly polished. Somewhere, here, is my great grandfather. We check the book, plot 1364, Isadore Goldblatt, died 1933. And there it is. It's the biggest stone in the place, seven foot high, red and brown stone, stark black letters unmissably read GOLDBLATT. In the near distance the office towers and strict grid of downtown, beneath my feet the red earth of southern Africa. Everyone's story has to start somewhere. Mine starts here.

Johannesburg, 11.01.96, 7.00pm

The freeway heading East to Jo'burg International. The signs rushing by overhead still say Jan Smuts. Grant laughs and violently exhales the last of his joint. 'Don't worry, you can say goodbye to all the Heindrik Verwoord Avenues... when they get around to it'. We are speeding through rain so dense that the endless line of heavy trucks beside us is hidden by a curtain of driving water. The huge plates of rain that have covered the road in front of us are invisible until we feel the car shuddering through them. Grant makes me nervous. 'Where are my Stuyvesants?'. His bare knees hold the bottom of the steering wheel as he stretches across the dashboard, blindly tapping around on the black plastic shelves for the packet. My feet press harder on imaginary brake pedals. The weight of traffic is only revealed by a massive streak of lightning. Transvaal storms are epic. The black and purple arches of the sky are rent every few seconds by a fork of crackling white lightning. My eyes are pinballs from lightning to speedometer to sky to the road to Grant grasping his soft pack and lighting up, knees still on the wheel.

On our left is Sandton - another paranoid suburb. But not just any other suburb, this is Jo'burg's Beverly Hills. As Sheila said to me 'The best people live here. The best hotels are here and oh, Frankie, look. There's that new cluster compound, its almost finished'. Frankie, 'Boy, that'll cost you, that'll cost you.' Sandton also boasts the most luxurious and fortified mall in the northern suburbs, Sandton City. You can't get in on foot. The complex lies in a maze of dual carriageways and slip roads without pavements. Brick ramps run up into the portcullis entrances of the first and second floors. Arrow slit windows dot the giant walls of the complex. Only high above, in the crenellated towers and walkways, do proper panes of glass appear. Inside it's wall to wall cappuccino, expensive shopping and squeaky clean courtyards framing a square of sky. On our right - Alexandra. One of the few inner-city townships to escape the bulldozer, it remains in the heart of the Jo'burg suburbs. A quarter of a million people crammed into a bowl half the size of Sandton and one of the most organised and militant centres of The Struggle in the Greater Johannesburg area. The dense lattice-work of street lights in Randburg and Sandton gives way to a pool of darkness. Only the two main roads that bisect Alex are lit. Along the horizon the last of the sun leaves an intense red strip illuminating the slow swirls of coal smoke. They disappear into the canopy of smog that hovers above.

Metisse Narratives

Jayne Ifekwunigwe

Jayne Ifekwunigwe *discusses the testimonies of women of 'mixed race' parentage in the English-African diaspora.*

It is out of chaos that new worlds are born

Audre Lorde

In the world through which I travel, I am endlessly creating myself

Frantz Fanon

Two little six year old girls have been separated from their peers for disrupting the Nando afterschool project on the outskirts of Thatchapee. Sandra has a white English mother and a black Jamaican father. She has blonde curly hair, hazel eyes and a complexion the colour of milky English tea. Her comrade Aneya has a white English mother and a black Libyan father. She has black curly hair, dark brown eyes and colouring reminiscent of roasted almonds. I am sitting at the table with them as they talk about their friends, various members of their family, as well as what they are going to do over the weekend since today is Friday. Aneya says to Sandra, who has been talking about her father who lives just outside Bristol, 'He's White isn't he?' She knows Sandra's Mum is White English like hers, since the two families often play together. Sandra says, 'No, he's Bl...' She begins to say 'Black', and then says, 'I mean dark brown'.[1]

Rather than representing a portrait of *métisse* ('mixed race') girls as unruly, at age six Sandra and Aneya have exposed the major problematic of 'race'. Their

---

1. Thatchapee is the fictional name for the multiethnic community where from 1990-1992 I conducted ethnographic research on the politics of identities for multigenerational *métis(se)* ('mixed race') families in Bristol.

discussion highlights the cultural paradoxes of 'race' and colour which multiple generations of women, men and children in England silently negotiate in their everyday lives. These individuals descend from lineages which cut across so-called different 'black and white' 'races', ethnicities, cultures, and classes. Their roots are both endogenous and exogenous.

In varied cultural and historical contexts, countless terms are employed to name such individuals - mixed 'race', mixed heritage, mixed parentage, *mestizo*, *mestiza*, *mulatto*, *mulatta*, creole, coloured, mixed racial descent, etc. I deploy the terms *métisse* (f), *métis* (m), *métissage* which more appropriately describe generations of individuals who by virtue of birth and lineage do not fit neatly into preordained sociological and anthropological categories. In England, at the moment, there are a multitude of terms in circulation which describe individuals who straddle racial borders. More often than not, received terminology either privileges presumed 'racial' differences ('mixed race') or obscures the complex ways in which being *métis(se)* involves *both* the negotiation of constructed 'black'/ 'white' racial categories *and* the celebration of converging cultures, continuities of generations and over-lapping historical traditions. The lack of consensus as to which term to use, as well as the limitations of this discursive privileging of 'race' at the expense of generational, ethnic, and cultural concerns, led me to *métis(se)* and *métissage*.

In the French African (Senegalese) context, in its conventional masculine and feminine forms, *métis(se)* refers to someone who by virtue of parentage embodies two or more world views, i.e. white French mother and black Senegalese father. However, it is not exclusively a 'racial' term used to differentiate individuals with one black parent and one white parent from those with two black or white parents. *Métis(se)* also pertains to people with parents from different ethnic/cultural groups within a country: i.e. in Nigeria, Ibo and Yoruba or in Britain, Scottish and English. That is, the term recognises the specificity of ethnicities as they are maintained and redefined within national borders. By extension, *métissage* is a mind set or a shorthand way to describe the theorising associated with *métis(se)* subjectivities: oscillation, contradiction, paradox, hybridity, polyethnicities, multiple reference points, 'belonging nowhere and everywhere'. *Métissage* also signals the process of opening up hybrid spaces and looking at the sociocultural dynamics of 'race', gender, ethnicity, nation, class, sexuality and generation, and their relationship to the mechanisms of power.[2]

The traditional stance is that this 'condition' requires theorising which is both psychopathological and victimising. Rarely are viewpoints articulated which frame *métis(se)* individuals' or families' lived daily realities from the vantage point of agency and empowerment. By demonstrating the myriad everyday ways in which first generation *métis(se)* individuals and their families in Bristol transcend and blur racial, ethnic, national, class, gender and generational boundaries, this article begins to crack the so-called 'mixed race' conundrum. The personal testimonies of project participants point to the many contradictions in state and popular 'thinking' about, 'race', nation, culture, and, most notably, family. Each of their stories transforms conventional British and English notions of place and belonging.

The rich marrow at the centre of this complex concern is the alternative identity narratives created by the recovery and reclamation of interwoven, multiethnic and multicultural histories. These reinterpretations run parallel with the master discourse of biological racism, which is predicated on perceived physical (phenotypic) differences rather than genetic (genotypic) inheritances. Moreover, within this master discourse, there is no scope for differential family forms which emerge from the convergence of different languages, religions, and cultures - that which is frequently subsumed under the heading of 'different races'.

This article confronts head on the 'bi-racialised' - one is either 'Black' or 'White' and never the twain shall meet - and lived challenges facing polyethnic, polycultural, post-imperial Britain and England as we limp towards the twenty-first century. I will be drawing on the project participants' narratives of identities, as well as theoretical developments in feminist/postmodernist theories. The testimonies signal the retrieval of cultural memory and identities. They also exemplify non-hierarchical discourses of differences and alterities which remain critical of the binary idioms of colour and the pseudo-scientific paradigms of 'race'.

I want to introduce the textual strategy of the *griot(te)*. In so doing I wish to acknowledge and work with inherent tensions in ethnography between the spoken and the written word. *Griot(te)* (*griot* (m) and *griotte* (f)) is a West African term which describes someone who functions as a tribal poet, storyteller, historian or genealogist. Their role is to recount culturally specific and provocative parables of

---

2. See Jayne Ifekwunigwe, *Scattered Be-Longings: The Cultural Paradoxes of 'Race', Nation, Gender and Generation in the English-African Diaspora*, Routledge, London forthcoming.

daily life. My claim is that, because of contradictory bi-racialised classification in Britain, *métis(se)* individuals' narratives both reflect the gender, generational, racial, and ethnic tensions of the society within which they live, and are located outside them in an imagined but not imaginary 'grey' space. And I argue that the women I worked with tell their stories as newfangled *griottes*. They simultaneously construct dual narratives, which embody individual and collective historical consciousness. They tell their own lived stories. At the same time, their memories preserve and reinterpret senses of past interwoven cultures. These recollections provide scathing sociopolitical commentaries and cultural critiques of contemporary English African Diasporic life, and its manifest bi-racialised problematics.

The *griottes* of Bristol

Collected and audiotaped over a two year period in Bristol, the personal narratives of twenty five women and men are the pivotal points on which this kaleidoscopic portraiture of An-Other Britain turns. Their evocative testimonies illuminate many of the cultural paradoxes in received thinking about 'race', nation, gender and generation in the English and British-African Diaspora.

However, in order to illuminate the intricate nuances between sisters, and the indelible impress of the mother or mother-surrogate, this text will shine the spotlight on six of the twenty five participants. The featured storytellers include two sets of sisters: Northumberland-Yoruba Bisi and Yemi; Scouse Irish-Bajan Akousa and Sarah, and two women who grew up in children's homes - Nigerian-English Ruby who grew up in London and German-Tanzanian Similola, brought up in Cardiff. Though the dialogic re-telling of these narratives of identities took place in Bristol over a two year period, the actual settings of the six featured narratives are urban working-class Liverpool and suburban London; the outskirts of Cardiff and middle-class post-independence Ibadan in Nigeria.

This is a very old story: recollected events reflect the decades of racialised folly in Britain, Barbados, Nigeria, and Tanzania. Historically in these regions, forced and voluntary mating between the black African and Amerindian 'hosts' (primarily women) and their white European/British 'visitors' (primarily men) spawned previous generations of *métis(se)* people. In sixteenth, seventeenth and eighteenth century Britain, the 'bi-racialised' tables of gender turned when imported black servants (primarily men) consorted with the local English population (primarily women). It is by navigating these murky historical waters that one discovers earlier generations of *métis(se)* communities in Britain, which pre-date the emergence of late nineteenth and early twentieth century longstanding sea-faring *métis(se)* communities in Liverpool and Tiger Bay in Cardiff. These former acts of 'transgression' are visible in the immense phenotypic diversity of Caribbean and African American people, and to a certain extent in continental African people (i.e. the coloured communities in Namibia, Zimbabwe and South Africa or the creole communities in Mauritius or Madagascar). This historical fact is tucked away in official accounts of so-called intercultural 'contact'.

Yet this oversight produces a profound paradox which underpins my entire intellectual project. That is, how can one talk about hybridity and so-called mixing, when the so-called black and white populations that are 'coming together' have not been 'pure' for centuries? I do not seek a way out of this quandary in the vagaries of 'race' science. Rather, plausible explanations are located within a postmodern logic which assumes that 'race' is an imaginary social and cultural construction. This invention of 'race' wields enormous power. 'Race', in its invidious operationalised form, produces racism, which as a mindset creates 'bi-racialisation' - power and prestige for some and disadvantage and discrimination for others.

This article showcases the lives of six extraordinary women - Ruby, Similola, Akousa, Sarah, Bisi, and Yemi. Through their black continental African (Nigerian or Tanzanian) or black African-Caribbean (Bajan (from Barbados)) fathers and white British (Irish or English) or white European (German) mothers, they claim rather than acquire both indigenous and exogenous roots. They belong both and neither 'here' and 'there'. By virtue of lineage, they can situate themselves within at least two specific and yet over-lapping historical narratives. However, rigid and irrational 'bi-racialisation' in Britain deems it possible for them to own just black - *not and white* - social identities.

Nonetheless, their powerful narratives of identities and families form the foundation for their individual constructions of place and belonging in post-slavery Bristol. In specific historical, social and cultural contexts, each *griotte* names herself as a dynamic agent actively engaged in the shaping and moulding of her identity. Within her repertoire, she describes strategies for resisting societal attempts to contain her, and addresses Diaspora(s)-driven tensions among being and becoming 'black', being and becoming African or Caribbean, and being and becoming English and/or British. In turn, by writing themselves back into the centres and not the margins of histories, their stories function as heightened representations of the individual and collective angst facing all people living in the (African) Diaspora(s).

Ruby

Many factors influence the ways in which white women accomplish the task of bringing up so-called *black (métis(se))* children. The circumstances surrounding the birth of the *métis(se)* child, the prevailing attitudes towards *métis(se)* relationships, class background, all affect the uniqueness of experiences. Ruby is white English and black Nigerian and was brought up in a children's home outside London until she left at age sixteen, even though both her birth mother and other blood relatives were alive. Their rationale for placing her there was they wanted her to 'have a proper growing up experience'. However, there was an overwhelming shame surrounding her birth. Her father was married and black African, which made it impossible for Ruby's birth mother and grandmother to fully accept her. From childhood to adulthood, the consistent thread running through Ruby's narratives is the relentless search for a place to belong which resulted from this early rejection. In the following excerpt, she recounts the ways in which, within her own family, that is among her husband and children, she remains an outsider, branded by her 'Blackness':

> The politics of 'race' is different for each of us. It's one thing to me, it's another thing to John, it's another thing to each of the children. Before John met me, I was aware that most of his girlfriends had been non-English. At that time I didn't really think much of it, but after I was married to him and had lots of years to reflect, I thought, I wonder what that's about? John likes black people. More than most people I guess. Now I know him very well, it would be very logical for him to marry someone non-white. He would be the first to admit that he gets a lot out of it. He probably gets a lot more out of it being married to me than I get being married to him, from that point of view.
>
> At the time that I married him, I didn't know any black people anyway. So it wasn't the case that I knocked around with black people and white people and made a conscious decision to marry a white man. It wasn't like that. It was that he was in the circle I mixed in, which was all white. 'Cause up until that time, I had always lived in a white situation. I had always been the odd token black. So, I hadn't had any thoughts about making conscious choices about white men or black men or black communities or white communities. It just hadn't come up in my life.

When we had children, I fully expected my children to be black. At least to be dark, apparently non-white. My first daughter Pauline is about the darkest of them. She has Afro features, in as much as she has dark curly hair. It's not curly like mine though, it's much more like the perms Europeans go to have done - pretty little curls. She has very dark eyes, but in fact she looks more like John's side of the family. She doesn't have particularly negroid features, although people think she looks most like me when they don't look very closely. Just because of the colouring, that's all, because she's dark. The other two are fair, so they are not apparently like me at all.

She was born. First of all, she was my daughter, and that was the most important thing. I was surprised that she wasn't darker than she was. When the second one was born, she was outrageously fair - she had very blonde hair and looked very much like John - not a bit like me. When the third one was born, Jake, what I first thought when he came out, when I saw him, was 'Oh, it's me Dad.' Because he just had a very negroid face. He's as white as the rest, but he has a very negroid face. He does have curly hair, but it's fair hair. Well, in fact it's light brown now, but when he was little it was very blonde. But he has got negroid features. I suppose it's only as they have been growing up that it came to me. That I was the one black member in a totally white household. Even though it's my husband and my own children, it still left me as the only black person in the household.

Similola

Similola is white German and black Tanzanian. She grew up in a Welsh children's home wherein she was made to feel that being white and whiteness were the ideal standards by which she should measure her self worth. In the long run, she knew she could never be completely white and being white-identified always seemed to lead to disappointment and rejection for her. The following testimony addresses this pain:

When I was growing up, the main influence was the house mother in the children's home, who totally dominated my life up until I was sixteen years old. Her views were my views. She was a very strict disciplinarian, very very strong, and also very very racist, and she made me have a low opinion of myself. She had never had any black children in her care before. She had me when I was very very young.

Obviously they considered me to be very cute and pretty and I was spoiled. In fact the other children used to hate me because I was so spoiled and always got my own way. As I got older - you know what children are like - they start being naughty. Then you get to be a teenager and you want to assert yourself. I couldn't do that. She'd built me up into feeling like a wonderful competent person. Because of all that attention I had been getting and because I was pretty and cute and did everything I was told. Then, when I started rebelling, probably from about the age of eight, she turned on me.

I'd never noticed before I was about twelve that I was that different from the other kids at school. It never occurred to me. I was always treated as being white. I don't remember being treated any differently until twelve, thirteen, and suddenly my hair was wrong, my lips were too big, my temper was because of the black blood in my veins. Everything that I did that was wrong was somehow related to my colour. I didn't have friends because people didn't like me...this is what I was told. I took all this in and it was very difficult to come to terms with. It's quite a shock when you're that age to suddenly realise you are very different from everyone else, and it seemed to be hitting me from all sides.

I'd realise that there were teachers at school that would pick on me for no reason and I'd think why, and of course it started falling into place, it was because I was different from the other kids. I wasn't white, and kids started calling me names. I'd be walking along the road and I'd get called 'Blackie', and 'jungle bunny' and 'chocolate drop'. These names cut through me. I was the only person in the whole town who was being called these names and I felt very singled out and couldn't understand it.

I felt very hurt and also humiliated. When I realised that was going on, I just wanted to crawl into a shell and die. Instead of seeing the positive advantages of being mixed race all I could see were the worst sides. I used to literally go to bed at night and cry and pray to god to let me wake up white. I used to do that because I was getting such heavy shit all around me, and I'd changed from being a happy outgoing child. I became very inward looking and detached.

One day I was coming down the stairs and heard my housemother talking to her friends. I noticed she'd stopped taking me out so much any more. I think it came up in conversation with her friend. Her friend said, 'Are you taking Similola?' or something. I heard her say, 'Oh no, people might' - she must have watched a programme on TV or something because it suddenly came to her - and I heard her say 'I can't because people might think I'm married to a black man'. So, she made it sound so disgusting and she never ever ever took me out after that. She never did.

If I had been black rather than half-black I'd either have been totally crushed or I'd have known I didn't have to identify with white people and found my own identity, because I knew I was different. But because of that, she made me want to deny half of my identity. I did, I really wanted to. Why, why, why? I've been punished by god. Why do you do this to me? It's as if he said, 'You can have some of being white but not all of it'.

Akousa

Akousa is white Irish and black Bajan (from Barbados) and grew up in Liverpool amid a strong African Caribbean community, and with her white Irish mother and her brother and sister. She is a Rastafarian woman and yet not everyone sees her as a Rastafarian. She sees herself as a 'light-skinned black' woman, and yet certain members of both black and white communities refuse to accept her as black. Consequently, most of Akousa's commentaries on her emergent bi-racial consciousness bring to the forefront what I refer to as 'the social chameleon' phenomenon. In general, 'a social chameleon' has strategically adapted and adopted different 'presentations of "race"' to correspond to particular societal assumptions, norms and expectations. In particular, *métis(se)* people such as Akousa, with so-called 'ambiguous' phenotypes - i.e. very fair complexions, blue, green or hazel eyes, more 'pointed/sharp' facial features, light coloured or straight hair - can 'change colour' from one social context to the next. In light of contradictory 'English' and related 'non-English' attitudes towards 'race', colour and citizenship Akousa has described herself or has been described as *métis(se)*, white and black:

Gettin' into me late teens, I didn't think much about meself because of all these conflicts that were startin' to come up from the past. Also new ones that were comin' in from other communities - black communities - that were really shockin' me. I mean there were times when I wouldn't show me legs. I'd go through the summer wearing tights and socks. Cause I thought they were too light and too white-lookin'. There was a lot of pressure. I remember one day I was leanin' up somewhere and this guy said to me, 'Boy, aren't your legs white.'

I just looked in horror, and felt really sick and wanted to just run away. I was thinkin', God why didn't you make me a bit darker? Why did you make me so light? It took me years to reconcile that.

Because of what happened in the 1970s in terms of the Black Power movement, especially in this country, if you weren't black like ebony then you just didn't have a chance basically. The other thing was the Marcus Garvey philosophy - at the end of the day Marcus Garvey was a man of his time, I could understand where he was coming from. But I'm sure he would have seen things differently now. It was the most difficult time of my life - trying to sort out who I was now. Whereas, before, I thought I knew who I was. My family comes from the Caribbean. I never brought me Mum into question. She seemed to take things in her stride. I kept comin' home and I'd say to her, 'I hate all white people...Tonkers, or honkies, or whatever.' There's me Mum sittin' there, and I just didn't think about it. It's hard work, but she's me mother. I don't think of her in terms of ... 'me Mum, she's white, I shouldn't be sayin' these things'.

But on the other hand, me Mum never told me that I was 'half-caste' or 'half-breed' or anythin like that. She saw me as a whole person. She told me, 'When you go out in the street, they're goin' to call you "nigger", they're not goin' to call you "light-skinned" or somethin' like that. They'll call you "black bastard". No matter how light or how dark you are, that's the vibe'.

So, I didn't really think about it. I could think now, at a certain point in time, it really must have hurt her. She managed to deal with it somehow. I don't know. I think she sat back and waited for me to work my way out of that and begin to understand people more. She's got an understandin' of people, because of her own experiences. She kept sayin' to me, 'People are basically all the same.'

In some respects, I can agree with that. But, as a black person, there are other issues involved. Her own experience was in terms of white people rejecting her; and certain sides of the black community. She'd go to a party with me Dad, and nobody would look at her, they wouldn't serve her a drink, wouldn't say nothin'. She'd sit there at this party all on her own. She had the experiences of the whites as well. To her, what's the difference at the end of the day?

Basically, you've got the same kind of attitudes except comin' from different standpoints. I could see what she said, but at the end of the day, with me

Mother and with the family, we've had more black friends in the family and
more black people. One or two white women I would call Aunt. That was Aunt
Celia, who was married to a black man, and another woman, who used to come
and do somethin' with me Mum.

...School was an experience. School wasn't too bad. There were a lot of
Chinese kids and black kids - everyone called each other 'Four-Eyes' or 'Fatty'.
It wasn't so heavy, there were certain racist undertones, but because you had
other black kids there, you had a bit of alliances with other people and things
like that. But round the school, some of the streets we couldn't walk up. 'Cause
the kids would come up, just particular streets, and call us 'nigger' or 'black
bastard'. So we never walked up that street, we'd have to go two more streets
down. Just avoidance, scared round it.

When I went to secondary school, it was like a horror story for me. I wouldn't
go to that school again, I wouldn't do my school career over again. People
reminisce a lot over their school days (kisses teeth). My Mum thought she was
doin' a good thing, she was sendin' me to a girls' school - secondary modern
school. Half of it was boys, half girls. We didn't mix, but we shared the hall,
which was in the middle. I was the only black girl there. The whole area is a
white area. They called you 'nigger' and 'coon' and 'you need to get back where
you came from.' All those things were goin' on in school.

I remember in the first couple of weeks of school I missed the bus stop. It was
only a simple thing, just one bus stop, but cryin' me eyes out. I was totally
terrified to walk up any of the streets to get to school rather than the way that I
normally walked. I was frightened some white people might come out and pick
on me. I never told me Mum. I don't understand why it was never discussed
with me Mum. Why I never discussed it with me Auntie. Me Auntie said to me
- I talked to her a couple of years ago - 'Why didn't you tell us?' I can't figure
out the reason why as yet.

You'd go in school and people would be tellin' you that your house stinks, you
haven't got any good clothes, black people are this, black people are that, black
people are the other. Basically gettin' called names, gettin' spat at. Stuff like
that went on throughout the years of my schoolin'. I was standing next to this
white guy and he started to call this black girl a 'nigger' and I said 'Who are

you callin' "nigger"?' 'Oh, you're all right Akousa, there's nothin' wrong with you. You're fine.' I said, 'Listen love, if you're callin' her a "nigger", you're callin' me a "nigger"'. And I walked away.

Sarah

White Irish and black Bajan, Sarah is Akousa's younger sister, and her recollections of her childhood and adolescence in Liverpool are remarkably different from Akousa's. Many of her recollections are interwoven with vivid descriptions of the houses she and her family lived in, and they become signposts along her journey. In the following narrative, Sarah recounts the way in which she found solidarity and a sense of belonging among other young *métisse* girls who did not fit in:

School... when we were young we went to primary school. All the schools my Mum sent us to were like mainly dominated by white people. But they were working-class schools; they weren't middle-class schools...they were very working-class schools. It was really awful at school because I never felt that I fitted in. I always felt odd - really odd. I was quite big as well. I wasn't like a skinny little girl who had knobbly knees...I always wanted to be like that and I was never like that.

So, I wasn't white and I wasn't like the shape that you know a little girl should be - knobbly knees. It was really hard. My friends at school - I had a friend who was white, and then she moved to Mobley, which was this new housing estate that they built. I had one friend who was Indian - Esther Pajit. She was really big, very big. She was mixed race as well. She was half Indian and half English. Her Mum was English. She had this hair that was really thick that went really down to her bum - really thick, thick, thick head of hair. She used to always have it in a thick plait going down her back. She's really big and she's quite like a...she was like a tomboy. Quite masculine; she wasn't, you know, like - huh ha hoh ('feminine' gesture) - she was very Uhhh ('masculine' gesture).

Then, I used to have another friend, let me see if I can remember her name...her father was Nigerian and her mother was English. I can't remember her name, maybe it'll come back. I saw her when I was in Liverpool - I hadn't seen her in years. Ngozi - that was it - Ngozi. She was really tall. You know, like somebody who's too tall for their age. Ngozi - and she was big as well (joint laughter).

And I was the smallest one among them (more joint laughter). So, we used to hang round together. 'Cause we were all just - we didn't fit in. Do you know what I mean? All three of us were from mixed race families, and the three of us were all funny shapes and sizes - for what little girls are supposed to be. So we used to kind of hang around and find solace...with each other. We did have our arguments...

Bisi

Bisi was born and grew up middle-class in Ibadan, Nigeria, with both her white Northumberland English mother and her black Yoruba Nigerian father, as well as two older sisters who were both born in England. The configuring of England in the colonial and postcolonial imagination is a dissertation in and of itself. However, here, Bisi presents dual conceptions of place and home which involve the natural world - the weather, landscapes, birds.

The landscape in England - in a way it was like hearing Doris Lessing talk about growing up in South Africa. She says, although she's there, where the earth is red, what she sees in her mind's eye is fairies, and little green fields and daffodils, because she's brought up with those fairy stories. England becomes the mythical prototype of land and country. Maybe it's the land beyond the rainbow. Right? You can only get to heaven if you're just like England. Okay?

Things my Mum said about being homesick, like, 'Oh, well, I have never heard the birds singing like they do in England.' I know they just make the same twittering noises. I try hard not to say to my children, 'You're calling this grass? Wait 'til you see the grass in Nigeria.' Because you're just going to give a reinforced impression. 'Call this rain? You haven't seen rain yet. Wait 'til you see hot rain, real lightning, like they have it in Ibadan.' So there was that sort of sense of expectation of coming to England - the Promised Land, where milk doesn't come out of tins, it comes out of cows. Where you can buy strawberries. Strawberries or things like that.

Where, actually, if you had ten odd years of looking forward to this fruit called a strawberry, by the time you get to the strawberry it's not going to be like you imagined. By that time, you imagine the strawberry like a quintessential mango, like a piece of ambrosia, not like the sort of rather watery taste - it has a good flavour but not a great deal of taste - that it really is.

Yemi

Yemi is Bisi's older sister and recounts very different, and less joyful, experiences, growing up in their English-Nigerian family. The following extracts exemplify the differential and relative meanings of 'race' and colour. Her recollections of her 'dark skinned black American' friend's encounter with local Yoruba market women in Nigeria also raise interesting questions about authenticity and affiliation:

> I went with an English girl to the wholesale market to buy haberdashery - sewing machine things. They started speaking in Yoruba. There was a girl there, a thin, very black young girl, and she said to the others, 'Let me show you how black I am. I am going to stand next to these white women'. They had lumped us together. She and I were both white. She stood next to us and compared her skin and 'You see now?'. It was unbelievable.

> ...I had a black American friend in college, who was quite dark. He was really, really dark. He was not black, very black. He was quite dark and he looked a bit like a Yoruba boy. His name was Anthony and he had a friend, William. William looked like a half caste. He was tall, had an afro and was yellowish. He was really tall and slender, like a basketball player. Anthony was short and squat and muscular, like abeketi man. Like a farmer man, muscles on his legs. They call it ishu - yams.

> He and William would go to the market. They'd be asking 'How much is this? How much is that?' Asking questions like tourists or Americans would do in the market situation in Africa. 'Mama how much is this one?' The market women would be abusing Anthony. 'You stupid boy, because you are with this Negro (they called black Americans Negroes then) you are pretending you don't speak the language anymore. You useless boy, speak to us in Yoruba.' Anthony would almost be in tears. 'Mama, I'm from America.' 'You see, you useless boy.' Whereas William was okay, because William obviously was not a typical Yoruba boy...But poor Anthony. We're talking about the early 1970s. This great balloon of black consciousness. So they would wear tie-dye shirts or something like that to the market, instead of American clothes, and have maybe leather bags. You know proper African sort of thing. There's Anthony trying really hard to look like an African, but unfortunately the women think that he is one.

Overall, the six *métisse griottes'* remembrances, located in both colonial and postcolonial contexts, shed light on the complexities of African and African Caribbean Diasporic social and cultural life which are too often distorted by historians. They also successfully re-frame much of the racially polarised and essentialised negativity which usually dominates most depictions of our lived experiences. Their transnational identities represent their family constellations as well as their individual experiences. These transnationalities challenge the very notion of the English-African Diaspora as a static and unitary formation, one which does away with differences of culture, nation, ethnicity, region, and class, among others; and one, of course, which ignores inter-racial collaborations. Stuart Hall's definition of cultural identity dovetails with this fluid notion of identities:

> Cultural identity...is a matter of 'becoming' as well as 'being'. It belongs to the future as much as to the past. It is not something which already exists, transcending place, time, history and culture. Cultural identities come from somewhere, have histories. But, like everything which is historical, they undergo constant transformation. Far from being eternally fixed in some essentialised past, they are subject to the continuous 'play' of history, culture and power. Far from being grounded in a mere 'recovery' of the past, which is waiting to be found, and which when found, will secure our sense of ourselves into eternity, identities are the names we give to the different ways we are positioned by, and position ourselves within, the narratives of the past.[3]

Similarly, by naming their gendered, class-bound, regionally specific and generation-centred experiences as those of *métisse* women, the *griottes'* personal stories become political testimonies. They re-insert themselves as active subjects, creating their own place in the re-telling of English-African Diaspora histories. A mosaic of cultures and histories is emblematic of their multiple reference points. This multicultural and diachronic scheme reflects, and cannot be separated from, the complex realities of all postcolonial, transnational people in the English-African Diaspora.

Akousa, Sarah, Ruby, Similola, Yemi, and Bisi are all products of history, the by-products of colonialism and imperialism. Their black fathers are from Nigeria,

3. Stuart Hall, 'Cultural Identity and Diaspora', in Rutherford (ed), *Identity*, Lawrence and Wishart, London, 1990, 225.

and Barbados, formerly under British colonial rule, as well as Tanzania, formerly under the auspices of Germany. Their white mothers are Irish, English, and German. The unresolved postcolonial struggles between Africa and Europe, blackness and whiteness, black man and white woman, are all permanently inscribed on the faces of these *métisse* daughters.

Eternal gratitude to Ruby, Similola, Akousa, Sarah, Bisi and Yemi without whose powerful testimonies my ideas would have existed as mere theoretical abstractions. My thanks also to the other ten women and nine men who participated in the original research project.

Complexity, Creativity, and Society

Brian Goodwin

Science is engaging with new ways of understanding and relating to the world of complex and unpredictable phenomena. This article explores some biological and social implications.

Every once in a while the dialectic of science carries ideas in unexpected directions that connect with wider social movements, revealing the deeper relationships between the two. Current concerns about health, environment, community structure and quality of life in general (as opposed to quantity of consumer goods), all reflect shifts of focus: from the individual to relationships and the collective, the part to the whole, and from control of quantity to participation in quality. This article is about new ideas in science that are connected with the recent remarkable proliferation of books and articles on chaos and fractals and their relevance in diverse areas of science and society. The broader context of these developments is the study of complex systems, which we all know are the reality which we experience, rather than the simple models of reductionist science. So, in a sense, science is finally coming of age, and as it does so it is going through some fundamental soul-searching. There is no consensus yet about where we shall end up, except that it will definitely be somewhere else. What follows is my own assessment of the significance of the new developments for the future of science and some of its social consequences.

The discovery of strange attractors

Complexity has a multitude of colloquial meanings, none of which corresponds precisely to its use in the area of study that has come to be known as the science of complexity. There, it refers to the potential for emergent order in complex and unpredictable phenomena. This science grew out of puzzling problems concerning planetary motion that were uncovered by the great nineteenth century mathematician and physicist, Henri Poincaré. He noticed that something as apparently simple as three bodies interacting, such as sun, earth and moon, gave rise to very strange dynamic motion that appeared to carry a distinct signature, a pattern that had new and unforeseen properties. Working out the precise characteristics of that signature has occupied mathematicians for nearly a century.

However, the study of a rather arcane problem in planetary dynamics is not itself sufficient to bring mathematics to the attention of millions: the maths has to connect with human experience. This connection was made when Edward Lorentz, a meteorologist at the Massachussetts Institute of Technology, discovered the same complex behaviour as Poincaré had while studying, in the 1970s, the solutions to equations describing weather patterns. The difference was that Lorentz had a computer, so that he could get it to trace out the solutions on a screen. Using Poincaré's method of mapping complex dynamic patterns, he observed a new and beautiful mathematical object, now known as the Lorentz attractor (see opposite).

Lorentz realised that he was dealing with a radically new type of behaviour pattern whose properties led him to an immediately graspable metaphor: a butterfly flapping its wings in Iowa could lead, via the strange dynamics of the weather, to a typhoon in Indonesia. Stated in another way: very small changes in initial conditions in the weather system can lead to unpredictable consequences, even though everything in the system is causally connected in a perfectly deterministic way. The way this works in relation to the diagram is as follows. Suppose you choose any point on the tangled curve in the diagram as the starting point, corresponding to some state of the weather. This will develop in a perfectly well-defined, though complex, manner, by following the curve from the (arbitrary) starting point in one direction, which is prescribed by the equations. Every successive state is clearly defined - i.e. everything is perfectly deterministic, since this is what dynamical equations describe. However, suppose there is a small disturbance that shifts the weather to a neighbouring part of the system, to a point on a nearby part of the tangled curve. Then, comparing the

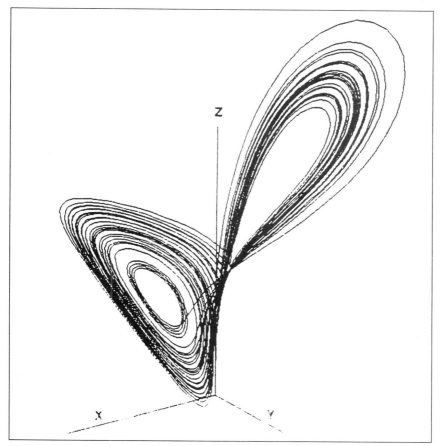

The Lorentz attractor

state of the initial weather system with that of the disturbed system as they both develop along the curve, a basic property of the strange attractor is that they move away from each other exponentially fast. That is, knowing what the weather is now is no predictor of what it will be a couple of days hence, because tiny disturbances (the butterfly effect) can produce exponentially divergent behaviour. This is the signature of deterministic chaos, now identified in a great diversity of mathematical equations whose dynamic properties are described by strange attractors, of which Lorentz' attractor is an example.

The consequences of this mathematical discovery are enormous. Since most natural processes are at least as complex as the weather, the world is fundamentally unpredictable in the sense that small changes can lead to unforeseeable results. This means the end of scientific certainty, which is a property of 'simple' systems (the ones we use for most of our artefacts such as electric lights, motors, and electronic devices, including computers). Real systems, and particularly living ones such as organisms, ecological systems and societies, are radically unpredictable in their behaviour, as we all know. Long-term prediction and control, the hallmarks of the science of modernity, are no longer possible in complex systems; an appropriate relationship to them is to participate with sensitivity in their unfolding, since we are usually involved in their dynamics in some way. Insight into the processes involved is now assisted by a precise hypothesis about what may underlie this complexity: they may all live dynamically on strange attractors, obeying dynamic rules that lead not to stereotyped but to unexpected behaviour.

This is where another aspect of the complexity story enters. A typhoon may well be the unforeseen consequence of the butterfly innocently seeking nectar in the fields of Iowa. But a typhoon is not itself a chaotic weather pattern: it has a highly organised dynamic structure. That is to say, a typhoon is one of the possible patterns that emerges from the complex behaviour of the weather system. So the dynamics of the weather combines both order and chaos. They live together. Although we cannot predict what will be the consequences of a small disturbance, we do know that one of a limited set of possibilities will follow - a typhoon, a high pressure region with sunny skies, a low pressure front with rain, and so on - a large but not indefinite set of possible emergent patterns. This is the signature of *complexity*.

Complexity and the edge of chaos

This approach to understanding complex processes is now being applied to many areas of study: to evolution, for instance, to economics, and to the dynamics of social change. All of these combine unpredictability with order in distinctive ways. Organisms of different species - kestrels, badgers, oak trees, columbines - all have distinct properties that express a specific intrinsic order that we use to recognise them as a 'type', a species of organism. However, both the emergence of these species in the course of evolution and their extinction are fundamentally unpredictable events. Developing models of these processes is the concern of 'complexologists' interested in biological phenomena.

The same approach can be used to study physiological activities *within* organisms, looking at the dynamics of the immune system, for example, or of the heart. Medical cardiology is undergoing something of a revolution as a result of applying ideas from complexity theory to the study of normal and abnormal heart beat patterns. Nothing is more orderly than the rhythmic beating of your heart as you sit reading this, you might think. It is the paradigm of physiological regularity on which your life depends in a most immediate way. However, combined with this order there is a subtle but apparently fundamental irregularity: in healthy individuals, and particularly in young children, the interval between heart beats varies in a disorderly and unpredictable way. If the interbeat interval is

'Complex adaptive systems function best when they combine order and chaos in appropriate measures'

regular - either constant or itself rhythmic - then this is a sign of danger, indicating that the heart may be prone to fibrillation leading to cardiac arrest, or some other arrhythmia. Cardiologists such as Ary Goldberger, working at the Beth Israel Hospital in Boston, consider that the healthy heart beat is embedded in a sea of chaos which both reflects its sensitivity to the activities of the rest of the body and its capacity to respond appropriately to the continuously varying demands made upon it as we go about our diverse activities and experience different emotions. Too much order in heart dynamics is an indicator of insensitivity and inflexibility, just as rigidity in other patterns of behaviour indicates stress and incipient danger. An intuitively attractive idea follows: complex adaptive systems function best when they combine order and chaos in appropriate measure.

This idea was in fact one of the earliest suggestions to come from the analysis of complex systems. While studying the dynamic behaviour of cellular automata, which are particularly useful for modelling complex systems, Norman Packard and Chris Langton had the insight that the 'best' place for these systems to be so that they can respond appropriately to a constantly changing world is at 'the edge of chaos'. Here order and disorder are combined in such a way that the system can readily dissolve inappropriate order and discover patterns that are appropriate to changing circumstances. This fertile suggestion has been subject to severe criticism, as should any proposal that attempts to capture a generic property of a whole new class of systems. However, the basic idea that creative, adaptive systems are most likely to function best at the edge of chaos is proving to be a robust insight, despite the difficulty of pinning it down precisely (mathematically, logically). One of the foremost contributors to the elaboration of this concept in a variety of contexts, all of which relate to basic biological processes such as the origin of life, gene activity patterns in organisms, and the evolution of species, is Stuart Kauffman.[1]

From competition and survival to creativity

There is a very interesting paradox about evolution that emerges from this approach, which has significant social resonances. In the Darwinian perspective, what drives evolution is competition for scarce resources between organisms that differ from one another in their 'fitness', their capacity to leave offspring. The survivors of this struggle are the better adapted, those that can function better in their environment. However, the evidence from studies of species emergence and extinction during past geological ages, and from models that simulate these processes, is that species do not become extinct because of failure to adapt to changing circumstances, or because of cataclysmic events such a meteorite impacts or volcanic eruptions. Although these have undoubtedly contributed to the disappearance of species - the dinosaurs, for example - it appears that there is an intrinsic chaotic component to complex systems such as interacting species in ecosystems, which results in intermittent extinctions that vary from small to large, with a characteristic distribution; and these occur independently of the sizes of external perturbations. As David Raup put it: species go extinct not because of bad genes but because of bad luck.[2] There seems to be an unpredictable dynamic to creative processes such as evolution that involves inevitable extinction or destruction with a characteristic pattern of survival that is not due to individual success or failure but to the interactive structure of complex processes. The game of life, we might say, is one of creative emergence and extinction; the reward is not long-term survival but simply transient expression of a coherent form, a revelation of a possible state of life which we call a species, whose value is intrinsic to its being.

Clearly the metaphors are shifting here, from competition and survival to creative emergence and expression of appropriate novelty. These are not necessarily in conflict. They express different ways of seeing complex processes, the latter viewing the dynamics of the whole while the former expresses the perspective of a part. In fact, the science of complexity has been characterised as a holistic science which seeks to describe the properties of complex wholes. For example, whereas a

1. Stuart Kauffman, *At Home in the Universe*, Oxford University Press, Oxford 1995.
2. David Raup, *Extinction: Bad Genes or Bad Luck?* Norton, New York 1991.

knowledge of parts and their malfunction gives the medical model of disease, a study of the dynamics of the heart described earlier provides an example of how one can assess the health of the whole body from a study of the behaviour of a part, the pattern of the heart beat.

D iagnosing the state of the whole from a study of a part is of course the procedure used in a variety of complementary therapies, such as pulse diagnosis for acupuncture treatment, reading and treating the body via the feet as in reflexology, and so on. It is the traditional therapeutic approach. The science of complexity may provide useful diagnostic procedures based on a similar conceptual model, in which the relationship between whole and part is so intimate and integrated that the dynamics of the part reflects the condition of the whole body. However, the concept of a whole within the science of complexity is something new and involves an apparent contradiction. Because of the mixture of order and chaos that is involved within a complex whole, the parts simultaneously have significant freedom while expressing order. Put metaphorically, the next heart beat can occur whenever it likes (i.e. whenever the heart 'decides' is the appropriate moment within the current situation that it experiences within the body, and in terms of its own complex dynamics). The only constraint is that there be an overall average rate of beating for any particular physiological state (sleeping, sitting, running, together with the emotions experienced). More precise statements of this paradoxical condition of maximum freedom of the parts, together with coherence of the whole, can be given in terms of entropy, and concepts derived from the quantum mechanical definition of coherent states.[3] This holistic view has developed independently in a variety of contexts, including quantum mechanics itself.[4]

Creativity and society

These concepts are now being applied to a range of complex processes, from ecosystems to social organisations. Business corporations have been among the first to see the potential relevance of these ideas to management structure and creative organisational change. Since their everyday experience is 'living on the edge', any insights into dynamic structures that facilitate adaptive response are welcomed. The suggestions of complexity theory for business practice are a flattening of the management hierarchy, distribution of control throughout the system with fluid

3. Mae-Wan Ho, *The Rainbow and the Worm*, World Scientific, Singapore 1993.
4. David Bohm and Basil Hiley, *The Undivided Universe*, Routledge 1993.

networks of interaction between the parts, and the necessity of periods of chaos for the emergence of appropriate new order. The move towards a more anarchic, spontaneous dynamic is clearly threatening to the controlling manager, but it appears to be the path to creativity and diversification. This in no way guarantees survival, just as there is no long-term survival granted to adapted, adapting species in evolution. What it allows for is innovative expression, which has intrinsic value for the members of the enterprise, as well as providing the best chance of the organisation's persisting in a constantly changing corporate world. All the participants in this sector of social organisation can then experience a higher quality of life, since they have greater freedom, more opportunities for creative play, and richer interactions - good for them and good for the organisation. The primary goal would not then be to survive through maximisation of profits, but to make possible a fuller and more creative life for all members of the company and thus to maximise the chances of appropriate collective response to perpetually changing circumstances. The shift of focus here is towards quality and away from quantity as the goal of a more mature society. In fact, the science of complexity may be seen as a significant harbinger of change, from the dominant science of quantities that has characterised modernity, towards a science of qualities that is emerging in the post-modern era.[5]

Naturalistic ethics

This shift of perspective in science clearly has many implications for our understanding of the natural world and our relations to it. One of the most profound concerns the relationship between scientific knowledge and ethical action. Logical positivism, the philosophical basis of empirical science, which rose to dominance in the early twentieth century, completely severs any connection between 'facts' and 'values' by asserting that no human mental components should contaminate the pure observation of reality by the senses. Rom Harré is a cogent critic of logical positivism, arguing both that it stifles science, and that it is immoral. He comments:

> It was positivistic in that it restricted the content, source and test of scientific knowledge to the immediate deliverance of the senses. It was logicist in that it confined the task of philosophers to the laying bare of the logical form of finished scientific discourse. The immoral character of this viewpoint hardly

5. Brian Goodwin, *How the Leopard Changed Its Spots*, Weidenfeld and Nicholson, London 1994.

needs spelling out these days. It is highlighted, for example, in Habermas's protest against the importation into human management of those favourite concepts of the positivist point of view, 'prediction' and 'control'. It is the animating philosophy of the morally dubious authoritarianism of Skinnerian psychology.[6]

Harré's philosophy of science is a form of realism in which explanation of phenomena depends upon the construction of models or theories that go beneath the level of appearance, to the generative processes that describe the real underlying causes of phenomena. An example of this is the theory of fluids (liquids, gases) that is used to describe the phenomena of the weather. The theory of fluids - like other similar approaches to science - uses the fundamental concept of a field, a domain of relational order in which the state of one part of a fluid is connected by a precise mathematical relation to the states of neighbouring parts; so that the whole weather system consists of a single three dimensional field which unfolds in time according to particular laws. Similarly, Poincaré's original studies on planetary dynamics involved the use of gravitational field theory to describe the motions of three interacting bodies as an integrated whole.

This is the basic stuff of science, and Harré is actually rescuing its philosophy from an aberration. But he has added some distinctive components, in particular a rethinking of causality in science.[7] This allows us to escape from the curious impasse imposed by David Hume, in which we are unable to perceive necessary causal connections in natural processes and can do no more than register correlations between causes and effects, which at any moment could change. This is the ultimate fragmentation of atomism and the denial of our ability to participate in and grasp natural processes. Harré and Madden restore the notion of causal powers to nature, which is then reinvested with 'powerful particulars', which underlie the appearance of specific structures such as the motion of the planets, weather patterns, and the strange attractors of chaotic dynamics. These powerful particulars are the real underlying causal powers of natural phenomena, particular to each type of field, such as the force of gravitational attraction, of electromagnetism, or of fluid dynamics.

With the concept of generative processes comes the concept of natural kinds, those structures that we identify as having distinctive types of intrinsic order such

---

6. Rom Harré, *Varieties of Realism*, Basil Blackwell, Oxford 1986, p21.
7. Rom Harré and Edward Madden, *Causal Powers*, Basil Blackwell 1976.

as the elements in physics (carbon, copper, gold, etc), weather patterns (such as typhoons), and species of organism (kestrels, badgers, oak trees, human beings, etc). This argument is developed with clarity and force by Roy Bhaskar in books that develop the realist philosophy of science in both the natural and the social sciences.[8] With the concept of natural kinds comes a naturalistic ethics. This depends on our relationship to what we take to be the truth, insofar as science reveals it to us, and is counterposed to the excessive relativism of much postmodern theory which is disabling for both science and for ethics. If we believe that we have some insight into the true nature of something, then this influences our behaviour towards it. For example, if we believe from the evidence that certain foods are beneficial to human health and others are detrimental, and we are in a position to influence diet, then we will experience some compulsion to encourage the consumption of healthy rather than unhealthy foods. If we believe that children have a basic need to play (i.e. this is a necessary expression of their nature), then in general we allow space and opportunity for them to play. Likewise if, from close examination and study of the behaviour of chimpanzees, particularly in the wild, we become convinced that to express their natures they need conditions such as life in social groups and an environment with adequate freedom of movement, then we will discourage the confinement of chimps in isolation or in severely restricted circumstances. The same type of argument holds for whatever understanding we may have of any other species.

Andrew Collier, discussing these issues in an admirably clear book, puts the argument for the social sciences as follows.

> Social sciences, then, generate practical emancipatory projects by showing there to be (a) a need, (b) some obstacle preventing its satisfaction, and (c) some means of removing this obstacle. This is not a matter of mere technical imperatives, coming into play only *if* you want the projected good; given that a social science can tell us not only about the means of satisfaction but also about the need itself, it may ground *assertoric imperatives*,i.e,. *since* you need this, remove that obstacle thus.[9]

---

8. Roy Bhaskar, A *Realist Philosophy of Science*, 2nd edition Harvester Press, Brighton 1978; and *Scientific Realism and Human Emancipation*, Verso, London 1986.
9. Andrew Collier, *Critical Realism*, Verso, London 1994.

Furthermore, according to Bhaskar, 'for emancipation to be possible, knowable emergent laws must operate', thus linking us back firmly into scientific realism.[10] This is necessary because without principles of emergent order from complex systems there is no real nature that is expressed and nothing intelligible for us to understand, everything being totally accidental and contingent. Then all possibilities would have equal logical status, and we could rationally argue that there is no violation involved in depriving children of play and requiring them to work; or that we can design chickens and cattle to have extra muscle which prevents them from moving 'naturally', since we can also design cages that can support them. The realist argument also connects directly with the programme of research in the sciences of complexity, in which a primary goal is to understand the generative processes that give rise to the diverse forms of emergent order that arise in evolution (biological and cultural) .

It thus becomes clear that the move from control and manipulation of nature, to participation in and understanding of the creative expression of nature in emergent forms, has significant consequences in a variety of contexts. Among these are our relationships with the environment and our use of plants and animals as commodities for manipulation by genetic engineering and biotechnology. The realist argument that different types of organism have natures means that, insofar as we understand these natures we are in a position to remove obstacles to their expression.[11] Only when organisms are able to express their specific natures will they be healthy. If we are to consume these organisms (lettuces, cabbages, fish, etc) as food, then food quality depends upon the health of the organisms and hence on the conditions under which they live.

We are currently manipulating species more and more, both through changes in their environments (soil conditions, use of fertilizers, herbicides, pesticides, etc) and their genes, in order to increase quantity (of product and of money). In so doing we are disturbing complex systems in unpredictable ways that result in epidemics such as BSE in cattle and innumerable food allergies. We are pushing species to the brink of their stability, where they suffer disease, such as the increased mastitis in cattle treated with growth hormone to increase milk yields. What is so absurd about this example is that milk production was adequate before the new

10. *Bhaskar, Scientific Realism and Human Emancipation*, see note 8.
11. These ideas are developed in Gerry Webster and Brian Goodwin, *Form and Transformation*, Cambridge University Press, Cambridge 1996.

technology was introduced, so it was quite unnecessary. Quantity goes up, quality goes down, and these complex living systems are driven beyond their intrinsic stability (their natures) into states of propagating instability that manifest as epidemics and disease.[12] Frequently there are alternatives to these processes that are ecologically safe and maintain health; but, because they are not patentable, they are not attractive to the food industry. Biotechnology has a role to play in food and drug production. But companies need to act responsibly, with adequate biosafety controls and regulations. These may well require periods of testing to extend beyond ten years, because of the slow response times of complex genetic networks and gene transfers between species in ecosystems, which need to be studied intensively under controlled conditions before transgenic varieties are released. Without these, human health, and that of the ecological networks on which we all depend, will be put continuously at risk, with periodic devastating epidemics. In the past, only litigation after severe damage has forced responsible behaviour. The more sophisticated understanding of complex systems which is now emerging encourages us to take precautionary measures to avoid such disasters, reflecting sensitive participation in the processes in which we are immersed, rather than continuing with the fiction that we can exert control from the outside as objective, detached observers with predictive knowledge of the outcomes of manipulations.

The potential influence of a new science that invites participatory engagement in complex systems, whether physical, biological, social, corporate, or economic, is very great. I have touched on only a few of the issues that are coming within the purview of new developments that could link science more closely, and more responsibly, to major social issues.

---

12. See Mae-Wan Ho, 'Unravelling Gene Biotechnology', in *Soundings* 1, pp 77-98.

Mediaworlds

Mediaworlds

Nowhere is historical time moving with greater rapidity than in the world of the media. In contrast to the domain of formal politics, where the post-Thatcherite thaw seems interminable, the media and cultural industries are leaping ahead with ever more spectacular bounds, defying the realms of the possible with breathtaking regularity. The constraints of time and space, even of the human brain, appear merely humdrum when confronted with new communicative hyper-highways and concocted virtual worlds where simulation is as good as the real thing.

This acceleration of historical time is genuinely impressive. New digital technologies even now are bringing to an end the classic era of the television age, which itself is of relatively recent historical origins. True, by the end of the 1930s British children - or London children, more accurately - could watch *Mickey Mouse* on TV (whilst drinking Coke and eating crisps). But the television *age* in Britain was a moment which was inaugurated much later - in the late 1950s or even in the 1960s - transforming the entire national culture, as Sarah Benton suggests in her discussion of the making of politics and political news. A uniform system of national broadcasting is, in the 1990s, giving way to a much more complex network of communications - which is both more globalised and administered and (at the same time) at least potentially more local and interactive. It is these conflicting pressures which confront us now.

In the face of these rapid cultural movements, intellectual comment has often been at best faltering, at worst, banal. Many of us still inhabit the cosy mental world of the television age, over-awed by a future which looks so bewildering. Much public debate still turns on a few, well-worn, sceptical motifs - patrician regulation vs commercial free-fall; politics vs the shamanistic spookery of the spin-doctors; authentic cultural meanings and critical reflexes vs glitz, style and junk eroticism; decency vs Murdoch.

In this debate New Labour holds an ambivalent position. On the one hand, for all its newness, it speaks a language of an archaic moral authority spectacularly cut adrift from the realities of the new cultural and demographic formations which are now so palpably present. This Angela McRobbie demonstrates with verve. But on the other hand, for all its oldness, the party is condemned for embracing all the trickery of image-consultants and the photo-opportunity, championing 'the sound-bite' over 'the issues'.

Clearly, politics *has* become more image-driven. But there is too a kind of innocence which underlies the arguments of the critics, and which underlies too such a dichotomous view of things. There never has been a time in the twentieth century when mass politics, or the cultural relations of citizenship, have not been deeply imbricated in the institutions of the mass media. There never was a time when politics - the issues - existed in pure form, free from the desires and fantasies inscribed in mass culture and the mass media. Or, to say this more emphatically, a new kind of citizenship was *made possible* by mass culture and by the mass media - even at the point when these were being denounced by the politicians, of left and right alike.

The purpose of the articles which follow is - put simply - to break through this kind of manichean thinking, which places the old in one corner, the new in the other. It is the fluidity and unexpectedness of the new mediaworlds which are both most enticing, and most worthy of scrutiny. The new, as Kevin Robins shows in relation to the virtual democracies fanfared by Bill Gates and Al Gore, can reproduce where least expected a weary traditionalism. The old, carried in new conditions, can surprise, humour, and even elevate. Who could have thought, in this moment of cybernetic image-invention, that two plasticine figurines would have become pop icons? What kind of symbolic world has come into being when press headlines mourn the loss of Wallace and Gromit in a Manhattan taxi?

Or to turn this around: old debates - Angela McRobbie discusses feminism for young women - can be revived and transformed in the most unlikely locales of an unashamedly commercial culture. It is the contingency of these forms which is most striking.

And it is these complexities, in which the old and the new are fused together, which James Curran discusses in more formally strategic, or policy-orientated, terms - opening up the question of public regulation of the new mediaworlds which are upon us. To evacuate the territory of public regulation, as some on the current cultural avant-garde seem to propose in the name of a profane populism, would be - Curran believes - a kind of folly, marking the moment where a cultural leftism becomes indistinguishable from the fantasies purveyed by the PR oligarchs of the market. What *kind* of regulation is a different question, and one which is pressing. Even on the cusp of the newest of new mediaworlds, the old problems are never entirely extinguished.

Yet what kind of possibilities the burgeoning media systems will bring to the refashioning of citizenship - as earlier in the twentieth century the mass media expanded the sphere of political life - remains an open question, with everything to play for.

Bill Schwarz and David Morley

Media soundings

James Curran

We still need public service, insists James Curran. It needs to be free and open, representative and diverse.

Media historians will recall Tony Blair's pilgrimage to Australia in 1995 to pay court to Rupert Murdoch and the massed senior executives of News Corporation as a key moment, in much the way that medieval historians remember King Henry IV's homage to Pope Gregory VII in the snow at Canossa in 1077. Both occasions symbolised political obeisance to a new power.

New Labour has since evolved from being a courtier to becoming a champion of media moguls. Blair's team attacked the Conservative government from the right for failing to abandon - rather than merely liberalise - media monopoly controls in the 1966 Broadcasting Act. An astonished Virginia Bottomley, Minister of National Heritage, had to make the case for defending media 'plurality and diversity' in the interests of a healthy democracy. In contrast, the Opposition talked of the need for media groups to get bigger in order to compete successfully in the global market, and tabled an amendment opposing a Bill which 'treats newspaper groups unfairly in their access to broadcasting markets'.[1]

New Labour was responding on this occasion not to Murdoch but to Montgomery's Mirror group. The Broadcasting Act retained a block on press giants controlling more than a fifth of the national press from buying up land-based TV and radio companies, and thus frustrated the Mirror Group's desire to become a leading popular broadcaster. However, Labour's stance encapsulated its new thinking about media policy: win as much goodwill from media kingmakers as possible.

---

1. *Parliamentary Debates*, 16 April 1996.

This has been combined with an aggressive and proactive news management strategy. Labour's spin doctors now match their Conservative counterparts in promoting their agendas and news angles through a combination of charm, exclusion and intimidation. Public clientelism is combined with private flak.

New Labour thus has a coherent media strategy, shaped by an all-consuming desire to win the next election. The right has also a clear political project - the marketisation of the media. Its latest initiatives are to sell off Channel 4 which has now gained official approval, and the conversion of the license fee into a voluntary subscription to BBC services which has the backing of influential Conservatives, and if implemented would fundamentally undermine the BBC.

But on the left, there is an eerie silence. It goes along with libertarian legal reform (Freedom of Information Act and reform of the Official Secrets Act) which is part of the centre-left consensus. But in relation to other media issues, the left is mute. Unlike the right, it does not have a project.

Alternative approach

If the free market strategy of the right is to be answered, it has to be countered by an alternative that is more appealing than the current practice of public service broadcasting. This alternative needs to be insulated from state pressure, and to respond more readily to the full diversity of British society. It needs also to create new spaces for innovative programme making.

This need for change is prompted by cumulative evidence that seventeen years of single party rule has weakened (though not destroyed) the political independence of public service broadcasting. No less important, the decline of political parties as representative and formative institutions makes it necessary to change the ground rules of reporting and commenting on public life in the broadcast media.

Political parties have lost much of their mass membership, compared with their heyday. They no longer command the same degree of partisan allegiance and identification among the electorate that they once did, and have consequently lost influence over their social constituencies. Above all, they are the products of class formations which have been ruptured and transformed by economic and cultural change, and are no longer representative institutions - the natural vehicles of cohesive social blocs - that they were, to a much greater degree, during the 1930s. Yet while their place in society has declined, their influence on broadcasting has, if anything, increased. They continue to monopolise avenues of access to television, and in the process crowd out other collective organisations. A way has to be found of weaning public service broadcasting from party domination, from its fixation with the symbolic processes of Westminster, and enabling it to respond more fully to wider social movements and trends in society.

Reform needs to foster creative programme making. Public service broadcasting (in the sense of publicly regulated or owned channels) is partly insulated from the market pressures that make for uniformity and blandness. Its programme range has expanded with the introduction of Channel 4. But public service broadcasting is still dominated to a remarkable degree by a metropolitan culture. The increased centralisation at the BBC, and increased commercialisation of Channel 3, is also making the core system more culturally conservative, more inclined to fall back on heritage programmes and tried and tested formulae.

In short, the way to respond to the challenge of the new right's market project is to develop a public service alternative that is free and open, representative and diverse.

Broadcasting independence

The system of government appointments to broadcasting authorities has become corrupted and debased. It is weakening the political independence of the broadcasting system. All those appointed to chair the BBC, for example, during the Conservative ascendancy were known Conservative supporters. Indeed, the previous longstanding chairman of the BBC, Marmaduke Hussey, was a brother-in-law of a cabinet minister: his predecessor, Stuart Young, was the brother of one.

A better method of making appointments than the present unmediated system of government patronage needs to be found. The proposal currently advanced by the Labour Party in an internal document - for a Parliamentary Select Committee to interview and recommend new appointees to broadcasting authorities - is only a partial advance. It keeps decision-making firmly in the political arena. Choices would be determined in effect by a committee of MPs, of which the majority would normally come from the governing party, and the government of the day.

Yet, an alternative, left-wing proposal for direct elections to broadcasting authorities is even less appealing. Political parties are the only organisations with the resources available to mobilise large numbers of people to the polls. Consequently, direct elections could result in the governing party gaining legitimated control over broadcasting authorities, and using this power to bring broadcasters to heel - the very opposite to what most left-wing reformers actually want.

The best solution is to establish an independent appointments committee, including some representatives from the broadcasting industry. It should guard against not only government but also Establishment 'packing': eight out of twelve BBC Governors in 1992, for instance, went to three universities - Oxford, Cambridge and London. In the selection process, the appointments committee should invite representative organisations to advance names, and interview a short-list. The convention of broadcast authority members acting as representatives of the nation rather than of sectional groups should be retained. But the objective should be to ensure that those appointed really are broadly representative of the country, and have the qualities needed to make a positive contribution to the public oversight of our core broadcasting institutions.

Another way of safeguarding the independence and future of the BBC is to finance it more adequately, and in a way that makes it no longer beholden to government. There should be automatic increases in the license fee linked to increases in national earnings. To mitigate their effect, license fee exemptions could be introduced for low income households compensated by Treasury grant.

Reinterpreting public service

A stunted definition of public service broadcasting is upheld by the law, the BBC's Royal Charter and by what may be called the 'official literature' of public enquiry reports and government consultation papers. It is inhibiting the renewal of public service broadcasting.

Certain key concepts have a very restricted meaning within this official canon. Thus, 'social access' is discussed primarily in terms of access to broadcast signals in outlying areas. It is about a right to reception rather than expression, the right to watch and listen but not to be heard.

Similarly, the notion of 'diversity' is understood in an unduly narrow and limiting way. It is conceived solely in terms of a mix of programmes that caters for minority as well as majority tastes, offers a balanced cultural diet (including 'quality' fibre) and serves different needs (including children's education). It is not about ideological pluralism, and extending the right to communicate. Moreover, diversity is discussed primarily in relation to non-political programmes. When political programmes are under review, the main concern is objectivity. As the *White Paper on Media Ownership* (1995) noted succinctly: 'programme requirements are focused on securing qualitative objectives or ensuring the accurate and impartial reporting of views and opinions, rather than securing plurality'.[2]

This astigmatic view stems from an inadequate understanding of the wider role of broadcasting. No attention is given to who is included and excluded in broadcast debate because broadcasting is not conceived in terms of mediating the collective dialogue of society. Indeed, this notion is mocked with patrician disdain by the Annan committee as the equivalent of wanting broadcasting to be a 'Witenagemot' (the king's advisory council in Anglo-Saxon times).[3]

> '"social access" is discussed primarily in terms of access to broadcast signals in outlying areas'

Nowhere in the last two Broadcasting Acts, the BBC's Royal Charter or the report of the last major enquiry into broadcasting is widening social access to collective debate identified as one of the purposes of public service broadcasting.[4]

This omission matters because broadcasting operates in the context of an elite political culture and a highly centralised system of government. There are very strong pressures on broadcast journalists to internalise uncritically the Westminster-Whitehall consensus, take their bearings from the leaderships of the parliamentary parties, and rely on the 'authoritative' and 'accredited' as their sources of information. A conscious policy of resisting these pressures is needed, if the collective conversation conducted through broadcasting is to be broadened to include non-elite groups.

Yet within the broadcasting community there has long been an unofficial tradition committed to extending the range of voices and perspectives heard on the airwaves. This has been central to the radical social-realist tradition of TV drama.[5] It has given rise to the adoption of new programme formats such as radio phone-ins and audience participation talk-shows,[6] and resulted in Channel 4 widening the ideological spectrum of broadcasting in a way that was not specified

2. *Media Ownership*, HMSO, 1995, p.17.
3. *Report of the Committee on the Future of Broadcasting*, HMSO, 1977.
4. Broadcasting Act 1996, HMSO, 1996; Broadcasting Act 1990, HMSO, 1992; 'Constitution' in *Guide to the BBC*, BBC, 1992; *Report of the Committee on Financing the BBC* [Peacock Report], HMSO, 1986.
5. G. Brandt (ed.), *Television Drama*, Cambridge University Press, 1981.
6. S. Livingstone and P. Lunt, *Talk on Television*, Routledge, 1994.

in its legislative brief. This unofficial 'access' movement is besieging even the citadels of conventional broadcast journalism. 'Involve a wider range of experts and members of the public. Reflect the country, get away from white men in suits, get away from the M25 [London's ring road]', commanded one internal BBC memorandum in 1995.[7] This was translated by young feminist journalists on *Newsnight* into a series of remarkable reports which placed the marginalised at the centre, and gave eloquent voice to the voiceless.[8]

This unofficial movement should be given recognition and legitimacy by becoming part of what public service broadcasting seeks to achieve. To the 'due objectivity' requirement should be added a 'pluralism' requirement. Licensed broadcasters should have a public duty to give adequate expression to a plurality of perspectives and viewpoints, and to facilitate the participation of different groups in the collective dialogue of society. This obligation should be entrenched in law, incorporated into the Constitution of the BBC, and become part of the public service duties that the ITC and Radio Authority uphold.

This is a more effective strategy of reform than seeking solely to construct an alternative, 'non-state' media system or to multiply access programmes where the pressure for reform can be confined and quarantined. It means seeking to change the commanding heights of the media system, where the main formative conversations of society take place. This innovation, combined with an independent appointments system, will also strengthen the democratic credentials of the public broadcasting system at a time when it will be fighting for funding and public support. It is a way of ensuring that public service broadcasting really is, in practice as well as in theory, independent, representative and committed to empowering all sections of the community - in striking contrast to a press that is owned by big business, unrepresentative in its views and committed to furthering private agendas and interests.

Re-inventing tradition

Channel 4 is a successful innovation, an imaginative way of reinterpreting the public service tradition. But it was introduced in 1982. Since then new technology has multiplied the number of television channels, yet all these have all been defined

---

7. '*Newsnight* Objectives 1995/6', internal BBC memorandum, 1995.
8. J. Curran, 'Television Journalism. Theory and Practice: The Case of *Newsnight*' in P. Holland (ed), *Television Handbook*, Routledge, 1997.

by a market logic.

How, then, should the repertoire of public service broadcasting be extended, particularly now that digitalisation makes possible the introduction of new public service channels? What new conception and structure should be introduced to add a further dimension to the public service tradition? In casting around for an answer, it is perhaps worth tuning in, paradoxically, to the conversations of backward-looking traditionalists. When they argue that the British system allows programme-makers more autonomy than either the American market model or the politicised public service models of continental Europe, they have a point. At best, the British system fosters both creativity and craft skill as a result of the relative freedom it allows broadcasters at the level of producer.

However this celebration of the British tradition also contains an element of self-deception. Even in the so-called 'golden age' of broadcasting during the 1960s, there were always checks and controls. These were rooted unobtrusively in the many ways in which broadcasters were socialised into corporate convention, as well as in the more obvious and explicit discipline of 'referring up' of controversial decisions to a higher level of management.[9] Individual autonomy has since been reduced by the Birtian revolution at the BBC, and by the increased market orientation of commercial, public service broadcasting.

However, myth can be the mother of invention. The much vaunted strengths of the British system, arising from the operational freedom it allows its creative staff, can be maximised through the introduction of a new form of public service broadcasting. After all, an idealised view of the small 'independent publisher' partly inspired the original conception of Channel 4. Another idealised image, that of the free and unshackled programme maker, should be the inspiration for another kind of public service organisation responsible for the 'Free Channels'.

A small public corporation should be established which would run one national minority TV and radio channel. It would be exposed to a different social and political culture from that in London and the south-east by being based in Glasgow and Liverpool. It would be publicly funded (perhaps from a tax on TV

9. See in particular, P. Schlesinger, *Putting 'Reality' Together*, Constable, 1978; T. Burns, *The BBC: Public Institution and Private World*, Macmillan, 1977; K. Kumar, 'Holding the Middle Ground: the BBC, the Public, and the Professional Broadcaster', *Sociology* 9:3, 1975.

subscriptions and videos) in order to shield it from market pressure. It would also be free from any prohibition or restriction other than the law of the land. In effect, it would be the only broadcasting organisation in the world which would be completely free from both regulatory and commercial controls. Its remit would be, simply, to make good programmes.

Civic media sector

Reform of public service broadcasting leaves untouched deregulated media. Here, priority should be given to promoting the civic media sector. In this context, political parties should be seen not as a problem (with too much airtime at the expense of others) but as one exemplar among others of a democratic culture.

The civic media sector consists of media linked to collective organisations like environmental campaigning groups, and social constituencies such as sexual minorities and immigrant groups. They range from party newspapers to ethnic radio stations, union videos to feminist magazines, music independents to campaign newsletters. They are a significant, if largely uncelebrated, part of our media system. They can help communities of interest to coalesce by providing a unifying focus, as well as positive group images and identities. They can also facilitate communication between members of the same organisation or group, and provide an outlet for disseminating ideas and information to a wider public.

The case for supporting the civic media sector is similar to that for providing financial support for political parties. It is a way of sustaining collective organisations as a counterweight to private interests, and supporting the basic building-blocks of the democratic system. Self-organised groups are the key means by which people lobby for their collective interests, and express their sense of what is right. They constitute the life force of civil society, sustaining a culture of public accountability and freedom.

This approach also represents a cheap but efficient strategy for increasing media diversity. A small amount of public money can go a long way because the civic media operate in low cost sectors. It can also have a ripple effect since civic media can be a significant source of ideas and talent for mainstream media. Thus, relatively small sums invested in reviving the political magazine press may be a more effective way of injecting new diversity into the national press than investing in new high-risk and high-cost newspaper ventures, some of which are likely to fail.

Admittedly this approach can be criticised for setting its sights too low. In principle, something should be done about the wall of economic exclusion that surrounds major media markets. It costs over £10 million to establish a national cable TV channel, some £20 million to establish a new national newspaper, and many times this to start up a new, transnational satellite TV service.[10] Without some form of public intervention designed to assist market entry, control over major commercial media will continue to be confined to the economically powerful.

Something more than fostering internal democracy within national newspapers is also needed in order to effect a major change in the national press.[11] One key to understanding why the national press is more right-wing than its audience, and why it distorts the political system, by under-representing the left, is the economics of the press. This both blocks market entry by resource-poor groups, and proscribes general minority newspapers serving low-income as distinct from high-income groups. Only a launch and selective subsidy system, directed towards nurturing and sustaining innovation and redressing advertising inequalities, will change this.

But this is ruled out by the current climate of political opinion which is hostile to public intervention in the 'free market', save in the form of watchdog regulation. This political consensus is doubly inconsistent. It turns a blind eye to far-reaching intervention in the broadcasting market. It also ignores the existence of continuing subsidies, often targetted towards the richest corporations (such as VAT zero-rating on newspapers which benefits the strongest newspapers with the biggest sales). But however illogical, it is a fact of political life. To be effective, it is necessary to advance schemes that have a chance of being implemented.

Media 4 (named after Channel 4) should be set up, with modest aims and endowed with modest funds from the National Lottery. It should have two briefs: to provide start-up and development aid for a small number of new projects in low-cost, niche markets, and to advise the government about ways of assisting the development of the civic media sector (such as action to enable minority publishers to gain access to oligopolistic newsagents). Media 4 would have all-party representation, and would support only those projects which,

---

10. These estimates are based on the launch of the *Independent*, Live TV and B Sky B.
11. For ways of doing this, see J. Curran, *Policy for the Press*, Institute for Public Policy Research, 1995.

on the basis of professional assessment, have a reasonable chance of success. It would also only help those applicants (1) without extensive media interests, (2) with a demonstrable need for public venture capital, and (3) whose proposed enterprise would add significantly to the diversity of the media system. Its most significant area of impact is likely to be in local radio, specialist book and magazine publishing, and independent music production.

Retrospect

Doubtless, many other - and more valuable - initiatives can be proposed and argued for. But the key point is that the left now has to think concretely about what sort of new media developments it wants to see, and make a case for them in the public domain.

For too long a radical culturalism has held sway, at least in the radical specialist literature, that assumes that media organisations are unconstrained vacuums - 'contested spaces' - that are shaped exclusively by wider social forces in society. The media will be changed, it is argued simplistically, only by transforming the society of which they are a part. The trouble with this approach is two-fold. It is blind to how the political and economic organisation of the mass media in fact influences their content. And it ignores ways of reforming media structures in a form that will make them more responsive to wider social movements and contribute to progressive social change.

The right has not made this mistake. It has promoted a clear agenda for change, based on rolling back public service broadcasting, in a seductive and universalistic rhetoric of giving people what they want and setting broadcasters free. In Britain, the progressive response to this challenge has been defensive, based on blocking and parrying new proposals from the right (with, as it happens, some success by comparison with some other European countries). But now that the climate in the country is changing, it is time also for the left to change and come up with some new ideas.[12]

---

12. Current alternatives are outlined in Campaign for Press and Broadcasting Freedom, *Media Manifesto*, CPBF, 1996; J. Keane, *Media and Democracy*, Polity, 1991; and J. Curran and J. Seaton, *Power Without Responsibility*, 4th edition, Routledge, 1991.

Political news

Sarah Benton

What's the story?

What's the story, what's the story? Death, disaster, fire accident, randy bishop and his secret love child, ferry sinks, bomb explodes, Charles and Camilla in secret love tryst. That's the story. Got the pix? Hold the front page.

What's the news? Major calls for moral crusade. Paddy says Liberals have no hope of forming government. Blair says Labour isn't socialist. Heseltine attacks Labour-union link. Clare attacks 'dark forces' behind party leader. Redwood demands Major stands firm on EMU. Blair calls for moral crusade. That's *news*? Tell me another; I knew all that already.

Of course you knew that already. Most of the time, there is no political news. There are only old stories which we all know already. The reason we know the political news already is not because nothing ever happens in politics that's worth knowing, or because nothing ever happens that is new, or that changes how our state works. We know it all already because information about politics only becomes the news when it can be fitted into a story that we know already. 'There are only two stories in the media', Tony Benn said with taut weariness in September 1996: 'did it embarrass the Prime Minister or did it embarrass the Leader of the Opposition. If it doesn't fall into either of those categories, it isn't news'.[1]

These do happen to be the stories of our time; but it is generally true that if potential news can't be fitted into a story, we don't understand it; we don't know who the good guys and bad guys are, don't know the sequence of act and punishment, or act and reward, which constitute a story. The mass readership of newspapers created the story as the principal vehicle for imparting political information. Without it, we don't know the significance of day-to-day decisions taken by Ministers of State, here or abroad. Only specialists, professionals, experts know the meaning of those small events. Almost all of the information generated

---

1. *Panorama*, 30 September 1996.

in and about the European Union sinks without trace. It's never news. We only
know two stories about the EU: will it rip the Tory Party apart, cause the downfall
of someone or other? will brave little Britain be shamefully exploited/destroyed
by vengeful and envious foreigners? Any little detail that can be made to fit this
story - John Redwood scratches his nose when he could have been applauding
Kenneth Clarke - will be 'news'; anything that can't will evaporate in the British
press. Not because they're 'anti-Europe', but because there isn't another story
about Europe. (Unlike widgets made in Birmingham, newspapers made in Britain
have no significant export market; no other industry of this size is so dependent
on a home market, and therefore has such an interest in cultivating its home
market as *intrinsically* unexportable. The coverage and foreign sales of the *FT*
and *Economist* prove this rule.)

I t used not to be like this. Once upon a time there was no political news, as we
understand it. There were stories of death, disasters, accidents and crimes,
horrible and trivial. These manifested what people knew to be the random
cruelty of life, or the vulnerability of unprotected women, or God's revenge on
wickedness, or the fearsome power of machines and Nature. There was what the
leading newspaper, *The Times*, called 'political intelligence'. The same term was,
and is, used by the state 'intelligence services'. In *Times*-speak, political intelligence
meant information about events that were germane to one's tactics or strategy;
only a very small elite needed political tactics or strategy, which they anyway usually
kept inside the high command. So 'political intelligence' might be a short item on
an inside page reporting decisions and divisions in a party leadership. There were
also long columns of reports of parliamentary debates. And there were records of
bills and committees. But there wasn't any political *news*.

Political 'news' as a mix of state chronicle and quasi-military 'intelligence' was
generated by nineteenth-century social and political relationships; these, as well
as the organisation, financing and technology of newspaper production, determined
its reach. One might have imagined that the mass franchise and mass political
parties from the late nineteenth century would have revolutionised political news.
Following the argument of Alessandro Pizzorno, that the new mass parties had the
effect of making people citizens, drawing them into the purlieu of the state,
newspapers would have been active agents in this politicising process. For the first
time, the mass of men, at least, needed to know about the workings of the state,
the decisions of national governments, the relations of power. This - the era of

Taylorism, Ford, and mass armies - was not the time for cultivating individual opinions about politics; it was the time for marshalling mass political opinion.

To a limited extent the growth of mass newspapers does indeed follow the curve of enfranchisement. The journalist W.T. Stead, editor of the *Pall Mall Gazette* in the 1880s, wrote that the telegraph and printing press had 'converted Britain into a vast agora, or assembly of the whole community, in which the discussion of the affairs of State is carried on from day to day in the hearing of the whole people'.[2] From the 1880s, the more popular papers provide a fitful and meagre ration of political news with a heavier counter-tow of the stories about the threatened collapse into disorder of this new mass society, terrifyingly unpoliced by the natural order of masters and servants.

Still, most national newspapers did not respond to this 'objective' need for political information - which in part explains the development of a partisan press. The revolutionary 'Northcliffe technique', applied to his invention, the *Daily Mail* (b. 1896), provided snippets of news, and put them on the front page; but the innovation was the judicious mix of crime, scandal and bizarre events as standard newspaper fare, rather than a revolutionary popularising of politics. Northcliffe, said the PEP's 1938 report on the press, assumed that news was intrinsically dull, and must be 'sugared' with the introduction of irrelevant details such as 'the girl'.[3] The Northcliffe technique became a byword in Fleet Street, his paper a model for all popular papers which did not want to provide that essential fuel for a radical citizenry - political information.

The conclusion drawn then, in the inter-war years, about the people and politics was pretty much what it is now: that the people don't like politics and won't read about it (so don't print it); but they have an insatiable appetite for anything about sex, so print everything. That says it all about popular papers and political news. Which doesn't explain why one journalist recently with a humdinger of a sex story couldn't sell it to a tabloid but probably could have sold it to a broadsheet. The story was of illicit video pictures taken of women in hotel bedrooms and lavatories, then displayed on the internet. This wasn't salacious, romping 'sex', tabloid style; this featured actual women doing actual bodily things, like using the WC. The journalist, Jonathan Margolis, was told by the *Sun*: 'It's a bit strong for us mate.

2. Quoted in Anthony Smith, *The Newspaper: An International History*, Thames and Hudson, 1979.
3. *Report on the British Press*, April 1938, Political and Economic Planning.

Sex is OK, but toilets ... no. It's a bit Internetty as well. We avoid that stuff'. And the *News of the World* said: 'the toilet stuff is a bit much for our readers'. [4]

Popular-media 'sex' is an invention. It is a cultivated creature which must be constantly patrolled to keep it in the control of its creators, and to keep out reality which would shatter the glittering illusion.[5] The paradox is that sex, the most personal of all matters, provides the most universal of stories. A story about sex is intrinsically more interesting, and engaging, than an account of the clauses of the Maastricht treaty for most people. But then *anything* 'personal', especially love and death, is by its nature universally engaging and has what earlier political news lacked - a story which anyone could understand. It was only when political leaders became personalities that we had a medium for stories that we could all recognise and understand.

The broadsheet/tabloid distinction then is not of politics v sex, is not even, now, one of left versus right, but more matter of whose mythical world the reader can enter into - one in which all women are aged 17-27, have bouncy breasts and never defecate, urinate, menstruate and all men can and will do it five times a night; or one in which all matters of importance are defined and dealt with by elected politicians.

From the beginning, it was left-wing papers, with their reach limited by the reach of the party or organisation that sponsored them, which propagated political news. Most of these were weekly or monthly publications, and only the adherents of the cause were likely to make much sense of it. For thirty years after the mass *Daily Mail* was launched, the right-wing papers were distinguished by their disdain for political news. The start of radio news broadcasts by the BBC in the 1920s rattled the complacency of most of the popular press. Radio provided political news for the masses; although the BBC adopted the authoritative, impersonal tone of the broadsheets, the speaking voice and the brevity of the items fashioned an appeal for listeners, creating a new mass audience for some sort of political news. However, the voice of authority did confirm that 'news' was remote and impersonal and neither did, nor should, engage the passions of the masses.

But the masses, in the inter-war years, did push their way into politics, marshalled by those leaders, impelled by those passions, which the guardians of

4. *Guardian*, 16 September 1996.
5. The media word always used to describe such fragile creations is 'robust'; it became a buzz-word of 1990s politics, always tossed in to cover the sound of the seams splitting.

democracy so feared and despised - and discovered new, equally despicable passions, in the people's palaces of 1930s cinema. One of the few who went out to meet the new need for political information was the documentary film maker, John Grierson, who recognised where the problem lay: 'The more we look for a world market in the matter of entertainment, the more we are limited in our formulae', he wrote in 1936. 'We must find the common factors for appeal over a heterogeneous mob of differing interests... We are forced in fact to the more or less exclusive pursuit of sensation and romance.' The answer was to use serious films, shown outside the commercial circuit, to find a 'better audience ... a better species than the people who go to theatres' (i.e. commercial cinemas). No, not simple snobbery; for as Grierson stressed: the people who go to theatres are *the same people* who go to halls, meeting rooms and discussion clubs. 'The difference is one of mood. When we go to the theatre we go for the most part to be amused. In the halls we come less to be amused than for discussion.'[6]

'The right-wing papers were distinguished by their disdain for political news'

Mass society, a mob of heterogeneous differing interests, could absorb information in one of two ways - one, if it was homogenised by the simple common denominator of sensation and romance; or two, if it took place in the context of active discussion. The latter route has never been taken by newspapers which have always treated their readers as inert consumers (whose desirable inertia is concealed under the new fancy of consumer choice); the first seemed all that was left. It took a long time for the press to learn that political news could be converted into The Story, for The Story, unlike sex, truly has universal appeal. But for as long as political news remained the preserve of august statesmen - unless it was besmirched by the vulgar masses - there was no story.

In the 1930s, *The Times* , the *Daily Telegraph* and the *Daily Mail* still devoted their outer pages to ads. (*The Times* did not put news on its front page until 1966.) By the 1950s, the *Daily Express* had become the leading paper, in the sense of dominating the market with its news-style and shaping of public opinion. Since the 1930s, *The Times* had only been the 'leading' paper in its identification with a

6. 'The New Cinema in Teaching Citizenship', *The Citizen*, October 1936.

political elite of civil servants and politicians whose interests it supplied. The internal view of its role, and therefore the news it should provide, was summed up in an anonymous memo by senior staff following the writing of the critical Cooper Report in 1957: 'Obviously, Great Britain cannot function without a strong, educated, efficient, informed governing class. *The Times* is the organ of that class... A country like Great Britain depends for its administrative efficiency upon its politically intelligent and professional men; these in turn depend upon *The Times* for the material upon which to reflect, and, ultimately, act'.[7]

As the mass newspaper-reading market increased during this century, so the interest of that elite was to procure concealment and containment. To allow *any* information which they had not sanctioned to be published was tantamount to allowing day trippers to open the cupboards in your stately home and finger your drawers. (The same view shaped Buckingham Palace's relation to the media.)

This impulse prevented *The Times* seeking political hegemony through news coverage - a fact recognised by outsider Rupert Murdoch and his first editor, Harold Evans (1981-82). Evans, when editor at the *Sunday Times*, had pioneered the technique of telling a highly complex story, often with scientific or forensic facts, in a readable *narrative* form. It was a lesson which Evans was unable to apply on *The Times*. It is a lesson that few papers on the left ever learned, irresistibly drawn as they have been to the tone of moral instruction larded with fact-texts.

The Times stood for imparting that information which it thought a wider readership ought to know (e.g. the sterling work in committees that officers of the state performed), for protecting the anonymity of its workings, and for concealing from the vulgar gaze the workings of politics. The public interest of the ruling class came to be the pursuit of dignity, at all costs. This created its counter-force in the press - to destroy that dignity, regardless of cost.

Political news was pioneered by left/liberal papers. The simple reason for this was that they thought the actions of a wide range of political actors - trade unions, left-wing parties and the Labour Party, campaign groups for the unemployed and, by the 1930s, students and women's groups - were worthy of newspaper coverage. Because they were treated as political actors, they *were* political actors.

---

7. Oliver Woods and James Bishop, *The Story of The Times*, Michael Joseph, 1983. p344. The Cooper Report was commissioned from the accountancy firm, Coopers Ltd, to explain *The Times's* falling profits and circulation.

Without political actors, there is no political news. There are only anonymous and impersonal state decrees. Thus while *The Times* and *Daily Telegraph* stalked stiffly through a decade of uniquely strong political passions, the *News Chronicle* thrums with reports of the new horrors of the Nazis as well as brief reports of protests about unemployment and health insurance, against Mosley's blackshirts and for disarmament and 'peace'. It also covers in considerable detail the deliberations amongst Liberals over their relations to the National Government before 1935. It could carry daily reports of the Reichstag fire trial in 1933 because by then its readers already knew the story - that the Nazis were brutal barbarians, nonetheless empowered by a virile vigour. Nazism endangered a democracy hampered by cumbersome niceties and marked by effeteness. How come there's such a difference between the universities of Berlin and Oxford, asked one of its reports. Because, replied a quoted German student, German men are virile while the British are supine.

This 'myth' became increasingly persuasive during the 1930s, generating much hand-wringing amongst intellectuals and organisational work amongst a new political class - the officials of municipal and educational institutions - to persuade public opinion that boring old civic democracy had much to be said for it. But there was no heroism in this, no drama, and while it created an appetite for political news, it did nothing to create a story for a newspaper. It failed to become a hegemonic news agenda because there were few who could turn Democracy into an admirable, vigorous hero. Papers of the right were animated by their admiration for the vigour of the dictators Franco, Mussolini and Hitler. For all the broadsheet appeals for Education in Citizenship, it was the possibility of British men fighting, using violence, which finally gave the papers their political stories.

However, even the national exigencies of war did not create a uniform political story. Again, it was largely a matter of who were the actors. The *Daily Mirror* created a new working-class voice and working-class audience in its promotion of the ordinary soldier's tale. The cartoonist David Low invented the character of Colonel Blimp for the *Evening Standard* in 1934,[8] but it was the *Daily Mirror* which most effectively used this caricature of the hopelessly reactionary and incompetent 'brass hat' as a running, explanatory

8. David Low was a New Zealander, not the first nor the last colonial to lead the British people through the newspapers in contempt for the dignified parts of the British establishment.

symbol of the British establishment and its military failures. It was only the war itself and mass mobilisation which allowed this character to be a principal actor in the political tale.

The activism of the British people incurred by total war made them actors in the story. After the war, the split between left-wing and right-wing coverage was as marked as ever, although for the first time papers from the *Daily Herald* to the *Daily Mail* agreed on one of the dominant stories: the Soviet threat to Britain. The war had left various actors in the national story hanging about without a clear role to play - communists, trade unionists and women. The tension about all of them simmers through the press coverage of the 1950s.

The cold war was the first truly hegemonic tale of British press coverage. But the primary actors in the story were often not politicians or even the principal parties. Because the Soviet threat moved in menacing and mysterious ways, so it could only manifest itself indirectly. And it was only a *British* story in so far as either Britain was an indistinguishable element of an organic western capitalist whole, or Britain offered a peculiarly vulnerable entry point to the heart of western capitalism.

What doesn't simmer through the coverage of the post-war Conservative era is the words and deeds of politicians. Days go by in which no MP appears in news pages. They are not important people. Visiting Russians, the AGM of the Co-op, trade union conferences, get more coverage than do politicians; as for women, they are everywhere and nowhere. It is surprising, looking back, to find how central to that era were issues of equal pay as well as of being a housewife - how far newspapers of all politics cultivated the image of the woman as a being apart from the business of daily life. (The new sex goddesses of the Hollywood film industry thrust through these grey pages like another life-form.)

The change comes in 1963. Philip Larkin was right; sexual intercourse begins then, when the fumbling, unspoken world of sex leaves off.[9] So does mass political news, in a way we would recognise it. Politicians are named. The events of state are more closely linked to the acts and words of real, living breathing, sexual-intercourse-having politicians. It is in 1963 that the *Daily Mail* introduces its strap 'Political News' to differentiate a page of reports largely based on the doings of parliament and politicians

---

9. *Annus Mirabilis*: 'Up till then there'd only been/A sort of bargaining,/A wrangle for a ring./A shame that started at sixteen/And spread to everything.'

from foreign, city, sports and general news. Before then, politics - like sex and women - were everywhere and nowhere. By 1963, it has become possible and desirable to report the Profumo affair. By 1963, a new TV programme, *That Was the Week That Was*, was stunning and delighting a new audience with a sort of running, animated cartoon show about actual politicians. It is difficult to convey just how shocking and revealing it was for a citizenry who had only dimly seen their politicians through the thick protection of well-buttoned suits from which the polite questions of the day resiled like so much confetti.

'Popular-media "sex" is a cultivated creature which must be constantly patrolled to keep it in the control of its creators'

Once unbuttoned, the box could not be closed again. With television, in particular, we get politicians' body language, and, as Milan Kundera says in *Immortality*, there are more people than there are gestures, so we all learn to recognise and interpret the same few, universal gestures. Television magnified the politicians as political actors, and extracted from their words that which commanded universal recognition. It also magnified the information politicians had previously concealed.

But for lasting change to have occurred - which it did - the media could not be the only player which changed. The relationships between politicians, media and people all changed, setting in train, amongst other things, the development of the political news story in a way that is familiar to us.

The next transformation is pioneered by the right. It is above all they who harness the familiar myths and shape them into stories about actual parties and politicians. If their habit before had been to ignore popular politics as intrinsically dissident - as far as was consonant with being a national newspaper - they now learned to adapt topical politics to the form of popular, narrative myth. This is an ancient art. Why do you speak in parables, the disciples asked Jesus. Because, he answered, 'it is given unto you to know the mysteries of the of heaven, but to them it is not given'. From which develops the exegesis of the parable of the sower and his seed. To them who have already - in this case, knowledge and insight - shall more be given; and those who have not - in this case, either knowledge or insight - even the little they have shall be taken away. That is they shall become more ignorant. 'For this people's hearts waxed gross, and their ears are dull of hearing, and their eyes have been closed.'[10]

The key to creating popular political myth as the shaping force for political news is to focus it all on heroes and villains; we carry in our heads more stories about leaders, about princes and dragons, than we do about ordinary people. The more the mythical dominates political news, the less actual information there will be, the more the news will be about the qualities and tests of leadership.

These are not always universal archetypes; stories are made out of actual events, or particular national legends. In Britain 'news' which echoes the stories of Wat Tyler or of Robin Hood, of the Battle of Britain or evacuation of Dunkirk, of adventurous sailors, of the march from Jarrow or the compassionate prince, resonate more than do stories of bold assassins, of the masses storming the citadel, or of ordinary men taking up arms and forming militias. But universal legends do play a role - the little people neglected at the hearth by the indolent old father-king while the ugly sisters go to the ball (weak Callaghan and the selfish Labour government); the lonely heroism of the pilgrim on his journey (Margaret Thatcher in 1982 and David Owen in 1985); the traitors in the cellar and the barbarians at the gate - all these structured political news from the late 1970s, pulling the masses into a hegemonic interpretation of events, in lieu of the varying, and divisive, degrees of information and analysis that were the alternative.

To become story-makers, leaders must be battling against ill-fortune or malevolent forces on their way to victory. The myths therefore have to tell us who the powerfully malevolent forces are. There is no story in defeat unless, as in the evacuation of Dunkirk, an heroic quality can be imputed to a defeat, the story thus turning into one of moral victory. Political stories are therefore stories of the leaders' valiant attempts to secure victory and to ascribe reasons for any apparent failure.

Myths are, in part, recurring stories, or stories with recurring motifs. That is how they work. A few elemental examples come quickly to mind:-

- Behind every leader there are dark forces; if the leader is weak, the dark forces are really in control. The archetype for this relationship is the Tsar and Rasputin; it has been fondly believed about Stalin; and it reverberates, in weaker form, in British newsreporting today.

- A great leader is hampered and surrounded by buffoons. This is said about many generals, and was said about Margaret Thatcher, cruelly let down by men weaker than her.

---

10. Matthew Chapter 13 - a good starting point for any theory of communications.

- Leaders are always beset by conspiracies. These provided the stories of the last years of the Labour government at the end of the 1960s - 'Attempt to replace Mr Wilson may be imminent.' Scoffing at stories of conspiracies is merely a way of shouting boo at the bogeyman who we *know* is hiding in that dark patch on the stairs.

- The job of the *young* leader is to wake the inert people from their long sleep into which they have been cast by a malign force.

And while the conceit of leaders may be that they are in search of the Holy Grail, the real quest is that defined by Oedipus - to uncover the crime that has cast society into its present state of decay. This quest has to be carried out, not by leaders, but by truth-seekers, that is, by journalists.

At first glance, the many political stories about the Family and its threatened defeat by the forces of misrule and disorder do not seem to fit the bill; except that the stories of the Family are really stories about the forces of misrule and disorder. Disorder always hovers, in mass civic society, in which natural masters cannot impose order. Where there is a citadel there must always be barbarians at the gate. It is impossible to overstate how powerful this sense of menace is amongst Conservative Party members, for whom menace is ever present, if protean, in form. In the 1980s, it came in the form of - successively - trade unionists, marxists, muggers, miners and Militant. Now the menace is even more mysterious, and therefore that much more menacing. A poster depicting Tony Blair as a demon in disguise captures perfectly Tory perceptions of what Labour is all about - and the only reason newspapers, and especially the BBC, do not propagate stories giving the true facts is because all journalists are secret socialists.

The *Daily Mail* has been the champion of this take on politics: politics *as such* is a menacing imposition on the business of everyday life conducted by good citizens (and their families). The family, says its columnist William Oddie, 'is essential for our society if our culture is not to disintegrate into a random collection of alienated and predatory individuals.' The story here is *not* the family. It is the danger of anarchic predators, of which the sub-text is young, male and black. The same paper's campaign (news-led) against the Divorce Reform Bill hailed the Bill's defeat as 'a major victory for the family' and in the next sentence wrote: 'It was also a great humiliation for the Prime Minister, into which he was led by the worst Lord Chancellor in living memory, and final proof - if it were needed - of how utterly incompetent the Government has become as handling its affairs.'[11] Here the story is again *not* the family, but the Bad Adviser.

Once the governing myth has been established, the heroes and villains identified, then the frame is set into which any story can then be fitted - and believed. Thus, with the GLC led by Red Ken identified as a band of marauding loonies, any story about the actions of such loonies can be printed, and believed. They build up such a momentum that at a point what begins as a common joke - they'll be banning black bin-liners next - becomes a news story. It becomes common sense. The office of the European Commission in London has, in the last few years, decided to respond to the 'news stories' about the nefarious dictates of the Commission with its own counter-information, a series of leaflets headed *Do You Believe All You Read in the Newspapers* (1994) and *Do You Still Believe All You Read in the Newspapers* (1995) and *Do You Know...?* (1996). Journalists, says the office, rarely bother to check their facts; it was just common sense that the Commission would ban something so intrinsically, so authentically British as London's double-decker bus.[12]

Similarly, it has become common sense that ex-Royal Wives will stoop to any indignity to have their fun; lacking the first requirement of the upper-class wife - impregnable continence - they have become archetypically incontinent loose women. It isn't easy to trick the press with hoax stories about their incontinence, but it's possible. As Roy Greenslade said of the Di-video hoax on the *Sun*'s editor Stuart Higgins, it 'fitted perfectly with his preconceptions'.[13] So does any story about the madness of Prince Charles. Or the paranoia of Lady Thatcher; or the venality of directors of privatised utilities and of Tory MPs. We already know that Princes of the Realm are unstable creatures, that the madness of political princes is paranoia, that greed is the driving force of capitalism and condemnation for greed the moral price that the rich have to pay. *Of course* Labour will raise taxes, whatever Blair and Brown say; for Labour must wreak revenge on the corrupting, exploitative rich on behalf of the masses, or they are nothing. It's that or building the New Jerusalem; those are the only people's victory stories we know.

11. *Daily Mail* 26, April 1996.
12. A recent pamphlet, *The European Commission in Britain Today*, says that up to 1994 it had to refute an average of 36 'Euro-myths' a year; in the twenty months to September 1996 there were thirty-two items of misinformation needing correction.
13. *Observer*, 13 October 1996.

Wallace and Gromit: an animating love

Esther Leslie

Wallace and Gromit have become national heroes.
What's it all about?

we're all found of our anmal matter.
James Joyce, *Finnegans Wake*[1]

One man and his dog

The success of Nick Park's *Wallace and Gromit* animations may be down to their proverbial premise: the renowned affinity between an Englishman and his dog.[1] Such rapport between human and canine, while famed, is a modern liaison, and culturally specific. Delving into it gives vent to some sonorous ideas inspirited by the bond between Wallace and Gromit. John Berger, in 'Why Look At Animals', registers the historical nature of the man-pet affiliation.[2] It is, he claims, a fraught relationship, anchored firmly in the industrial epoch. In a broad mapping of human-

---

1. Success is understood here in terms of public and critical recognition. As measure, here is an indication of the variety of awards and accolades won by the three films in the *Wallace and Gromit* series. *A Grand Day Out*, Park's graduation film, won a BAFTA. *The Wrong Trousers* won an Academy Award and over thirty other awards and wins a position in the International Animation Festival's shortlist of all-time animation favourites as voted by a jury of five animation experts. Apart from its Oscar, *A Close Shave* won a succession of prizes at the 1996 British Animation Awards: Best film over 15 minutes; Best scenario; Public choice favourite film; Public choice funniest film. On Christmas Eve 1995 10.62 million people watched *A Close Shave*, comprising BBC2's highest audience that year.
2. *About Looking*, Writers and Readers, 1980.

animal relations across time, Berger notes how animals, once resident at the centre of the human world, subjected but also worshipped, endowed with magical significance and anthropomorphised, 'disappear', during the process of urban industrialisation in the nineteenth century. They re-surface, first as machines, and later as raw materials - meat, leather and horn. Exotic animals become inmates of public zoos. Used up or caged in, animals' special and equal relation to humans vanishes. A chasm opens up between people and nature, which is really a gulf within nature. However, simultaneously, the 'marginalisation' of animals is revoked by the invention of the household pet. Pets, asserts Berger, are but animals reduced and drained, 'mementoes from the outside world', lodging in the hermetic family-home, along with pot plants and romantic landscape paintings. The owner's relationship to the pet is corrupt, because the animal is corrupted. Pets resemble their owners for they live lives like them, but in as much as they do this, they lose their animality and autonomy. In such a filiation, nature, lost to people of the urban era, is regained in compromise form.

Wallace and Gromit dovetails with audiences because it reflects upon the dynamics of a commonplace, yet remarkable, relationship. But while Berger is appalled by devaluation of the animal in its debasement to pet-status, the home life and frolics of Wallace and his dog demonstrate how fulfilling and equitable such a partnership may be. Their animated antics recast an abusive and unequal coupling in utopian form. In pulling together to combat time after time an evil that is technologically-enhanced, the two act out the idealised interconnectedness of humanity and nature.

Since the nineteenth century, children have been surrounded daily by likenesses of animals; toys, pictures, cartoons. These animal icons are frequently cute and often humanised. It is a peculiarity of the industrialised world, and it ensconces early on in life the fantasy that to be at one with animals is to inhabit a lost paradise. Images of reconciliation rescind recollection of an ongoing instrumental violation of animals - as initiated by Descartes, who conceived animals as soulless machines. In order to prove that animals have no soul, Descartes nailed his wife's dog by its four paws to a board and dissected it alive, thereby installing a common practice for scientific researchers at London's Royal Society. Live animals, flayed and dissected, appeared to the vivisectionists as watch or clock mechanisms. Ostensibly activated by wheels, ratchets, springs, gears and weights, they were conceived as automatons. It is here that the cuddly toy and the faithful pet submit their counter-claim, voiding the justification for cruelty and overriding its actuality. Here Gromit, as toy (for us) and pet (for Wallace), with his resourcefulness and fidelity, rehumanises or re-animates (from *anima*, Latin for soul or spirit). And he seems all the more human when confronted by the truly automated Cyberdog in *A Close Shave*. The pet is vindicated, the pet-man relationship sanctified. But, at the same time, the punishment meted out to animals in industrialism is never completely screened out. Gromit is falsely put behind bars in

'To prove that animals have no soul Descartes dissected his wife's dog alive'

A Close Shave, and in *The Wrong Trousers* the diamond-thief penguin ends up in what seems to be a prison, but when the camera pulls back it is revealed to be a zoo. As Berger insists, the fact that those Victorian institutions, prisons and zoos, are so alike reveals at one blow our affinity with animals and our tragic species-isolation. To keep a pet may be, however misguided, an attempt to overcome this breach.

In a radio lecture for children, titled *True Stories about Dogs*, Walter Benjamin notes that the dog is the only animal (with the possible exception of the horse) with which humans have been able to establish a bond of intimacy.[3] Benjamin attributes this familiarity to the victory of humans over animals, secured long ago, when animals were tamed and became dependent on people. Not for Benjamin Berger's idea of a pre-industrial golden age of animal-human relations, when humans depended upon animals, and so had to respect them. For thousands of years, Benjamin insists, dog has been slave and humanity master. But man's victory is not absolute, and dogs retain traces of their untamed and self-sufficient origin. Caught between wolfish past and devotion to humans, the dog straddles the line between nature (animality) and culture (humankind). Like any domesticated dog, then, Gromit oscillates between two worlds; from kennel to bed, from dog-bowl to dining-table. Gromit's frequent sojourns in the human world demonstrate the fantasy of pet-lovers. Their dogs are their friend and their mirror. When favoured by Wallace, Gromit lives a human's life. He knits, he does d.i.y., he listens to music. And he reads the philosophy handed down by a doggish antiquity; Pluto's *Republic*. He might more gratifyingly read Aristotle's

---

3. *Gesammelte Schriften*, VII.1, Suhrkamp, 1989.

History of Animals - a work which ascribes moral qualities to animals, noting that, like humans, they are capable of mildness or ill-temper, courage or timidity, fear or confidence, high spirits or low-cunning, and they exhibit something akin to sagacity. True to Aristotle's vision and countless Disney films, Gromit's appeal, like the appeal of the pet, is that he is just like us. He is anthropomorphous.

The plastic arts

Aardman Animations, the studio that took on Nick Park while he was still a student at the National Film School, emerged into public consciousness in 1976 with a clay creature whose very name hinted at the essence of animation: Morph. This cheeky homunculus was animated using a process known variously as 3-D, clay, stop-motion/stop-frame animation. Patronage by the advertising industry and the music business brought about a flourishing of British animation. Aardman Animations were commissioned to experiment with stop-frame techniques. These forays led to the notable *Sledgehammer* video for Peter Gabriel, and memorable advertisements, including Nick Park's theriomorphic series for the Electricity Board. The *Creature Comforts* animals, animated to the sounds of documented human voices, allowed Park to hone his skills in clay animation, and initiate the mundane but cute regional characterisations that have become his trademark. The tiniest movements, idiosyncratic and yet familiar ticks and quirks were reconstructed. *Wallace and Gromit* continued this exploration of the point at which English ordinariness segues into eccentricity. It combines familiarity and cliché with high adventure and suspense, just as it also synthesises a demented irreality with naturalistic observation.

The rendition of Englishness in *Wallace and Gromit* oozes with sentiment and nostalgia. The routines of toast and jam for breakfast, four o'clock tea and day-trips at the weekend are irresistible, the simple pleasures being always the best. Framed photographs testify to past good times and companionship - recognition of the photos' motifs arouses our own private familiarity and knowledge of the storylines, as does the generic and intertextual playfulness. The theme-tune,[4] an oompahing ditty, sets up the tradition-seeped scene, echoing simultaneously the

---

4. Apart from deploying suspense-movie techniques, including Julian Nott's Bernard Herrmann style compositions, intertextual references abound. In *A Close Shave*, for example, there are references to *Brief Encounter*, *Indiana Jones*, *The Third Man* and *Alien*.

regional peculiarity of a colliery brass band and the empire-oriented World Service signature tune. Wallace and Gromit reside in West Wallaby Street, a sort of Coronation Street of Victorian back-to-backs in a Northern town. Art director Yvonne Fox travelled to Manchester to capture ideas for houses and skylines. While the skylines that surround their urban domicile do not omit the tower blocks and gasometers of late twentieth century cityscapes, the Victorian terrace-house setting chimes well with prevailing ideas about pre-modernist, post-towerblock solutions to city habitation. Nostalgia abides too in the technical vision. Wallace's self-built mechanisms issue from a pre-electronic age. Even though they are built to visit the moon or execute complex industrial tasks, they look mechanical rather than electrical or digital. Both the moon rocket of *A Grand Day Out*, and the multi-tasking machine in *A Close Shave* resemble old-fashioned copper brewery distilleries. But *Wallace and Gromit* does not simply present a twee parochialism or mourning for a lost era. It plays with those themes, unleashing them in the context of modernity. The episodes follow a pattern borrowed from the conventions of Hollywood action movies. At a certain point the chase sets in and anything can happen. There are no boundaries to what might occur and how the available implements will be used. Wonderment at Wallace's inventiveness and Gromit's good strokes (i.e. Park's ingenuity) taps cinema's very essence.

The figurines, Wallace, nine inches, and Gromit, five inches high, are made of a concoction of plasticine, a shinier and more colourful American modelling clay, beeswax, and dental wax for extra sheen or hardness. The clothes are fashioned from foam latex. Non-moving parts are moulded from a modelling clay that can be baked hard, and the swirling eyes are wooden beads, whose holes in the pupils allow adjustment using the tip of a paperclip. Inside the figures is an articulated metal skeleton, and magnets are used to maintain balance. The models are constructed to maximise morphability. This morphing of objects into real and non-real states fixes a utopian and infantile edge to the clay-animation form.[5] The chunkiness of the plasticine world and its slightly over-sized objects, evoking a childlike perception of scale, combines with the material's unjaded utopian and surreal faculty for moulding the potential

---

5. Childlike connotations persist with the clay form despite the adult-oriented efforts of Bruce Bickford or Xhonneux's *Marquis*. See *Frank Zappa presents the Amazing Mr. Bickford*, Honker Home Video/Barking Pumpkin Records, 1989 and *Marquis*, ICA Projects, 1989.

mutability of all things into all other things. Clay-animation appears as realisation of Coleridge's esemplasticity, the imaginative law of a world where everything is made of the same stuff and everything could be everything else. This perfect unity of the universe and its contents is underscored by the similarity of our duo's features, their oblique foreheads, their squeezed together ping-pong ball eyes.

Watching inanimate objects metamorphose induces immense joy. Roland Barthes accounts for this effect in an article on plastic in *Mythologies*. Here he analyses the alchemical and miraculous associations of mouldable, infinitely transformable materials. He describes:

> the reverie of man at the sight of the proliferating forms of matter, and the connections he detects between the singular of the origin and the plural of the effects. And this amazement is a pleasurable one, since the scope of the transformations gives man the measure of his power, and since the very itinerary of plastic gives him the euphoria of a prestigious free-wheeling through Nature.[6]

In tandem with eliciting the exhilaration of an unfastening from nature's necessities, the building matter of stop-frame animation's mouldable universe draws upon potent associations. In *Genesis* God is cast as the original animator, who forms man of the earth's clay and exhales into his nostrils the breath of life. The poetic meaning of the word clay takes up these religious resonances, standing for the material of the human body. The formation of these clay bodies intimates an originary aspect of creation, and asserts the existence of the human.

Some have claimed that the special thing about animated puppets is that - unlike cel-animation - they tender something akin to live-action. 3-D animation is essentially vital. Such an inkling coincides with Aardman Animations' philosophy of 'shoot and light' as if the animation were a live-action movie. Everything is designed and built around the camera. The clay world and the clay-puppets possess an undeniable reality. They are not shiny clean like 3-D computer animations. They cast actual shadows and throw around real weight. This morphing parallel world *is* a world, not a sliver of painted celluloid or a digital fantasia.

---

6. *Mythologies*, Paladin, 1973.

Love and craft

In 'Plastic' Barthes remarks that this infinite material can never perfectly imitate the triumphant smoothness of nature. The same might be said of Park's plasticine figurines. They are handmade, literally. It is possible to see fingerprints on the figures' bodies. In the context of an industrialised society wherein crafted goods exert a fascination, such manifest facture becomes an advantage in the quest for an audience. Imperfections place Park's animations in the realm of craft, and so by default, remove taints of self-serving commercialism. Not insignificant here is the fact that stop-frame

> 'Wallace and Gromit become plucky fighters against Disney corporate products'

animation was, prior to the Fall of the Wall, a tradition associated with apparently non-capitalist, i.e. non-profit-oriented, Eastern Europe. Much of the rhetoric around Nick Park and the three Oscars, 'gained for Britain', identified his output as homespun, virtually a craft product in comparison to the industrial machinations from Disney's studios. This domestic sensibility is reinforced by the connection to television, specifically to the BBC. Park's films all appear first on TV and, once for sale as home videos, they pointedly refuse aggressively to promote either the series or any other product. Wallace and Gromit, and Park himself with his shy persona, become plucky fighters against Disney corporate products. The process that produces the animations is artisanal in its methods. It is relatively low-budget. No expensive computers are needed for scanning in and out to film.[7] The characters' flexibility, their incessant movement that appears so effortlessly achieved, is in fact the result of an effort obsessional in its dedication. Each two syllable word spoken by Wallace necessitates six different facial expressions. Breaking movement up into tiny constitutive parts renders defamiliarising close-ups of the banal, just as Adrian Rhodes' close-miking of ordinary noise makes sound extraordinary. This is the closely-observed surrealism of actuality. Each second of film may involve twenty-four movements for every clay character or prop. Each day about three seconds of film may be completed. Such work emerges, it is said, from love, devotion

---

7. Of course success changes things, and processes industrialise. Thirty-odd people worked on *A Close Shave*, with Park taking on more of a director-role. The budget was £1.3 million rather than the £650,000 spent on *The Wrong Trousers*. Digital technology makes easier the execution of certain optical effects and enables previously unrealisable things to be done, such as the aeroplane scene in *A Close Shave*.

and obsession. The animation's theme also happens to be about love and devotion. Such a labour of love, in a tale about love, generates in turn its own devotees, as is testified by the internet's countless internationally-authored pages of fan stuff - all lovingly composed by adults who make it their business to broadcast quotations, images, scenarios, reviews. It is the stuff of d.i.y. and true amateurism.

Apparently low-tech, these animated lumps of moulded clay and wax dramatise questions of technology and control. Wallace, a Heath Robinson style inventor-hobbyist, self-builds or acquires his machinery, which in turn goes out of control, in some way or another. The narratives feed off rather routine fears of the techno-age. In *The Wrong Trousers* the ex-NASA techno-trousers are manipulated by the criminal penguin, and end up effecting Wallace's monstrous alienation from his own self-directed activity. He awakes upside-down, swinging from a museum's ceiling, about to undertake a diamond heist. In *A Close Shave* it is the Cyberdog who wreaks havoc. The narratives are driven by the attempt to regain control over technology run wild. In *The Wrong Trousers* the train set, a homely technology, is used to defeat the evil Feathers McGraw. In *A Close Shave* the wash-shave-knitting machine finally does the business of refurbishing the Cyberdog. Unlike Jan Svankmajer's animated surrealism, this is not a cosmic display of magic and the supernatural but demonstrates rather the extraordinary temper of technology and its alternating empathy with masters and slaves. The twentieth century fairy-tale involves the voodoo of machinery not the wizardry of goblins.

In 'The Mass Ornament' Siegfried Kracauer discusses fairy tales' intimation of genuine reason. Fairy tales, he claims, 'are not stories about miracles but rather announcements of the miraculous advent of justice'. He goes on to relate how in the fairy-tale, 'fidelity triumphs over the arts of sorcery.'[8] Truly in *Wallace and Gromit* it is fidelity, as 'personified' in the dog, that, in the end, triumphs over the mischievous diabolism of technology, and holds aloft the banner of love. Gromit always facilitates the victory, irrespective of Wallace's disloyalty in chasing money or seeking love elsewhere. Our pleasure in doggish fidelity signals a strong desire to be at one with nature; that is, to transgress the 'new solitude', so poignantly pinpointed by John Berger.

---

8.   *The Mass Ornament: Weimar Essays*, Harvard University Press, 1995.

Pecs and penises: the meaning of girlie culture

Angela McRobbie

From the Spice Girls to More! *magazine, images of confident and sexually assertive young women proliferate across the media. Is this new feminism? Or simply new fun?*

In February 1996 Tory MP Peter Luff presented a Private Member's Bill which sought to require that 'teen' magazines carry a sticker giving the appropriate age-range of readers. Luff had purchased a copy of the innocently-titled *Sugar* for his daughter and had been horrified by the contents. Instead of harmless boarding-school stories there was graphically illustrated information about sex, and about how girls can give and get sexual pleasure. At about the same time the family entertainment magazine *TV Hits* (purchased and read mostly by young adolescents) carried in its advice column a question, and fairly detailed answer, about oral sex. In the few weeks following, and running up to the presentation of the Bill, a moral panic of some scale reverberated across the media. This took the by-now predictable course of outrage and condemnation about the corruption of childhood innocence, followed by calls for 'something to be done'. In the event the Bill failed, as expected, but strong pressure was put on the publishers to set up a regulatory body to monitor their own practice and to ensure the appropriateness of the information given in the magazines. In itself this is not a bad thing, since it will force the magazine industry to account for itself. In the past, 'girl's and women's magazines have been considered so trivial that nobody ever thought to ask them to take responsibility for what they publish.

What was most noticeable, however, was how opinion was divided along the lines of gender. It was men like Darcus Howe, presenting Channel 4's *The Devil's Advocate*, who were most outraged and it was they who did not like the idea of their daughters finding out about sex in a way they did not think appropriate. It seemed as though men still thought that sex for girls and women should be presented in the guise of Barbara Cartland-style romance, in soft focus and without too many questions being asked. Anything more than this appeared to make them feel uncomfortable, as men or as fathers, even though they would in all probability expect their teenage sons to be reading *Penthouse* under the bedclothes. And of course in another guise it is men who provide the primary consumer market for explicit sexual material in films, magazines, and newspapers like *Sunday Sport*. At any rate these men didn't seem to like the new frankness and the rude jokes found on the pages of the new magazines.

There were, in contrast, very few women on the TV panels or in the studio audiences who took the same view. Most thought it better to know the facts at an early age to avoid unwanted pregnancy and to be confident enough to have sex without feeling forced into it. The information provided in the magazines,they argued, gave girls a bit of bargaining power. They would know what to expect, and they would be in a stronger position to negotiate new emotional and physical experiences. Counsellors from family planning agencies argued that magazines like these served a useful function, and were more effective at getting the safe sex message across than most other means. They also reminded us of how many young women still remain uninformed about sex and their own bodies. There even emerged a current of approval for the joky way in which sex was talked about in the magazines. The double standard for too long had meant that only men and boys could treat sex lightheartedly. Pleasure and enjoyment, fun and jokes on the subject of sex were hardly going to threaten the moral fabric of the nation, especially when 'dirty jokes' told to and by men had for so long been a part of male culture. This point was made by several groups of young women themselves, who held their ground against the formidable presence of Darcus

Howe by insisting that reading about different ways of having sex did not necessarily mean that 14 year olds across the country were going to go out and do the things they had just read about. It was also noticeable that the editors of the magazines from *Just Seventeen* and *Mizz* to *Sugar* and *More!* were also all-female. They too spoke in the language of what is now called 'popular feminism'. Female assertiveness, being in control and enjoying sex, are now recognised as entitlements, and the struggle for equality with men and boys starts young. Forced to defend the kind of features they regularly ran on masturbation, fantasy and orgasm, what was significant was the surprise, indeed shock, on the part of the men that women - and young women especially - actually wanted to read this stuff. It was as though they suddenly were forced to recognise that 'girls' were no longer sweet and innocent and that women were no longer 'ladylike'.

Commercial culture, in the form of the magazines, has devised a better way of 'doing' sex education than any of the official agencies. By developing a humorous language of 'pecs and penises', the magazines have broken the grip of clinical terminology. If, as Darcus Howe sharply pointed out, the magazines were doing more than educating young readers into the use of condoms, what kind of sexuality are the readers being presented with? Is it better or worse than the diet of romance and beaches-at-sunset which used to fill the pages of *Jackie*?

Although, set against the landscape of major political debate, issues like this are of minor importance, they nonetheless touch upon a bigger set of changes which have indeed exercised politicians. This has been most manifest in anxieties about young single mothers and the decline in family values. It has also surfaced in debates about young women becoming more aggressive. But what I am referring to here is the deeper change in consciousness which has affected the outlook, values and expectations of women and young women, from different social backgrounds, from different parts of the country, from different cultures. It is difficult to generalise across such a large sector of the population. It is not as though women share anything like a single set of values or beliefs. Nor has change affected women homogeneously. By exploring the climate of change in the culture of young women today one is tapping into something which exists in a state of disaggregated latency, a 'semi-structure of feeling', to re-phrase Raymond Williams, which surfaces at unexpected moments in unexpected ways. But its presence is a sure sign that there has been some deep and apparently irreversible shift across the whole social domain. These transformations find symbolic form in the consumer-culture of young people, and in particular young women's culture. If they strike a note of discord or discomfort among some feminists, as much as among the male moral guardians of left and right, then this does not mean that feminists of my generation should discount them as politically insignificant.

Indeed it is disappointing that feminists have tended only to see the negative dimensions in girls 'behaving badly' on the pages of the magazines and on TV programmes like *The Girlie Show*. It is not enough to write this off as girls simply becoming like boys. Yet even if they are playing at what it's like to be a lad, this in itself is an interesting phenomenon. Our own surprise at the apparent pleasure young women seem to get from subjecting men and boys to the kind of treatment they have come to expect, by virtue of being a girl, is a mark of just how unexpected this kind of response is. One young woman recently described to *Women's Realm* how 'we sit in a cafe on the quayside eyeing up male runners as they pass by. For years men have talked about women as though they're pieces of meat. Now we say "look at the state of that bum, 2 out of 10", or "Get a load of this crumpet"'. This kind of reverse sexism can also be seen as a riposte to an older generation of feminists whom younger women now see as weary, white and middle class, academic and professional, and certainly not spunky, vulgar or aggressive. Coming across as loutish and laddish is a provocation to a generation of feminists now established as figures of authority. This dynamic of generational antagonism has been overlooked by professional feminists, particularly those in the academy, with the result that the political effectivity of young women is more or less ignored. And yet various studies show, for example that the politicisation of older Asian women around issues of domestic violence comes from the agitation and encouragement of their daughters and by younger women in the community. To these young women official feminism is something that belongs to their mothers' generation. They have to develop their own language for dealing with sexual inequality; and if they do this through a raunchy language of 'shagging, snogging and having a good time', then perhaps the role this plays is not unlike the sexually explicit manifestoes found in the early writing of figures like

'The magazines defend against the critical voices of mothers, teachers and feminist academics'

Germaine Greer and Sheila Rowbotham. The key difference is that this language is now found in the mainstream of commercial culture - not out there in the margins of the 'political underground'.

Charlotte Brunsdon has recently argued that in commercial culture, particularly in Hollywood cinema, feminism increasingly plays a role as reference point; it informs a good deal of narrative action; but at the same time it is also disavowed, even repudiated.[1] In the end the heroine opts for marriage to some Richard Gere-like male. But this does not wholly invalidate the presence of feminism as a tension, a productive force for moving things on. Here feminism can be seen as having entered the public psyche. In a similar way teen magazines often seem deliberately to set out to provoke a feminist response, as a way of setting themselves apart from an older generation concerned with 'real-life-serious' issues. They do this by 'doing gender' in an exaggerated and ironic way. If '70s feminists argued that make-up and fashion turned girls and women into commodities, then these magazines overdo the make-up and the fashion, without resorting to the old sexist repertoire of female competition, anxiety and neurosis. As Brunsdon notes in relation to *Clueless*, the Hollywood film devoted to teenage female consumerism, cultural forms like these turn femininity into a performance. Gender is dramatised and girls can even play the old-fashioned game of romance so long as they know it's all a bit of a joke. Ironic distance works to give girls room to breathe; it gives them space to explore new emotional ground on their own terms. It designates a place of playful thinking and exploration, away from the watchful eye of their elders. The editors of the magazines understand this, partly because many of them are still in their twenties and close enough to their readers to recognise the need for separation and autonomy. This is the trick of the successful magazine: it intervenes in a space which attempts to defend itself from the critical voice of mothers, teachers and feminist academics. It is one thing to do 'women's magazines' at university, by which time many young women are thinking about looking for jobs in this kind of field: it is quite different to be 13 and have your culture ridiculed for not being serious enough, or for not covering the right kind of feminist issues.

Women's studies academic Stevi Jackson, for example, seems bewildered by the contents of the new magazines.[2] Her argument is strongest when she suggests

---

1. Charlotte Brunsdon, *Screen Tastes*, forthcoming, Routledge.
2. Stevi Jackson, 'Ignorance is Bliss; When You Are Just Seventeen', *Trouble and Strife* 33, 1996.

that the magazines still take heterosexuality as the norm. She deplores the ways in which female sexuality continues to be organised around fashion, beauty and personal appearance, as though only for male consumption. But she has to admit that many feminist lessons have got across. Yet even if heterosexuality is taken for granted in the magazines, does this mean that we consign them to the dustbin of patriarchy? Or can we see them as disruptive, more open-ended, more disputatious forms? Jackson is right to say that heterosexuality is the norm. It would be difficult to imagine *More!* (designed for 18 year olds but read gleefully by 14 year olds) carrying a 'Position of the Fortnight' feature for lesbians. This in itself shows how the magazines set their own limits, and in so doing also reveals how sexuality remains something continually inscribed within boundaries - but boundaries which are fluid and permeable. Lesbianism on these pages remains a social issue rather than a sexual desire. Even when *Just Seventeen* ran a piece recently on 'Girls Who Fancy Girls', the feature itself seemed strangely enclosed. It didn't tip over onto the fashion pages; it was as though the feature was describing a separate world. Lesbianism remains perhaps the touchstone, its existence marking the line between 'popular commercial feminism' and 'real feminism'. But there is no inherent reason why this too might not change. Consumer culture shows itself elsewhere open to those who can afford to participate, as the growth of the pink pound demonstrates. In the more sophisticated world of women's magazines, including *Elle* and *Marie Claire*, 'lesbian chic' now has an uncontroversial existence.

Nowadays there are many competing feminisms; who is to say which version is better than any other? Or at least let us put that question on the agenda. The tone in Jackson's article is that of the feminist expert, surveying the state of women's and girls' magazines from afar. Almost inevitably they fail to meet the mark. However the question that feminism rarely asks itself these days is what exactly is it looking for in young women? What does it expect of them, what should they be like? What should magazines be saying to them? What kind of relationship does '70s feminism envisage itself as having with young women growing up in the 1990s? More generally, how does feminism today connect with 'ordinary women'? What does it mean if, as I suggest here, 'ordinary women' are themselves set upon improving, often against the odds, their own lives and those of their daughters? How does feminism connect with this new emergent consciousness of women and girls? How does it relate to the kind of feminist issues daily debated on TV programmes, and even in the tabloid press? Are they just watered down, sanitised and de-politicised versions of feminism? Are they cynical attempts to up the ratings or the circulations by exploiting women's anxieties about sex, or are they actually capable of bringing about some change? How does one group of feminists, represented let us say by Stevi Jackson in one corner, respond to another group, of young women editors and journalists of magazines like *Just Seventeen, Mizz* and *Sugar*, many of them graduates of media studies and even women's studies, who also define themselves as 'feminist'?

I t is my contention that there has been, over the last few years, a terrific determination among women somehow to transform and improve the conditions of their own existence and to find equality with men at home, in work and also in leisure. This has often been a long and painful process, but the gains of it are being passed on to daughters and to young women. There is an exchange going on, between and across generations of women, in living rooms and behind closed doors, inside the family, where the idea that women can achieve a good life for themselves - and that they need not rely on men or marriage to achieve - is increasingly prevalent. This accounts for the tremendous degree of change in family life. Nowadays if a young girl gets pregnant and wants to keep the baby, her mother will encourage her to delay marriage rather than rush into it. In the old days it was a question of 'Will he do the decent thing and marry you?' Now it is more likely to be 'Stay at home and continue with your studies, marriage can wait'. This kind of shift in attitude shows just how far sexual politics has penetrated the private sphere of the family. Paradoxically it could also be seen as a sign that solid family values actually prevail, since research shows that it is in this kind of context that young single mothers and their babies do best.

T here is an enormous energy in the way in which sexual politics now bursts across our TV screens. From *Newsnight* to *Oprah Winfrey*, social issues of the day almost inevitably touch on changes for women in work, in the family and also even in the field of leisure. The private and public tensions around what it is to be a woman or young woman today also account for the energy and exuberance found in the popular cultural forms, like the magazines. Female independence has entered into contemporary common-sense, it is the very stuff of women's genres today; from women's and girls' magazines and TV sitcoms to radio programmes like *Women's Hour*. It has a particular resonance in British society where high divorce rates and the rising number of single-parent families have encouraged women to concentrate on careers and on organising their own lives, with or without men. Sex, having fun and enjoying a sense of freedom, is one dimension of this new independence. If women are marrying later,and if they are working hard for qualifications and good careers, then the idea of enjoying their leisure time becomes part of their social expectations. And if pleasure and leisure have left older women and mothers behind, they are not going to grudge their daughters the right to have some fun. I think in many ways it is this kind of sensibility which accounts for the hedonism and the rowdy behaviour on the part of young women, which has recently been brought to public attention. Beatrix Campbell recently explored the fashion for young women going out on the town and actively seeking pleasure.[3] If this includes drinking or drugs, they will make sure one of the group remains sober or clear-headed so that they can look after the others. Other writers have described how young women are as keen participants in the dance culture based on taking ecstasy as their male counterparts. As Sheila Henderson reports in *Druglink*, they quite openly talk about wanting to 'get out of their heads'.[4] Indeed in the days following the death of Leah Betts, an articulate 18 year old young woman joined a panel discussion on *Newsnight* refusing to condemn the drug, arguing that overall it was safer than alcohol, and that in terms of enjoyment it was 'a lovely drug'.

None of this is very appealing to politicians. The Labour Party has gone out of its way to support the family values platform and Jack Straw was predictably critical of the girls' magazines for encouraging the wrong kind of attitude. Women MPs from the Labour Party have had little to say of late on any of these issues, and it was up to the Tory Teresa Gorman to challenge her party leader last year for unfairly scapegoating single mothers. Pressure groups and self-help groups have been much more vocal and articulate. And yet for the Labour Party this truly is a lost opportunity. To recognise the role of choice and diversity in family life and in sexual identity, to address women on their own as well as in the context of the family unit, to commit themselves to improving further the career opportunities for women and girls, and to develop a set of social policies which take into account the transformed landscape of family life today, would hardly be more radical for women than we find expressed in contemporary commercial cultures. Indeed, if anything, Labour is more anxious

3. Beatrix Campbell, 'Girls on Safari', *Guardian*, 15.6.96.
4. Sheila Henderson, 'Time for a Make-Over' and 'Keep Your Bra and Burn Your Brain?' *Druglink* Sept/Dec 1993.

to break any conceivable connection with these kinds of ideas. The image of social respectability combined with respect for traditional family values leaves New Labour with nothing to say about current changes in family life. Questioned on these matters on the *Today* programme (following his speech on family values as necessary for the creation of a 'decent society' during a recent visit to South Africa), Tony Blair couldn't, or wouldn't, say the word gay in relation to family life - indeed he could hardly bring himself to say the words single parent. All he could do was repeat the fact that children were best looked after by both parents living in the traditional family unit.

'Older women and mothers are not going to grudge their daughters the right to have some fun'

It is the care of children which really is an important issue, one which seems to have completely slipped the political net. If parents are going to divorce and possibly re-marry how can ways be found of avoiding the children finding themselves absorbing the anger and disappointment that typically comes with the end of a relationship? Are there ways in which this kind of pain can be minimised, and can parents learn to act with the requisite responsibility? Should we not be looking for guidelines on these kinds of family values? Feminism has played a role in making it possible for women not to feel they have to remain miserable in marriage. Men too will often prefer to risk the emotional turmoil of divorce rather than put up with a partnership which is based only on antagonism and resentment. Is it not better that we recognise these as the new facts of life and try to think how children can survive and flourish when marriages dissolve rather than try and return to a situation where marriage is for life?

Underpinning this is an even more awkward issue. Do new family values really mean remaining sexually faithful to one partner for life? Is this what is now expected of us? In the highly sexualised consumer culture that we now live in this seems extraordinarily limiting in human and social terms. But if we have to abide by these new rules in adult, if not in adolescent life, do we simply retreat into the world of sexual fantasy? Where sexual pleasure is now regarded as a social entitlement, and where sexuality is so prominently a part of consumer society, can we now be expected to relinquish this expectation and rely instead on finding ways of spicing up a marriage which has gone stale?

Or must we confront something which really is a challenge to how we live as human beings today? How do we reconcile the diversity of sexual desires with our social responsibilities as parents? This poses a bold political challenge and New Labour might gain more respect by confronting such issues. Maybe Tony Blair is actually saying, without stating it, that sexual culture has gone too far and that we need to constrain desires and forego their dangerous currents in favour of the pleasures and rewards of everyday family life. The problem about developing policies based on values and ideals like these is that those who cannot fufil such ideals, who through no fault of their own cannot get the 'true happiness' package together, are condemned as failures.

Ask most men or women how they would like to live and the chances are they might describe a scenario not unlike the one envisaged by Tony Blair. But material and other circumstances simply don't allow that to be a reality for many people nowadays. Of course most women would want a husband who loved them stupid, had a brilliant job, was a wonderful father and a responsible upright citizen. But we at least have learnt that this is a Barbara Cartland fantasy. Breaking down the myth of romantic love which most women have been exposed to in popular culture - and in teen magazines as they used to be - has been necessary for survival and for participating in a much crueller and more disappointing world. It's been a hard lesson for women to learn. To now have these fantasies foisted back on us by the likes of Jack Straw is little less than insulting. In short, social and cultural change have moved further and faster than either the Labour Party or many feminists are willing to admit. We now have to run to catch up. The danger for feminism is that it remains unwilling to recognise that there are now many ways of being a woman or girl in contemporary society. The danger for Labour is that it fails to find a way of talking to women and to families at the same time. It also has to face up to the fact that the myth of the 2.4 family is as unrealistic as the belief that girls are still sugar and spice ...

The cultural politics of dance music

David Hesmondhalgh

*David Hesmondhalgh examines new forms of
production in the music business, and asks what we
can learn from the dance music boom.*

In 1990s Britain, dance music is at the very centre of contemporary youth culture.
But for many commentators, dance music is despicable, and its recent popularity
only makes it more so. Of course, it might be expected that the right would see
dance culture as dangerous, or banal, or both. But the left too has failed to engage
adequately with it. For an older generation of intellectuals, who located the politics
of music in lyrics, or in the public actions of rock stars, dance music's anonymity
and hedonism can seem regressive. Yet dance music culture in the 1990s has
enormous credibility amongst those still committed to the notion of 'oppositional'
popular culture, in a way that would have been unimaginable twenty years ago. So
how did dance music culture come to be understood as counter-hegemonic? How
do the politics of its production and consumption match up to the sometimes
utopian claims of its proponents?

The rising credibility of dance music in the 1980s

In the late 1970s, the dominant form of dance music at the time, disco, was the
target of derision for rock fans. The audiences and institutions of dance music showed
considerably less interest than the punks in the political issues of the day. There was
no dance equivalent to the Rock Against Racism movement associated with punk

and reggae, and punk garnered much more attention and credibility in left circles than dance music. Journals such as *Marxism Today* and *New Society* provided extensive and positive coverage of punk. But there was no such acclaim for disco.

For some sections of the left to embrace dance music culture in the 1980s and 1990s, a shift had to take place in the way the politics of popular culture were understood. At the centre of this change was a developing analysis by cultural studies writers of the relationship between pleasure, dance and politics in black music. Typically, this contrasted the subtle, pleasurable eroticism of black dance music with the thrusting machismo of rock.[1] This new politics of pop drew on feminist and gay activism's emphasis on the body as a potential site of 'resistance'.

Such concerns were reflected in the work of a highly influential generation of music and style journalists. In magazines such as the *NME*, *The Face* and *i-D*, writers such as Barney Hoskyns and Stuart Cosgrove (now Head of Arts and Entertainment at Channel 4) were propagating similar ideas about 'the politics of dancing'.[2] Rock's embarrassment about dancing was being slowly transmuted into a celebration of dancefloor sexuality. Music journalism and academic populism formed an alliance which found new kinds of authenticities in dance music, around not only class (as in rock) but in connection with sexuality, gender and ethnicity too. Partly as a result of these interventions, new cosmopolitan audiences were attracted to dance music, alongside the working-class and lower middle-class audiences who continued to attend discos and soul events.

So, when the dance boom hit Britain in 1987-8, dance music had already come to be construed as oppositional. The terms used at the time to describe the new dance culture, 'rave' and 'acid house', now sound as out-of-date as the phrase 'beat combo' must have done to early '70s hippies. But both draw attention to discourses which putatively gave dance spaces an added radical edge in the late 1980s.

The term 'acid house' was widely understood to be a reference to drugs. A tedious debate continues to this day about whether the term derives from LSD or from a more esoteric reference to the distorted bass lines of a dance sub-genre developed in Chicago. Whatever the origin of the term, imported American house

---

1. One influential example was Richard Dyer's 'In Defence of Disco ', first published in the magazine *Gay Left*, in 1979.
2. Many of these writers were intellectuals who referred to the names and theories most influential in British cultural studies at the time: Barthes and semiology, Hebdige and subculture, Kristeva and psychoanalytic feminism.

music and the more commercial British version became associated with illegality and marginality. 'Rave' was a term used for big, often unlicensed dance events, usually held out-of-town. In the early 1980s, parties in abandoned warehouses had been the subject of extensive and glamorous coverage in the UK style press. Raves extended this movement away from the restrictions of licensed city-centre premises, out into the unregulated outer-city and rural areas of Britain.

For many commentators, rave confirmed the subversive populism of dance. Its dangerous reputation was sealed by a 'moral panic' in the national press about the drugs associated with the scene, especially ecstasy. Accompanying this panic, though, was an especially strong utopian discourse of collectivism and equality within club culture, which stressed the breaking-down of ethnic, class and gender differences. Dance events had long been viewed as rituals of togetherness and inclusion, but the new dance culture went further, and the rhetoric at least was genuinely democratising: 'No performers, no VIPs, we are all special', was one typical slogan from a club flyer. Many dancers attribute the feeling of unity and love at late 1980s raves entirely to the physiological effects of ecstasy. Such pharmaceutical determinism ignores the crucial role of subcultural *discourse* in framing such events, but there can be little doubt that ecstasy did help to bring about a strong sense of collective abandon on the burgeoning scene. At many clubs, people started to dance in a much looser, uncontrolled way. The music comprised, at first, rhythmic offshoots of disco, imported mainly from Chicago, Detroit and New York City. House, techno and garage are the three terms which have stuck. Pop producers, increasingly dance-oriented since the early 1980s, picked up on these black American subcultural styles, and dance music's centrality to the most popular songs intensified.[3] This made the dance sound all the more loathsome to those within rock culture who still felt resistant to rave/acid house. Dance-pop production team Stock-Aitken-Waterman became a new metaphor for mass culture, both amongst those still affiliated to rock culture, and to dance audiences who preferred more 'underground', 'experimental' sounds.

Dance music culture and the left

Over the past fifty years, musical cultures associated with British youth have had a complex relationship with political movements. Punk represented an

---

3. *The Economist* (30 May 1992, p34) reported Gallup figures showing that dance accounted for 23 per cent of singles sales in the UK in 1988 and 33 per cent by 1990.

unprecedented overlap between the left and popular culture: the 'movement' produced its own organic intellectuals who drew on leftist thought; and it encouraged intellectuals to rethink their relationship to popular culture. (Punk was also, of course, contradictory: violently misogynistic at times, and appropriatable by far-right groups as an expression of working-class reaction.) The left in Britain has had a much more distant relationship with dance music culture. This is ironic, given that it was the central strand in contemporary subcultural music during a period when the left was congratulating itself, in the pages of *Marxism Today* and *New Socialist*, on having developed a new sensitivity to popular culture. In fact, the very split that such magazines sought to heal, between a political left (Labour Party and trade union activists, journals such as *New Left Review* and *Socialist Review*) and a cultural left (organic intellectuals in the style and music press, such as *The Face*, and academics drawn to postmodernism and/or post-structuralism) still seems to be with us. Both sides of this divide have failed to develop an adequate understanding of dance music culture.

The cultural left saw (and heard) the significance of dance music in terms of *innovation* (the music was centred on rhythm, far more than the voice-and-guitar fixation of rock) or as a matter of *a new collectivism* amongst club audiences. This focus on audiences was characteristic of a more general movement amongst intellectuals to reinvigorate left politics by looking to consumption rather than production, to leisure and play rather than work. So commentary on dance music from the cultural left has located its politics mainly in what happens in clubs and raves - the sites of consumption. At its best (for example, Simon Reynolds' work for *Melody Maker* and *The Wire* on the sexual politics of rave) this has popularised a sophisticated aesthetics of the body. But rave has also provided fertile ground for the excesses of postmodernist theory. Many journalists and academics have commented on the intense hedonism of club crowds, and on the adoption of childish symbols. The postmodernists read this hedonism, which they term 'disappearance', using the fashionable jargon of Jean Baudrillard, as offering more threat than mere oppositional activism to the established order. This is because, according to one academic collection, by refusing the whole idea of meaning, subcultures engaged in such regression refuse even to acknowledge authority.[4] But this crude romanticisation is by no means confined to academic

4. Steve Redhead (ed), *Rave Off* , Aldershot 1993.

comment: such views of the politics of hedonism run through the music and style press's coverage of dance music too. But when researchers started to bother asking dance audiences what they thought, it turned out that ravers saw the new dance culture as anything but 'meaningless'.[5]

But the political left's treatment of dance is equally lacking. It has treated dance music as a mere soundtrack for activism. Typical of this was The *New Statesman and Society's* treatment of the Luton activist collective, Exodus, during 1993-5. The magazine at least was prepared to give regular

> 'The political left has treated dance music as a mere soundtrack for activism'

coverage to the new 'politics of protest' - but dance music itself was treated as a new folk music, a means of rallying the troops. How the music sounded, what these sounds implied about the culture, and how the culture was made, sold and circulated were all invisible in such political-left coverage.

The principal theme, instead, was to treat dance music as the target of moral panic. In the most sophisticated work on dance music culture to date, Sarah Thornton has provided a critique of moral panic theory with regard to dance music culture.[6] Thornton argues that, rather than providing a threat to youth subcultures, unfavourable coverage by 'mainstream' media actually sustains them, by generating credibility amongst potential audiences. Moral panic theory, says Thornton, fails to take account of the way competing niche media (such as the dance music press) use tabloid outrage to muster what she calls 'subcultural capital'.

But Thornton's critique shows signs of the cultural left's intense suspicion of traditional left politics. She overlooks the degree to which such coverage can help to generate consent for the intervention of the state, in the form of police raids and road-blocks aimed at controlling youth leisure, and the introduction of parliamentary measures designed to increase police powers. Two laws have quite rightly been seen within dance music institutions as an attack on the 'right to party'. The first was the Bright Bill, eventually passed as the 1990 Entertainments (Increased Penalties) Act. The second was the Criminal Justice Bill, passed as the Criminal Justice

5. See Maria Pini, 'Women and the Early British Rave Scene', in Angela McRobbie (ed.), *Back to Reality? The Social Experience of Cultural Studies*, Manchester 1997, forthcoming.
6. Sarah Thornton, *Club Cultures*, Cambridge 1995.

Act in 1994. The aim of these new measures was primarily to control a new culture of free parties, political protest and 'alternative' lifestyle. In spite of her marginalisation of these political concerns, Thornton's argument is important. It criticises the functionalist view of the state and media held by many within dance music culture (who are not nearly so uninterested in politics as the cultural left claim). Her book is currently being snapped up eagerly by students and other readers hungry for intelligent comment on dance music.

The production politics of dance music culture: three myths

Thornton's study, however, is typical of a reluctance on the part of the academic cultural left to engage with issues of production. Indeed, cultural studies academics often claim that an interest in cultural production is a sign of an unreconstructed, old-fashioned Marxism (the cliché of the 'cloth cap' often emerges at popular culture conferences when the issue of capitalism comes up). And the political left has done little to discredit such facile links, at a time when the commodification of culture and information is becoming an increasingly important part of the strategies of globalising multinationals.

D ance music is a particularly compelling example of the need to think more carefully about the politics of cultural production, because those drawn to dance music culture feel strongly that its methods of production are counter-hegemonic. That so many dance fans are interested in the notion of 'underground' and 'alternative' production is significant: it suggests that dance music's utopianism is not confined to the club, the site of consumption many academics have been concerned with. Rather, it is common to hear a number of claims, which represent a set of hopes about how people might carry out creative work under capitalism. However, there are important omissions in the common-sense beliefs of dance music fans about how the music is put out. I dispute them here, in order to clarify, rather than to dismiss, dance audiences' views.

The following passage contains some of the most common characterisations of the way dance culture has supposedly democratised the production of popular music. (Ironically, it appeared in the former political left-flagship *The New Statesman*, written by a journalist who was keen to persuade the magazine's political left readership that their suspicion of dance music culture was misplaced.)

[T]here's a fundamental subversiveness at the heart of dance music ... No longer is pop music something produced and - crucially - *owned* by musicians recording 'original' tracks based on melodic and harmonic principles. Ambient and techno can be made on computers in bedrooms, and are more concerned with *texture* than melody. House music can be created purely by mixing together other people's records, using sampling technology. Many records central to E-culture aren't even available commercially - they're DJ-only 'white labels'. Much of what's played at clubs is created on the spot by DJs. There is no 'original'. Dance music can be imitated, even co-opted, but it remains, by nature, subversive.[7]

Three key, inter-related themes in discussions about dance music's production politics emerge here. Firstly, there is the idea that dance music production challenges notions of authorship and originality. Central to such claims is the practice of remixing - the practice of taking a master and altering the arrangement of sounds to create a new version of the record. This has an ambivalent status in claims for the radicalism of dance music culture. There is a tendency for dance music audiences to disparage the practice, but for some commentators remixing acts as a subtle deconstruction of the notion of the 'original'.[8]

Secondly, there is the image of the 'white label' as a form of recording which transcends or escapes commodification by being circulated only amongst DJs, or by resisting the personality cults associated with the star system. The 'white label' is simply a 12-inch vinyl record which contains little or no information about its contents. The prestige of the 'white label' has declined as the dance divisions of major record companies have flooded the market with promotional copies, but even in its heyday (1988-91) the practice seemed to confirm dance music's opposition to the emphasis on personality and 'image' in the rock and pop world. Thirdly, there is the increased access to music-making allowed by the 'bedroom studio'.

All these claims are difficult to sustain. In fact, remixing can best be thought of as an attempt to *extend* authorship, rather than to challenge or disperse it. By associating the name of a star DJ or mixer with an indie track, for example, the dance audience can be encouraged to buy, as well as the rock/pop fans. And the

7. Toby Manning, 'Meet the E-culturati', *New Statesman and Society*, 23 February 1996.
8. E.g. Simon Watney, 'Cover Story', *Artforum*, October 1994.

white label's radical status was very quickly undermined by its use as a promotional strategy by big dance companies. This is not simply a case of the major labels co-opting something authentically subcultural: the emphasis on obscurity and secrecy in dance subcultures was always convertible into a form of elitism, an attempt at distinction (this is the aspect of dance culture of which Sarah Thornton is most critical). Will Straw has pointed out how this investment in secrecy is a mark of a male-dominated culture of connoisseurship, rather than a sign of democratic egalitarianism.[9]

The 'bedroom studio' provides a more complex case. The images of access and decentralisation evoked by the notion of musicians working in their own living spaces are powerful ones, and are fundamental to the notion of democratisation in dance music culture.

If punk's metaphor of access (borrowed from American psychedelic pop-rock) was the garage, dance music's is the bedroom. The image refers to real changes in the availability, expense and sophistication of recording technology. But to what extent can these changes be thought of as *democratising* music-making, as many dance pundits claim?

Dance music and new digital technology

A number of important developments in the commercial organisation of music technology meant that it was possible by the late 1980s for records to be produced extremely cheaply. Together, *sequencers* and *samplers* add up to a radical reconfiguration of musical creation, by combining storage and composition. Sequencers are 'word-processors for music', which allow various instrumental tracks to be co-ordinated easily. Samplers allow extracts from other musical works to be transferred, without loss of quality. In the 1980s, the costs of these useful computer tools plummeted and by the end of the decade, semi-professional production in domestic studios was relatively affordable.

Because of the rising credibility of dance music outlined above, music journalists in the late 1980s were able to portray the compelling rhythm lines of house and techno as radical. Sequencing equipment meant that these repetitive beats could be reproduced relatively cheaply. Coverage in magazines of the speed and ease with which house-style records could be made encouraged musicians to 'have a go' themselves. Musicians would record their own tracks at home; perhaps test them out on DAT (digital audio tape) at a local club; press up 500 to 2,000 copies on 12-inch singles; and distribute these records informally to networks of specialist retailers in an area.

So there is certainly some truth in claims that dance music has brought about a new era of Do-It-Yourself music-making. But the bedroom and the cottage are romantic images of autonomous production, which evade the dialectical complexities of music as a commodity. The notion of the bedroom studio draws powerfully on the Internet-driven technological utopianism prevalent amongst the US libertarian left. It neglects the importance of distributing and publicising these cultural goods

'If punk's metaphor of access was the garage, dance music's is the bedroom'

to achieve significance beyond a small, self-contained niche. Beyond very small runs, large distribution firms are needed to get the product out, and to help publicise it - and many dance companies choose to collaborate closely with the major corporations they sometimes profess to despise. The early success of small dance labels was largely due to the low promotional costs allowed by the special subcultural credibility available for dance, through its connections with a rebellious youth culture. But dance music's move into the mainstream should not be understood necessarily by an authenticity/co-optation model, whereby the nasty majors polluted a pure, unsullied youth form. Rather, dance music always has had a profound ambivalence about being popular, about being a mass form. And the dance music press very rarely paid critical attention to fundamental issues of music production: co-operating to form new, long-term outlets for creativity, for example, or providing less exploitative contractual relationships than are possible in the major-dominated mainstream.

The politics of ethnicity in dance music

Ethnicity has been another area in which the claims of dance music insiders have been exaggerated and, again, left intellectuals have failed to provide coherent alternative analyses. For cultural left commentators, the post-house British dance scene was validated by its roots in the work of (often gay) black American DJs, and by the supposedly high degree of racial integration at raves

---

9. 'The Booth, the Floor and the Wall: Dance Music and the Fear of Falling' , *Public* 8, 1993.

during its 'golden age' (1988-1990). Whether or not rave really did bring about a temporary reconciliation of black and white dance scenes, there is little doubt about the very great degree of segregation between white dance music culture and black music institutions (sound systems, shabeens and blues parties) before and after these dates. This segregation is apparent in the British dance music press, which prints many pictures of white clubbers, but where black faces - other than those of American house DJs and musicians - are few and far between. Magazines oriented towards black readers (such as *Hip-Hop Connection* and *Touch*) feature hip-hop, R&B and reggae. Both British-Asian and British-Caribbean youth seem to have found more affinity with these other dance styles than with rave-related dance music culture.

Dance music started to fragment after its eclectic golden period in 1991. A sub-genre called hardcore techno started to use hip-hop-style breakbeats, often sampled from recordings, rather than the programmed rhythms of house variants. This meant that hardcore techno became the one part of British dance music culture which drew significant black audiences. Ironically, the dance music press (generally staffed by those brought up in the 'soul boy' tradition of dance music culture) reacted against the perceived lack of sophistication in hardcore techno, and the scene received very little publicity between 1991 and 1993.

But in 1993-4, the sounds which had been developed on this underground scene gained exposure, as the music press and the national media picked up on the latest subcultural trend (accompanied by a minor moral panic about guns at clubs). Hardcore techno 'crossed over', and as it did so, the term 'jungle' became widely used for it. Just as house music gained credibility from its origins in a black, underground scene, jungle gained much of its significance for white audiences from its roots in 'hidden' black British institutions: pirate radio stations, and dance clubs attended by predominantly black crowds. It incorporates some important elements of British-Caribbean subcultural production and consumption, previously confined to the world of reggae and ragga sound systems, such as the use of dubplates (tracks exclusively produced for a particular DJ) and the demand by dancers for 'rewinds' of favoured tracks.

Jungle/drum & bass is the most important black British sound and genre of the 1990s (though there are important and respected white musicians involved). In terms of the ways its commodities are produced and circulated, it has much in common with post-house dance music culture: it is digitalised, producible for relatively low costs, and is reliant on a network of dedicated shops, promoters and labels. And, significantly, it is being analysed by intellectuals in ways which recall the treatment of earlier forms, such as house and techno.[10] But the same questions need to be asked of the institutional politics of drum & bass, as of dance music culture: has it made a serious difference to who produces popular music, and where the money goes? Has it resulted in a democratisation in the making *and* distribution of recorded music in Britain? The greater sophistication involved in producing drum & bass breakbeats means that production costs are higher than in other dance forms. But the main problems facing drum & bass musicians and musics derive precisely from the genre's current status in media coverage as the most fashionable contemporary subculture. Drum & bass faces the same trap which has faced many other black music forms this century: as soon as the passage is made from margin to mainstream, the genre gains prestige, and produces pride for the communities creating it. But at the same time, the style becomes prone to appropriation and exploitation. 'Jungle' remixes of the most banal pop hits are now common. The music's combination of frantic percussion with smooth vocal and bass lines have seen it adopted as yuppie cocktail music. Nevertheless, drum & bass must not be dismissed: it is a distinctively black British style, expressive of new identities, an often thrilling mixture of the dark and the uplifting, of tender humanity with a street-tough demand for respect.

Meanwhile, in another lineage of dance music culture, a mystical anti-intellectualism prevails. The most absurd ramblings of neo-hippie rave culture portray the DJ and other artists as magical shamen, rather than people who earn a living through cultural communication.[11] Audiences are 'tribes' - and the pre-industrial term reflects a sentimental nostalgia amongst its users. In order to counteract such nonsense, it is important that intellectuals interested in popular culture work towards an integration of approaches. Whereas the cultural left have concentrated on textual innovations and on new forms of audience behaviour,

10. Benjamin Noys, for example, concentrates on formal innovation and audiences, and sidelines production. He insists on an analysis of jungle's textual features as the most important route for investigation. What he finds there is the 'refusal of meaning' supposedly present in house and techno (though he may mean simply that there are no lyrics); and, more intriguingly, new fusions of race and sexuality: 'Into the "Jungle"', *Popular Music* 14:3, 1995.

11. The New Age dance music figure, Fraser Clark has made many such claims.

the political left have tried to understand the relationship between dance music and new social movements. Of course, the distinction between these tendencies blurs at times: some dance music magazines, such as *Mixmag*, have covered political issues widely; and the political left are occasionally willing to publish articles about dance music (while, if *Red Pepper*'s recent issue on music is a reliable index, apparently believing that Britpop's retro-rock is the most important development in contemporary popular music). But more attention will have to be paid to unfashionable issues about commodification, and the place of cultural production within changing forms of profit-making. As the cultural industries become an increasingly vital part of the strategies of global corporations and national governments, it will be all the more important to understand where emerging cultural producers are pinning their hopes of developing alternatives.

Enter, stage right: Neoconservatism, English Canada and the megamusical

Jonathan Burston

Megamusicals and global culture: an international diet of McTheatre for the masses?

The megamusical and industrial transformation

The economic engine, geographical site, theatrical community and larger social imaginary known as Broadway is currently being transformed. The same matrix of social, material and ideal constellations we call the West End is also undergoing a slower if similar transfiguration. In both instances, this transfiguration is indicative of live theatre's very own industrial revolution which, in the late twentieth century, is necessarily transnational in both scope and structure. Though it is somewhat overdue in historical terms, significant portions of the commercial theatre in English speaking countries and elsewhere are now playing a frantic game of catch-up, deploying mass production models which are virtually unprecedented in the history of live theatrical production. We are witnessing a phenomenon that can only be described as the global-industrialisation of the musical theatre.

The motor behind this process of global-industrialisation is the megamusical - a common term in Canada and one gaining currency in Britain and the United States as well. Megamusicals are stage productions conceived and produced in a style born in the last fifteen years, and are exemplified by the long-running success of *Cats*, *The Phantom of the Opera* and *Miss Saigon*. Most industry insiders mark the megamusical's birth with the opening of *Cats* in the West End in 1980. Megamusicals are different in important ways from the merely 'big' musicals that preceded them (*My Fair Lady*, *A Chorus Line*) or that continue to run in the West End, on Broadway, and on tour internationally (*Crazy for You*, *Kiss of the Spiderwoman*). A large musical does not automatically qualify as a megamusical. Unlike their predecessors and contemporary close relations, megamusicals are big global business: capital investments are larger, markets are bigger, more international and more numerous, and stakes are higher than ever before in the history of musical theatre. With the arrival of megamusicals, we have witnessed the attainment of a level of standardisation in production regimes previously unknown in the field of live theatrical production.

Megamusicals thus share a number of essential criteria. These include, first, markets characterised by both rapid global expansion and marked internal growth since 1980. By itself, *Les Misérables* has been seen by over 40 million people. Second, megamusicals are produced and controlled by a select group of highly capitalised, globally competent and now even transnational players. Pioneer British megamusical producers such as Andrew Lloyd Webber and Cameron Mackintosh, each heading what are now large, diversified and global companies, have lately been joined in the market by Disney. Indeed, the broader field of stage musical production is crowded with new transnational players, including Polygram, Viacom and MCA.

The megamusical's third and most distinctive characteristic is its cultivation of specific commercial, technical and aesthetic models which ensure the meticulous replication of any given production across a number of international venues. The megamusical's rationalising, industrial logic - including a quality-control model implemented and supervised outward from a single metropolitan centre - reproduces technical and artistic production detail with such rigour as to significantly delimit the interpretative agency of local musical performers. Hence the increasing use of terms like cloning, franchising, and McTheatre to describe the megamusical business.

Megamusicals consequently afford a new vantage point from which to survey current trends towards the transnationalisation of cultural production. Here I will consider community responses to a changing theatrical economy in Toronto. In the 1980s Toronto became the world's third largest English-speaking theatre centre, and it did so precisely on the back of the city's success in staging megamusicals. The megamusical in Toronto has grown into a symbol of ideological choice and political action. Megamusicals have fuelled the already well-stoked fires of long-standing left-Canadian positions on American cultural imperialism by providing new flammables from an altogether unexpected source: the field of live-theatrical production. At the same time, for the new right they have come to represent the laudable outcome of an emerging and desirable economic order in the cultural sector.

Neoconservatism and changing climates of production

Using the elections of respective conservative governments as a practical benchmark, we can date the consolidation of neoconservatism within Britain, Canada and the United States from the early 1980s onwards. The megamusical's star likewise ascended during this period. Although I do not want to posit *too* close a correspondence between the megamusical (either as a genre or as an industry) and neoconservatism (either as a method of government or social regulation, or as an ideology), their attendant advances are not entirely coincidental. Though these connections can be seen in London, New York and Toronto (the megamusical's three most stable markets), Toronto's example is the most pronounced and complex. But before taking a close look at conditions in Toronto, we need to consider the broader effects of neoconservatism on cultural policy in all three countries where megamusicals have most prominently established themselves.

In Britain, in order to tilt the provision from public to private, traditionally subsidised sectors had to be destroyed or weakened, which in turn allowed a new inrush of private investment. Nowhere was this clearer, in the cultural ecology of the capital, than in the Thatcherite demolition of the Greater London Council in 1986. Indeed, the GLC's cultural policies provoked a particular hostility amongst true-blue Thatcherites. They may or may not have banked on the arrival of the megamusical; but there is no doubt they were determined to put an end to a range of democratic experiments in the cultural field which were on the threshold of becoming genuinely popular.

In the United States from 1981 onwards, the forces behind the Reagan administration supplemented deregulation inside and outside the cultural sector

'The megamusical's star ascended during the period of neoconservatism within Britain, Canada and the United States'

with sustained attacks on the National Endowment for the Arts (NEA), the most important of all government funding bodies for American theatre. Since the mid-1980s the NEA has been presented in neoconservative propaganda as a hot-bed of urine drinking, anti-American homosexual radicals, unworthy of public support. Sustained attacks both on the budget and on the moral credentials of the NEA proved effective in the long term, for it continues to fight for its life under the

Clinton administration. And the NEA is not alone. The American Corporation for Public Broadcasting (PBS) is also staggering under an ongoing war of attrition. Moreover, PBS's struggle to stay alive is now occurring in the context of new American telecommunications legislation which makes *de jure* the previously *de facto* revitalisation of trends towards corporate conglomeration in broadcasting.

Attacks like this on the public cultural infrastructure were not common in Canada until Brian Mulroney's first Progressive Conservative government in 1984. Once in power, the Mulroney Conservatives aimed their bureaucratic and fiscal arsenals at Canada's cultural institutions with a zeal unknown in the previous Liberal regime, in order to weaken the subsidised cultural sector to the point at which it was less and less able to present a convincing case for the social value of public subsidy for the arts. It was a strategy similar to that employed by the Conservatives in Britain during the 1980s and 90s, as outlined, for example, in the *Independent*.[1] The components of such a strategy can be outlined as follows: 1)Starve public cultural institutions of funds required to operate even at minimum efficiency. 2)Observe audiences and artists complaining about declining quality. 3)Pronounce all such institutions unfit to manage themselves, which in turn justifies futher budget cuts. In such a manner, the Canadian Conservative government managed to reduce grants to the Canada Council, the primary source of public subsidy to theatre, by more than 20 per cent in the course

1. See the editorial, 'A chronicle of mismanagement', in the *Independent*, 11 December 1993.

of its two terms. During the late 1980s and early 90s, as arts organisations across the country faced extended layoffs, severe pay cuts, or bankruptcy, it became clear that the sector's ability to produce work other than for the mass market had been badly weakened.

It was in this newly deforested cultural environment that Canadian productions of megamusicals began to take off, not only to packed houses in Toronto, but on tour in other Canadian and American metropolitan centres as well.

Broadway, the West End and Toronto

Although it is shadowed closely by London, New York is the largest theatre centre in the English-speaking world. Broadway's gross theatrical revenues topped US$356 million in 1993/94. Despite this impressive sum, Broadway has been lurching from financial crisis to financial crisis since the mid 1980s. Although Broadway has recently enjoyed increasing audience figures, belief in the financial impossibility of producing around Times Square remains widespread, driven largely by steadily rising entry costs. The omnipresence of British megamusical imports and the decrease in production of new, original non-musical plays have regularly been cited as reasons for rising production thresholds.

Set against this long-term picture of chronic instability are the dramatically improving fortunes of 'the road', a category which comprises all open-ended, limited and touring productions in North America. 1993/94 road receipts brought total North American gross revenues to US$1.044 billion. Despite the perilous nature of sectorial investment, the overall picture for Broadway's entire North American market is one of significant growth. Over the 1980s, as North American industry figures rose steadily toward the $1 billion mark, the live-theatrical (or 'legit') sector grew to sufficient size to interest Disney, Polygram and other transnationals - not only in relation to North America, but to Europe, Asia and Australia as well.

During the 1980s, the political economy of London's West End differed from that of Broadway. Although the West End theatre had traditionally benefited conspicuously from the influx of public money and new talent that was the legacy of Keynes and the post-war settlement, the West End's essentially commercial character had remained unchanged. Changing fiscal realities, however, had begun to damage the ecology of subsidised theatre in Britain. The conspicuous success of musicals was only one factor among several regarding the challenges facing contemporary British theatre. Because of the relatively well-entrenched position of the non-musical commercial play within the West End, rarely if ever was the musical ('mega-' or otherwise) positioned as a phenomenon that had the potential to alter the balance between publicly-subsidised and commercial production in Britain, to the irreparable detriment of the subsidised sector.

T his was precisely how the megamusical quickly came to be understood in Toronto, however. Theatrical imports have always possessed a singular resonance within English-Canada. This is because an identifiably Canadian theatrical scene only came into existence in Canada's largest urban centre with government support, and only as recently as the late 1950s. Prior to this, touring British and American shows comprised the greater part of Toronto's theatrical life. The commercial sector sponsored these touring shows, and state subsidies for theatre were virtually non-existent prior to 1957. Before then, Canadians only very rarely saw their own lives represented on Canadian stages. For these reasons, in English Canada more so than elsewhere, public theatre (benefiting from government subsidy) came invariably to designate indigenous theatre as well. It was in the context of this tradition that, through the 1980s and 90s, English-Canadian journalists, policy makers, theatre workers and audiences debated with increasing passion and regularity the merits and detractions of commercial blockbusters like *Cats*, *Phantom of the Opera* and *Les Misérables*. Public debate about the cultural significance of the megamusical went to the heart of the debate about the newly emergent 'free market for culture'.

All the world's a stage: Toronto's battle of the paradigms

At the forefront of these debates in Toronto was the prestigious conservative national daily, the *Globe and Mail*. Its 1993 editorial heralding the Toronto premiere of *Miss Saigon* exemplifies the contest for legitimacy between the city's newly maturing commercial theatre scene and its previously pre-eminent subsidised one. The editorial's first sentence announced:

> Last night's opening of Miss Saigon, the latest mega-musical to play Toronto, not only marks the launch of a new theatrical spectacle, but heralds Toronto's arrival as a major theatrical centre.[2]

Significantly, the *Globe* presented the contest between Toronto's two theatrical sectors as a zero-sum game, characterising each sector in oppositional terms. Ignoring the

---

2. 'The city a stage, and filled with players', *Globe and Mail*, 27 May 1993.

trend towards the presentation of more commercial productions within subsidised houses, the *Globe* portrayed subsidised theatre as a sclerotic integument from a previous era, stuck on a body politic otherwise newly invigorated by free markets in virtually every sphere of production. 'For too long', the editorial declared,

> too much of Toronto's theatrical community has behaved as if the theatre would be a wonderful thing if it weren't for the audience.

The *Globe* summarised the city's theatre history 'BC' ('before *Cats*') as elitist and irrelevant to its citizenry, offering up 'theatre as therapy', where - it argued - the people wanted real entertainment.

In contrast, commercial theatrical production was portrayed as inherently virtuous. The *Globe*'s depiction of the sector was exultantly populist, rejoicing in the fact that 'Toronto is suddenly bristling with large commercial theatres, most of them opened in the last decade and all of them seemingly packed every night'. In a manoeuvre consistent with neoconservative conviction, market demand was tendered throughout as the final arbiter of cultural value.[3] Thus the *Globe* celebrated 'Toronto's arrival as a major theatrical centre', notwithstanding the fact that this new major theatrical centre's successes were based upon the purchase and reproduction of theatrical spectaculars already running in New York and in London, and in Hamburg and Melbourne and elsewhere as well. As left-leaning commentator Rick Salutin observed the following day, the Toronto production of *Miss Saigon* would appear to herald the city's 'arrival', 'because we've got version No. 5 (after London, New York, Tokyo and Chicago)'.[4] In fact, insofar as market demand functions as a principal arbiter of social value within neoconservative thought, these very attributes heightened the megamusical's stature and celebrity.

The editorial also introduced an aesthetic comparison between government-built auditoria, in which many subsidised companies performed, and the newly-inaugurated theatre housing *Miss Saigon*, privately owned by impresario David Mirvish. Theatres built in the 1960s and the 1970s with public funds suffered from an 'institutional banality we have come to expect from public architecture.' In contrast, the *Globe*

3. A classic and concise Canadian formulation of this central tenet of neoconservative philosophy, observable in all three national contexts is elsewhere delivered by *Globe and Mail* editorial writer Andrew Coyne: 'When one pays for a work of art... that does not vulgarize or commodify it: it sanctifies it', *Ideas: Culture and the Marketplace*, Canadian Broadcasting Corporation, 1993, p45.
4. Rick Salutin, 'Miss Saigon, meet Stan Rogers', *Globe and Mail*, 28 May 1993.

described Mirvish's new hall as 'a humanist theatre, one that delights the senses at every turn' - driven, moreover, 'by the need for intimacy between audience and performers, not by the architect's ego'. State-supported theatrical production implicitly mirrored the dull, state-built theatres in which they could be found.

Perhaps most troubling to many in the theatrical community was the editorial's suggestion that the megamusical was developing a theatrical infrastructure in Toronto where none had existed before. According to the *Globe*, the megamusical was

> creating an infrastructure of theatrical talent: actors, singers, dancers, musicians, directors, producers, technical people, all of them developing their craft in an atmosphere of professionalism.

For many of those involved in the construction of recognisably Canadian theatre in Toronto from the 1960s, the suggestion that commercial theatre was the primary vehicle within which they developed their craft was dangerously unhistorical; the insinuation that only in commercial theatre was an 'atmosphere of professionalism' to be discovered, insulting. The history of theatrical production in Toronto was in fact widely acknowledged to be very different. Far from commercial capital providing a needed industrial platform, it was the very presence in Toronto of a pre-existing, publicly-constructed infrastructure - comprising both talent and fixed capital - that eventually provided the conditions which enabled the commercial theatre boom to happen. Even *Miss Saigon*'s Toronto producer, David Mirvish, accepts this interpretation of events, and proffers it in his regular lobbying for the reinstitution of adequate government support for Canadian theatre. On these occasions Mirvish insists, as does London-based megamusical producer Cameron Mackintosh in his own regular exhortations to British parliamentary committees, that the relationship between publicly-supported theatre and its commercial counterpart is symbiotic, rather than oppositional. Commercial theatre, Mirvish insists, continues to rely on the seedbed of skill and talent that the public-theatrical infrastructure supplies.

The *Globe*'s paean to the virtues of free-market theatrical production can thus be said to have outstripped the views and interests even of commercial producers in order to further a broader political agenda. In Toronto and within English Canada that broader agenda possesses one further distinctive attribute that requires illumination.

The megamusical as political marker

In English Canada, a complex set of conflations were fashioned into a simple opposition. On the one hand was the publicly supported cultural sector which was *Canadian*, and on the other a commercial cultural sector which was *global*. In a conspicuous homology, political discourse in English Canada during the 1980s came to position the English-Canadian left as explicitly 'nationalist', while Canadian neoconservatism was seen to be decidedly 'continentalist' both in its economic programmes and in its cultural predilections.

Until the 1990s, neoconservatism in English Canada, unlike in Britain or in the United States, was not characterised by strong appeals to the idea of nation, tradition or patriotism, appeals that had elsewhere sought to counterbalance the destabilising effects of deregulation of social life by calling upon allegiance to the imagined community of the nation. Nor were parallel xenophobic strategies regularly touted regarding the restriction of immigration; nor covertly statist ones invoked regarding the strengthening of policing; nor protectionist measures demanded against foreign imports or corporations. All of these strategies - save the last, which was and remains largely the objective of American supporters of Buchanan, Perot *et al* - were embraced by neoconservatives in Britain and the United States.

Instead, Canadian neoconservatism hitched its fortunes unequivocally to the wagon of deregulated trade with the United States, and to the idea of continental integration. Though they avoided overt discussion of political union, Canadian continentalist elites discussed - and continue to discuss - continental integration both in terms of economic policy and social programmes. Thanks in large part to the inability of the English-Canadian left to formulate coherent strategies allowing for a continental integration of national economies toward progressive ends the idea of continental co-operation congealed as the exclusive terrain of the pan-Canadian right, and a newly confident pan-Canadian business class. Appeals to any sort of - attenuated - nationalism virtually became the exclusive property of the English-Canadian left.[5]

---

5. Contemporary English-Canadian left-nationalism is uniquely configured. It asserts the value of state intervention in matters social and economic; it eschews conventional ethnic patriotism in favour of celebrating Canada's multicultural reality and its conspicuous, regional 'senses of place' from sea to sea to sea; until the 1990s it entirely embraced the task of building consensus between Quebec and English Canada; and crucially, it defines an ideal Canada in negative relation to the United States and its perceived jingoism and atomistic social philosophy. As a result of these composite characteristics, English-Canadian left-nationalism has been described by some as paradoxically post-modern. Readers interested in this aspect of English-Canadian left-nationalism might begin with B.W. Powe's (occasionally maudlin) poetic treatise, *A Tremendous Canada of Light*, Toronto, 1993.

It is within this larger frame of reference that the megamusical accrued its deeper meanings in relation to Canadian politics during the 1980s. Its supporters, mostly positioned on the continentalist right, did more than hail its emergence as a sign of a maturing cultural marketplace, its social value gauged in all-important market terms. As the first sentence of the *Globe* editorial implied, Canadian neoconservatives had additional cause to salute the emergence of megamusicals because the shows were laudably 'global' in both form and content - that is, similar if not practically identical to parallel productions in New York, Los Angeles, Vienna, London, Singapore and elsewhere.

Most of the megamusical's detractors were accordingly located on the nationalist left. Left *intelligents* were customarily disdainful of megamusicals because of their status as cultural imports from Canada's former imperial master; in other instances they were critical because their cultural value was gauged by the marketplace and not by the *polis*. But most important, the marketplace in which the megamusical's value was gauged was the *global* marketplace, and in Canada even more than elsewhere, global markets have been automatically understood as American ones. Thus until the arrival in 1995 in Toronto of the first American megamusical, *Disney's Beauty and the Beast*, British megamusicals often took on honorary status as American imports. This is entirely understandable, given that both Lloyd Webber and Mackintosh control their North American operations out of New York.

From early on, left-nationalist critiques of the megamusical were organised not only from the perspective of audience, but from the perspective of the actors as well. Members of the English-Canadian theatrical community were prominent among the critics of the megamusical. The term 'McTheatre' acquired cachet in this circle, invoking as much the new experience of working on what was perceived as a 'theatrical assembly-line' as it did the (often only imagined) experience of attending a show that conformed to the expectations of a cultural McDonalds.

In Toronto, *Les Misérables*, for example, was dismissed by most on the left as an exercise in the commodification and sterilisation of the revolutionary impulse; as homogenised in sound and utterance, utterly incapable of generating any significant meaning. In 1989, in the then left-liberal national magazine, *Saturday Night*, theatre critic Robert Cushman put forward a considered reflection on what he termed an 'international neutrality' pervasive in the aesthetics of the still-new megamusical genre. He went on to comment: 'Most of Act Two of *Les Mis* is devoted to revolution. Does anybody know who is revolting against whom, or why?'[6]

It was within the logic of this distinctive system of legitimation that the megamusical acquired two kinds of social value in Canada, each corresponding to broader positions on contemporary political issues. The English-Canadian left-nationalist position, intensely critical of the new genre and its connected industry, shares some characteristics with criticisms levelled at the megamusical in other locations, but it also possesses an additional level of analysis that is not significantly present in either New York or in London. The objection that Canadian critics share with megamusical detractors elsewhere is the 'McTheatre' critique, accusing routinised global cultural production of producing a concomitantly homogenised cultural product. Thus Cushman is able to speak of a 'pervasive blandness' permeating the works of the 'Lloyd Webber school', in much the same way as critics in Britain and the US.

In Toronto this critique has acquired a new twist, triggering discussion about the ways in which Canada's two imperial powers (the ascendant US and the declining UK) continue to exercise control not only over cultural production in the hinterland, but also its meanings and values. It also rejects the (global) market as exclusive arbiter of cultural value. The English-Canadian left-nationalist critique of the megamusical thus names a sector of cultural production previously unconnected with the drive of cultural imperialism.

In a similar fashion, right-wing Canadian champions of the megamusical share their general appeals to populism with megamusical advocates in other cities. But in addition, the megamusical functioned in Canada as a legitimating vehicle for the emerging commercial sector of live-theatrical production: its status as a globally celebrated commodity lent it its credibility.

---

6. Robert Cushman, 'Musical Chairs', *Saturday Night*, January 1989. It is worth mentioning that when David Mirvish moved *Les Misérables* from Toronto to Montreal and opened it in Quebecois French, other highly politicised groups immediately and wholeheartedly embraced the show as their own. According to Canadian company manager Eric Goldstein, significant numbers of *independentiste* actors and audiences interpreted what remained a highly standardised production - notwithstanding its re-translation - as a clarion call to the separatist cause. The English-Canadian left-nationalist characterisation of *Les Misérables* as a production void of any revolutionary impulse had fewer supporters in Quebec. Instead, Quebecois performers and their fans often chose to read *Les Mis* as a text charged with local, radical meaning.

Concluding confessions of a reluctant Broadway Baby

Despite my own long-held position as a Canadian cultural nationalist, I have always had a passion for Broadway. This ought to indicate a great deal, given the hostile, occasionally predetermined and characteristically English-Canadian response I regularly experience when confronted with the constant wash of American cultural products over Canadian airwaves, along cable, or on Canadian cinema screens. Yet as a teenager in Canada, when watching Broadway shows or those of the West End in the days prior to the megamusical, I rarely if ever found myself 'chafing under the bridle of an occupying power'. And in noting this absence, I know I was not alone. Despite the stark ideological and structural obstacles of colonial residualism (*vis à vis* the United Kingdom) or neo-colonialism (*vis à vis* the United States) that did objectively face Canadian producers brave enough to mount local work prior to the arrival of the megamusical era, a touring Broadway show, for many Toronto audiences and performers alike, rarely stood as an effective marker of *coca-colonization*. This almost certainly had something to do with its character as a live-theatrical event. Until recently, live theatre had a quality of singularity about it that seemed to exclude it from being seen as a force for global cultural homogenisation.

Yet it would be a mistake to adopt the cultural imperialism/McTheatre critique wholesale: within the world of the megamusical, neither aesthetic homogenisation nor wholly alienating work practices are universal, nor are they inevitable. And enquiries into the global-industrialisation of the musical need to scrutinise carefully those moments of nuance, interpretation and resistance to 'assembly-line' production that continue to occur.

But to ignore the forest for the trees would likewise be an error: despite moments of subversion, 'Fings Ain't Wot They Used t'Be' in the field of live-theatrical production. The global theatre industry continues to transform itself in ways that affect our lives to a degree still only properly acknowledged by its own players.

I want to thank my sister, Varda Burstyn, for her important contributions to this piece, and for the lifelong example she has set for me in activism and in scholarship.

The new communications geography and the politics of optimism

Kevin Robins

Is Bill Gates the future? Al Gore and New Labour seem to think so. Kevin Robins *thinks not.*

'We are going to a different world', said Candide, 'and I expect it is the one where all goes well; for I must admit that regrettable things happen in this world of ours, moral and physical acts that one cannot approve of.'

Voltaire, *Candide*

In his recent book, *The Road Ahead*, Bill Gates says that he is an optimist, and tells us why we, his readers, would do well to be optimistic like him. What drives his optimism, he tells us, is the prospect of a 'revolution in communications', associated with the Internet and its future transformation into a global information highway. 'We are watching something historic happen', Gates intones, 'and it will affect the world seismically, rocking us in the same way the discovery of the scientific method, the invention of printing, and the arrival of the Industrial Age did.'[1] From this historic event, he believes, we have everything to expect. 'The network will draw us together, if that's what we choose, or let us scatter ourselves into a million mediated communities. Above all, and in countless new ways, the information highway will give us choices that can put us in touch with entertainment, information, and each other' (p274). Of course, a revolution of this kind must confront some difficulties (described as 'unanticipated glitches'), but 'despite the problems posed by the information highway', Gates concludes, 'my enthusiasm for it remains boundless' (p272). Such is the force of his optimism.

Nicholas Negroponte, who is the director of MIT's Media Lab, also happens to be a self-declared optimist, indeed he is 'optimistic by nature'. And his grounds for optimism are pretty much the same as those articulated by Bill Gates. In *Being Digital* - the cover blurb describes it as 'the bestselling road map for survival on the information superhighway' - Negroponte tells us of his firm conviction that 'in the digital world, previously impossible solutions become viable.'[2] 'More than anything,' he explains, 'my optimism comes from the empowering nature of being digital. The access, the mobility, and the ability to effect change are what will make the future so different from the present' (p231). With enthusiastic conviction, Negroponte declares that all social divisions will be overcome by 'the harmonising effect of being digital': 'Digital technology can be a natural force drawing people into greater world harmony' (p230). Again, there is the tokenistic recognition that the yellow brick road might not always be an easy one. 'But being digital', concludes Negroponte, 'nevertheless, does give much cause for optimism. Like a force of nature, the digital age cannot be denied or stopped' (p229). Here, as is the case with Bill Gates too, optimism expresses itself in terms of the force of human destiny.

At this point, you might feel yourself being drawn to the summary conclusion that all of this is no more than a rhetorical smokescreen, obscuring the real motivation of Gates and Negroponte alike, which is to exploit the new communications technologies as a source of both corporate profits and personal gain. You might want to conclude that this techno-uptopianism is just the fancy marketing language of 'virtual capitalism' (or what Bill Gates terms 'friction-free capitalism').[3] But to remain

---

1. Bill Gates, *The Road Ahead*, Viking, 1995, p.273.
2. Nicholas Negroponte, *Being Digital*, Hodder and Stoughton, 1995, p.230.
3. The argument that Gates' motives are primarily economic and profiteering is made by Michael Dawson and John Bellamy Foster, 'Virtual capitalism: the political economy of the information highway', *Monthly Review*, 48:3, 1996.

content with such a quick judgement (whatever partial truth it may indeed contain), would, I suggest, be to ignore a great deal that is worth trying to understand in and about this discourse. I think that we have to accept the optimism and idealism of these writer entrepreneurs at face value. There seems no reason to doubt the sincerity and conviction of their belief that the new communications technologies will bring a better world into being. What moves them is, moreover, a vision that has considerable resonance beyond the world of enterprise; the project to develop the information highway has also become a central issue in the political agenda of the 1990s. And it must be taken seriously in so far as it has become perhaps the nearest thing we now have to a political vision for the future.

In the United States, both Newt Gingrich and Al Gore have made the new communications systems central to their political visions. The Democratic administration has taken steps towards the creation of a National Information Infrastructure (NII), and exhibits an optimism to rival that of Gates or Negroponte. Gore envisages that it 'will help educate our children and allow us to exchange ideas within a community and among nations. It will be a means by which families and friends will transcend the barriers of time and distance.' The new technologies are presented as a panacea for all that is wrong in national and international affairs. 'The GII will not only be a metaphor for a functioning democracy', claims the Vice-President, 'it will in fact promote the functioning of democracy by greatly enhancing the participation of citizens in decision-making. And it will greatly promote the ability of nations to cooperate with each other. I see a new Athenian democracy forged in the fora the GII will create'.[4] In the political domain too, then, extraordinary investments are being made in the redemptive potential of the 'communications revolution'.

And what is the case in the US is also true in British political culture. Here it is the Labour Party that has been most attentive to Gore's proclamations about 'virtual' town meetings and information democracy. The argument is put forward that 'new technologies give us the opportunity to extend our thinking about the form that democracy takes' - 'only a Luddite would ignore the possibilities that technological change offers for an extension of the

---

4. Al Gore, 'Forging the new Athenian age of democracy', *Intermedia*, 22:2, 1994, p.4.

democratic process'.[5] The 'Blair revolution' has involved the development of a policy document on the Information Superhighway: 'We stand on the threshold' of a revolution as profound as that brought about by the invention of the printing press. 'New technologies which enable rapid communication to take place in a myriad of different ways across the globe, and permit information to be provided, sought, and received on a scale hitherto unimaginable, will bring fundamental change to all our lives.'[6] In his speech to the 1995 Labour Party conference, Tony Blair conveyed his own vision of an information utopia, involving such visionary things as 'virtual reality tourism that allows you anywhere in the world', and 'computers that learn about a child as they teach them, shaping courses to their personal needs'. There is the confident sense of a technological and social revolution in the making. 'Blair is talking science fact', observed an approving Victor Keegan in the pages of the *Guardian*; this new 'digital socialism' is closer to the real spirit of 'socialism', he maintained, 'because it offers individual empowerment or equality of opportunity in knowledge'.[7] Through the new information and communications technologies, it is argued, political dreams can finally become everyday realities.

Now - as should already be apparent from my own rhetorical tone in presenting both the entrepreneurial and the political agendas - I find this common technocultural vision quite incredible. I personally cannot share this sense of anticipation and expectation, and I cannot be persuaded that, in this particular context, optimism is the appropriate attitude to adopt. As I listen to this discourse of revolutionary transformation, I find that nothing can convince me that these new technologies will change our lives in any meaningful way. So what, I am inclined to ask, is this investment in optimism all about? How is it possible that there are so many people who can (still) accept this narrative of progress, and can do so quite unproblematically (and we cannot doubt the integrity of their acceptance)? And what do they actually find themselves believing in when they affirm its validity? These are questions I want to put in the way of the politics of optimism, which presents itself as such a good and well-meaning thing, beyond any possibility of criticism or objection.

First, there is the activation of a new ideal of community. From just a casual

5. Peter Mandelson and Roger Liddle, *The Blair Revolution*, Faber and Faber, 1996, p.209.
6. *Information Superhighway*, Labour Party, 1995, p.1.
7. Victor Keegan, 'Labour on net', *Guardian*, 5 October 1995.

acquaintance with the politics of the information highway, it might seem as if the road ahead involved an uncertain step into the unknown, and that being digital was about becoming excitingly different from the way we are now. One might be led to think that new kinds of social interaction were being inaugurated, and new forms of social experience made possible in virtual communities. In part, this possibility is indeed what is being suggested. A little more scrutiny soon reveals, however, that this is far from being the only aspiration. Indeed, what quickly becomes apparent is that the reality of the technocultural imagination may be quite the reverse: what may, in fact, be proposed is some

'What is this investment in optimism all about?'

kind of electronic reinstatement of a lost order, a lost way of life, and lost values and ideals (the communitarianism of Amitai Etzioni is a crucial reference point). The imagination of the virtual society is commonly associated with the recovery of familial and communitarian principles, inspired by a nostalgia for 'traditional' forms of interaction, associated with the village pump or the town square. The imagination of electronic *Gemeinschaft* evokes a world of shared meanings and values, a world in which social interaction has the transparent simplicity associated with face-to-face encounter. Virtual political life is conceived in terms of the Jeffersonian town hall meeting (or in terms of a communitarian vision of the Athenian *agora*). What is on ideological offer is something familiar and reassuring, and the appeal of techno-community surely derives, to a large extent, from this sense of comforting restoration.

Alongside this construction of an ideal of community, there is a complementary idealisation of communication. Is not enhanced communication the very essence of the information highway agenda? 'The information highway makes all communication easier', says Bill Gates. 'Bulletin boards and other on-line forums allow people to be in touch one-to-one, or one-to-many, or many-to-many, in very efficient ways'.[8] 'Our goal', proclaims Al Gore, 'is a kind of global conversation in which everyone who wants can have his or her say'.[9] Now this may well be presented again in terms of new horizons and possibilities, but in fact it simply perpetuates a very old dream. As

---

8. *The Road Ahead*, p271.
9. *Forging the new Athenian age*, p6.

Armand Mattelart has demonstrated, this faith in the salutary efficiency of communication goes back to the Saint-Simonians, and has been reactivated with each successive technological 'revolution' since that time. What has been sustained over time has been 'the idea of communication as the regulatory principle counteracting the disequilibria of the social order'.[10] In certain respects, as Mattelart suggests, the ideology of progress has given way to the ideology (or perhaps religion?) of communication. Communication has always promised to bring people together (to put them 'in touch' with each other; to join them in an extended 'conversation'). It has been associated with increased intelligibility, then with mutual comprehension, and thereby with social solidarity and integration. It has seemed as if it must bring coherence to the social order. Who could be opposed to communication?

These closely related ideals of community and communication are central to what I have called the new politics of optimism. What is being invoked is the (only) kind of social order that could contain the projections of the committed optimist. And, as such, it stands in striking contrast to the recalcitrant and disorderly nature of the real world. What is called into being is a new world like Candide's Eldorado: 'It is probably the country where all goes well; for there must obviously be some such place'.[11] It is precisely a utopian space (a space apart). All goes well here because it goes on in terms of a radically diminished form of society and of sociality. The transparent and ordered space of virtual interaction is perhaps the ideal medium in which to cultivate Etzioni's ideal of 'responsive community'. But even more significant, I want to argue here, is the aspiration to transcend our human condition of living and being in dimensional space. It seems as if things will go better when it is no longer necessary to move in and through the real world, negotiating its complex spaces and engaging in contact with the others, who also have their places there. Why, it is asked, should we involve ourselves in such difficult encounters when community can be wired directly to us now in our electronic homes? The present optimism is directly related to this desire to abolish space and place, which have hitherto been the very ground of embodied (enworlded) experience and meaning.

---

10. Armand Mattelart, *Mapping World Communication*, University of Minnesota Press, 1994, p.36. For an excellent historical analysis, see Armand Mattelart, *L'Invention de la Communication*, Paris, La Découverte, 1994.
11. Voltaire, *Candide*, Penguin, 1947, p77.

We should reflect on this strange aspiration. An absolutely central preoccupation in projected scenarios for the information highway concerns the elimination or transcendence of distance - for is not distance that which keeps people apart, is not distance what prevents them from understanding each other? Thus, Bill Gates argues that 'the information highway makes geography less important', and suggests that this will make it easier for us 'to reach out to others with similar interests no matter where they are located'.[12] Nicholas Negroponte is an uninhibited visionary in this respect: 'the digital planet', he predicts, 'will look and feel like the head of pin', and 'the post-information age will remove the limitations of geography'.[13] Again what is invoked is the possibility of new kinds of social interaction: 'We will socialise in digital neighbourhoods in which physical space will be irrelevant ... Digital living will include less and less dependence upon being in a specific place at a specific time, and the transmission of place itself will start to become possible' (pp7, 165). The virtual condition is one in which it will be possible to transcend the parochial concerns of what we have until now called the real world:

> While the politicians struggle with the baggage of history, a new generation is emerging from the digital landscape free of many of the old prejudices. These kids are released from the limitation of geographic proximity as the sole basis of friendship, collaboration, play, and neighbourhood. Digital technology can be a natural force drawing people into greater world harmony (p230).

After geography, Negroponte wants to believe, there is the infinite possibility of a floating world - for 'the kids', at least - a world without gravity or friction.

In his recent book, *City of Bits*, William Mitchell - 'I am an electronic *flâneur*', he tells us, 'I hang out on the network' - pursues the same wishful theme. What he likes so much about the information highway is that it is 'profoundly antispatial', and makes possible the 'despatialisation of interaction'.[14] Again there is the pleasured observation that 'community has come increasingly unglued from geography'. Mitchell gives the example of a global teaching seminar he has himself conducted, one in which 'we scattered souls have become an electronically linked virtual community'. 'Bodily location is no longer an issue', he reports, 'for me, the

---

12. *The Road Ahead*, pp181, 263.
13. *Being Digital*, pp6, 165.
14. William Mitchell, *City of Bits: Space, Place and the Infobahn*, MIT Press, 1995, pp8, 10.

students in Hong Kong are as much part of it as are those to be found within walking distance of my office (p166).' Elsewhere, Mitchell shares with us his vision of the virtual city of the future:

> This will be a city unrooted to any definite spot on the surface of the earth, shaped by connectivity and bandwidth constraints rather than by accessibility and land values, largely asynchronous in its operation, and inhabited by disembodied and fragmented subjects who exist as collections of aliases and agents. Its places will be constructed virtually by software instead of physically from stones and timbers, and they will be connected by logical linkages rather than by doors, passageways, and streets (p24).

What is being envisioned is 'a new urbanism freed from the constraints of physical space' (p115). What Mitchell, like Gates and Negroponte, wants to make clear to us is that the new communications geography is, in fact, a post-geography.

The politics of optimism wants to be rid of the burden of geography (and along with it the baggage of history), for it considers geographical determination and situation to have been fundamental sources of frustration and limitation in human and social life. As William Mitchell puts it, 'geography is destiny' (p10). To understand the affliction of geographical existence must, then, be to strive to overcome the historical constraints of space and place. And now this long-standing desire for transcendence seems to have found the new technology that will finally bring about its realisation. Now the tyranny of distance is being technologically abolished, and we may communicate with others wherever they might be, forming new kinds of electronic communities based on interest and affinity (rather than the accident of physical location). This is the age of tele-presence, interactivity, connectivity, and of 'being in touch'. The new communications media make it possible to achieve greater closeness to others (to others in the virtual network, that is); they have become associated with ideals of intimacy, and with new possibilities of social communion and bonding. Where geographical distance is presented as an obstacle to communication and community, the achievement of technological proximity may appear as the solution.

This ideal of bringing people together and promoting mutual understanding seems to be self-evidently a good thing. This is what Al Gore appears to believe, and Tony Blair too. The social rationale for the development of the information highway is entirely predicated on such sentiments. I find it interesting - though in no way surprising - that this new virtual politics has such plausibility for, as I have clearly suggested in outlining the vision of Gates, Negroponte and Mitchell, it is a politics that is based on the most naive and superficial social analysis. Whatever the appeal of this futurological project - and clearly it does have very considerable social and political resonance now - it remains, nonetheless, a severely diminished and impoverished social imaginary. Those who are not so infatuated with technological futures, those who are concerned, rather, with the question of plural and democratic culture in actual societies, must surely find this vision and project deeply problematical. For what is involved is a fundamental disavowal - both intellectual and by technical means - of the real complexity and disorder of actual society and sociality. And thereby, I want to argue, what is entailed is a significant depletion and reduction of the resources of social and political culture. In so far as this is the case, the technocultural agenda that promises a new social order in fact constitutes a force of resistance to social and political transformation.

> Do you understand the sadness of geography?
> Michael Ondaatje, *The English Patient*

Let me just say a little more, in conclusion, about what it is that I find so deeply problematical about this technocultural politics. I want to make clear what it is that is facile in this understanding of technology, and to explain what I think is regressive in the desire technologically to transcend space and place.

Here I can do no better than refer to Martin Heidegger's famous essay 'The thing', written nearly fifty years ago, which considers the shrinking of distances as a consequence of both new transportation systems and new media technologies (radio and television). Heidegger's lucid observations are worth quoting at length:

> Man puts the longest distances behind him in the shortest time. He puts the greatest distances behind himself and thus puts everything before himself at the shortest range.
>
> Yet the frantic abolition of all distances brings no nearness; for nearness does not consist in shortness of distance. What is least remote from us in point of distance, by virtue of its picture on film or its sound on the radio, can remain far from us. What is incalculably far from us in point of distance can be near to us. Short distance is not in itself nearness. Nor is great distance remoteness.

What is nearness if it fails to come about despite the reduction of the longest distances to the shortest intervals? What is nearness if it is even repelled by the restless abolition of distances? What is nearness if, along with its failure to appear, remoteness also remains absent?

What is happening here when, as a result of the abolition of great distances, everything is equally far and equally near? What is this uniformity in which everything is neither far nor near - is, as it were, without distance?[15]

It seems to me that these observations have even greater pertinence with respect to the new communications technologies and ideologies. Heidegger works towards the deconstruction of banal and common sense beliefs about distance and the conquest of distance. What, he asks, is the problem about distance and remoteness? This is a question that is also pursued with considerable insight by Gabriel Josipovici, who reflects on the experiential possibilities of separation, and on what he calls the 'therapy of distance'. Sense and meaning must be made out of distance. Drawing on Walter Benjamin's concept of aura ('the unique phenomenon of distance, however close it may be'), Josipovici suggests that, rather than seeking its abolition, we might actually be concerned to 'bring distance to life'.[16] What is also made clear in the Heideggerian formulation is that mere closeness or proximity must be distinguished from true nearness. The technological erosion of great distances brings with it only an illusory intimacy: technological mediation can in fact insulate us against being touched by the other. We become content to live in a world of 'uniform distanceless', that is, in an information space rather than a space of vivacity and experience.

In his recent book *Cybermonde*, Paul Virilio gives this philosophical stance a political spin, raising serious questions about the technological neutralisation of our existential and moral relation to the world. Virilio is concerned, too, with the collapse of geographical distance, for he considers this to have been fundamental to our human liberty. 'The scale of the world is our freedom', he argues, and 'one of the first freedoms was the freedom of movement'.[17] The diminution of distance associated with the so-called global village represents, then, a kind of intellectual and spiritual enclosure. It

15. Martin Heidegger, 'The thing', in his *Poetry, Language, Thought*, Harper & Row, 1971, pp.165-166.
16. Gabriel Josipovici, *Touch*, Yale University Press, 1996, pp.65, 10.
17. Paul Virilio, *Cybermonde, la Politique du Pire*, Textuel, 1996, pp.43, 57.

also has profoundly significant implications for the way we relate to others in the world. Virilio challenges the myth of electronic communion, casting into doubt the ideal of virtual interaction. This he sees in terms, rather, of 'the loss of the other, the decline of physical presence in favour of a phantom, immaterial presence' (p45). Embodied and situated existence is fundamental to our political being in the world. Virilio is sceptical about the now common belief that one can, and should aspire to, communicate with those at a distance as one does to physically proximate others. It is possible to seek out the distant other, he recognises, 'without being aware that one hates one's neighbour because he is present, because he stinks, because he makes a noise, because he disturbs you and because he summons you - unlike the one who is distant, whom you can zap' (p42). The pleasures of remote control may exceed the obligation to embodied and situated others.

So, where does this leave us, then, those of us who happen to find ourselves unmoved and unpersuaded by the politics of optimism? How should we respond in the face of the social and political investments that are now being made in the information highway? This is not an easy matter. The intensity of the investment in the technoculture makes the articulation of dissent extremely difficult. To express doubts about the technological restoration of community and democracy is to be regarded as a pessimist. And being pessimistic is now regarded as self-evidently a bad thing, as being an optimist seems a good one. Jeremiahs are not welcome in an 'age of optimism' (Negroponte).

What we first have to do, I believe, is to resist this simplistic denigration of pessimism. As Joe Bailey emphasises, pessimism does not constitute a psychological disposition or problem, nor should it be seen as expressing some kind of metaphysical taste or sensibility.[18] It is, rather, a form of social thought and social valuation, which may be grounded in historical experience, and for the expression of which there may be very substantial grounds. Thus, given our long experience of previous new communications technologies, each of which was in its time supposed to herald a brave new world order, how could we not be suspicious of what is now being claimed for the information highway? Wouldn't it be exceptional if this technology could deliver what no other new technology could before? I would argue that a certain scepticism or pessimism is quite in order. But it should aim to be an active and transformational response - recall Gramsci's neat formulation: pessimism of the

18. Joe Bailey, *Pessimism*, Routledge, 1988, pp.vii, 5.

intellect, optimism of the will - engaged in disturbing the complacency and conformism of the technoculture. It should scorn the kind of shallow optimism which would have us believe that new communications technologies could of themselves create a new and better world. Paul Virilio points the way: 'I work in the "resistance"', he says, 'because there are now too many "collaborators" once again telling us about salvation through progress, about emancipation, about man being freed from all constraints, and so on'.[19] Without such a resistance, there would only be technological conditioning and acquiescence in the technological order.

But more than this is needed. We have to move the debate beyond the new technology agenda (where it is sadly the case that the banalities of Gates and Negroponte pass as prescient social thinking). For what is really at issue is the more fundamental question of creating a more plural and democratic culture, and we must not let this be reduced to being simply a technological issue. We have to come to terms with the embodied and situated world in which we live, a world in which difference and antagonism are inescapable, and we have to find the political means to negotiate this inescapable reality. And in this context, I maintain, virtual dreams are an irrelevance. The utopia of virtual order is based on the denial or disavowal of real-world disorder. The new virtual politics, the information highway project for example, substitutes for a real social and political vision. 'Life in pre-cyborg places was a very different experience', quips William Mitchell. 'You really had to be there' (p44). Precisely. And it was being there that was crucial. And not being there represents an evacuation of the political scene. The real antithesis to the politics of optimism is not, in fact, a politics of pessimism. It is a grounded politics, and a politics of complexity.

I would like to thank Armand Mattelart; many of the thoughts in this discussion were stimulated by conversations with him in London (nearly) in September 1996.

---

19. *Cybermonde*, p78.

Heat from a small fire

Tony Dowmunt

Hollywood meets Alice Springs?
Who has the last laugh? Tony Dowmunt reports.

A dark night in the Central Australian desert, twenty miles outside Alice Springs. Normally the only visible light would be the carpet of stars in the clear black sky. But tonight at Simpson's Gap, a spectacular gorge in the Mcdonnell Ranges, the stars are thrown into shadow: the massive orange-red stone walls of the gorge blaze under movie arc lights. A feature film crew are setting up the next shot: there are three 35mm cameras and crews, at least as many assistant directors shouting through megaphones, and a group of wardrobe and make-up people hovering around the star, Olympia Dukakis.

I had been invited to visit the location because I happened to be staying in the same motel in Alice Springs as the film crew. The director was George Miller (not the *Mad Max* George Miller, everyone kept explaining, the other one): I bumped into him in the motel laundrette, and remember being surprised - and impressed - that a big movie director would do his own washing.

I was in Alice for a rather different purpose: making a documentary with an Aboriginal media group for Channel 4, about Aboriginal television and video.[1] The visit to the feature film location was a fascinating glimpse of how the other half lived - particularly interesting as some of the Aboriginal people we had been working with on our programme had been hired as extras on the film.

For me the most important part of our project - and the most interesting sequences in the final programme we produced - involved the local TV stations (EVTV) on the Pitjantjatjara and Warlpiri lands, hundreds of miles outside Alice,

---

1. *Satellite Dreaming*, APT Film & Television/CAAMA, 1992.

in the endless, apparently empty desert of the 'Red Centre'. Both these stations had started out as illegal, pirate operations to resist the influx of white TV via newly launched satellites (AUSSAT) in the mid 1980s. AUSSAT was the result of a strong lobby by Murdoch, Packer and other media barons and, at the beginning at least, conceived of its audience as being white - the scattered and isolated farming communities across the continent's interior - and ignored the needs of the extensive Aboriginal populations in the area. But even before AUSSAT was on air, the Pitjantjatjara and Warlpiri community operations had developed an easy-going style of local programming: they covered events in their area, like any other local station, but also started to use video in a process of 'cultural maintenance', recording stories (*tjukurrpa*), songs and ceremonies in the areas of country to which they referred.[2] This wasn't a simple matter of heritage but a vital process reaching into the heart of cultural survival: re-infusing the landscape with their creation-myths in the act of singing, dancing and recording, reclaiming the country for the 'dreamtime' on video. This activity could also have more straightforwardly political consequences, especially in relation to claims for land rights.

The red desert isn't empty at all, of course: it's populated by what remain of the original inhabitants - scattered aboriginal communities, for whom the landscape teems with myth and meaning. For Topsy Walter, a member of the (Pitjantjatjara) EVTV board, Pitjantjatjara country is full of 'stories' : EVTV's mission is to keep these stories 'strong'. For some Warlpiri elders who are now too old to travel from Yuendumu, the mission settlement, Francis Jupurrurla Kelly of Warlpiri Media goes on trips to record distant landscapes of which they are the owners or custodians; the playback sessions that follow back at Yuendumu are often very emotional affairs - people being re-introduced to country that they left, or were forced to abandon, fifty or sixty years ago.

EVTV and Warlpiri Media figured out how they could interrupt AUSSAT broadcasts as they began to be beamed in from the satellites, and how to substitute their own locally originated programming - live or from pre-recorded video cassette. In both communities this process was and still is under the control of committees

---

2. This is described in more detail by Philip Batty in 'Singing the Electric', in Tony Dowmunt (ed), *Channels of Resistance: Global Television and Local Empowerment*, BFI/Channel 4, 1993. Warlpiri Media is discussed at length by Eric Michaels in *Bad Aboriginal Art: Tradition, Media and Technological Horizons*, University of Minnesota Press, 1994.

of elders whose interest is in the maintenance of traditional culture. It provides stark contrast to the way in which TV is used as a mass medium in most other parts of the world, not only because of the degree of local control: the traditional restrictions on the circulation of sacred knowledge mean that much of what they shoot can't be shown even to the small but general audiences of their stations. EVTV have a cupboard in which they keep all the women's ceremonies recorded by Pantjiti Tjiyangu, their camerawoman: they can be viewed only by groups of women in the community who have had children.

> 'The Pitjantjatjara women are supposed to somehow transmit their primitive power and arcane knowledge through their eyes alone'

EVTV invited us to film an expedition they were mounting to record on video a section of the Seven Sisters 'songline' at Kuruala - a remote site a couple of hundred miles drive across dirt tracks into Western Australia. On the way we picked up a convoy of old cars and a battered lorry full of people from the settlements we passed on the way. Some of these people were along for the ride, but most had ritual obligations in relation to the Seven Sisters recording: to be properly validated - a true record of the song, story or ceremony - these events have to be supervised by a range of people with particular kinship connections to the traditional 'owners' of the site, or custodians of the story. One of the custodians travelled with us in our Toyota on the last leg to Kuruala. He told us stories in Pitjantjatjara associated with the landscape we were passing: although I couldn't understand a word of what he was saying, it was fascinating watching his finger pointing at rocks and trees and tracing almost every contour of the land as he told us its story, its 'dreamtime' associations. When we arrived at Kuruala it was his job, as custodian, to narrate the story and direct the camera as it panned towards the women who were re-enacting the Seven Sisters as they fled from Nyiru, their tormenter.

It was members of this same group of women whom the Dukakis movie company had hired as extras - to perform a song in the background of the key scene of emotional revelation for Olympia's character. The film they are shooting - *Over The Hill* - is her story: an American woman, recently widowed, who goes to visit her daughter in Sydney. The daughter is married to a politician who is cynically exploiting ecological issues to win an election: they both reject Olympia, who - rather implausibly - 'goes bush': heads into the interior in her granddaughter's boyfriend's souped-up car. Through a series of encounters and adventures, she eventually 'finds herself' as an independent woman, and at the end of the film magically regains her daughter's love and respect. Her emotional transformation is signalled in two key sequences: one in which she swims in the sea with a dolphin, the other where she is led at night by a wordless Aboriginal woman to a women's campfire and is sent into a trance by their chanting. The film plays on a romantic - not to say racist - assumption about the 'natural' healing power of Aboriginal culture, parallelling it to that old stalwart new age symbol, the dolphin. The woman leading her to the campfire was played by Pantjiti Tjiyangu, the EVTV camerawoman, and the women round the campfire were all from her community, a good few hundred miles south of Simpson's gap on the Pitjantjatjara lands.

The contrast between these two representations of Pitjantjatjara culture - at Kuruala, and here at Simpson's Gap - couldn't be more stark. For the Dukakis movie the women are stripped to the waist and painted up to perform the traditional songs - but they are miles away from their own country and from the sites where traditionally these songs should be performed. The scene being shot features these silent but 'deeply significant' encounters between Olympia and the Pitjantjatjara women, who somehow transmit their primitive power and arcane knowledge through their eyes alone: the performers do a great job, but admitted afterwards they thought the whole idea was absurd and comical - unsurprisingly, since it is so clearly based on Western myths about their culture. Most distorted and strange of all - to the Pitjantjatjara actors - was the director's insistence they build an enormous bonfire to sit around and sing traditional songs, because big flames would 'work best for the cameras'. In Aboriginal culture (as with most tribal peoples living in areas where wood is scarce) large fires are taboo: normally they use just two or three small logs to last the night.

But there's another side to the story. As the flames from the fire leap ten, fifteen feet in the air, and the First Assistant Director tries to organise the women for the first take, a Pitjantjatjara man wielding a camcorder circles the encampment, joking with the women and filming the moviemakers' antics. This is Simon Tjiyangu, cameraperson with EVTV, and Pantjiti's husband. His jokes are about the spectacular waste of wood: the women joke back that they're grateful for it because they were getting cold waiting around half naked to be filmed. Simon videos these exchanges and the rest of the evening's shoot. When the movie work is done he returns to base with the women, and over the next few days he edits the footage and puts it out in the community news slot on EVTV.

Maybe because I started my work in TV in community-based video, I find it tempting to believe that the kind of indigenous peoples' TV represented by EVTV is somehow more culturally 'authentic' than our own uses of media in the West. But, of course both EVTV and Warlpiri Media are as much embedded in their particular social circumstances as we are in ours, and the myth of 'authenticity' is no more helpful than that of 'naturalness'. Nevertheless I still find the differences interesting, and challenging.

My own experience as a viewer of television is mainly of disconnectedness, of floating in a shallow, but increasingly global electronic soup. TV amuses me, may even occcasionlly stimulate or move me but it rarely goes very deep.Yet here in Australia are people who are creating their own community television at the same time as using video to deepen their connection to their own psychic and physical ground, their sense of place, rootedness, belonging.

Traditional Aboriginal people talk about the process of recording their stories on video as one of deep validation. It is true. The ancestors, dreamtime creatures, are here. They are the hills, the rocks, the sandbanks. Noli Roberts, the custodian of the Seven Sisters' site at Kuruala explained why he wanted it videoed: 'When people see it they will say, "It's true. I see how Nyiru and the Seven Sisters came to Kuruala".' Eric Michaels - the American anthropologist who helped to set up Warlpiri Media in the 1980s - refers to the 'centrality of the prohibition against fiction for Warlpiri oral tradition'.[3] In its conviction of absolute truth, its strict adherence to the law of the 'dreamtime' and the authority of its stories, Aboriginal culture represents the polar opposite of postmodern uncertainty. In our culture television is - thankfully - losing the ability to claim any such representative authority, as Reithian certainties recede; but we are also losing any sense of the social purpose, meaning or value of television in these new circumstances - a sense that these democratically controlled TV stations in the desert have in spades.

So I think that the real appeal to me of EVTV and Warlpiri Media has less to do with their particular function in representing indigenous cultures and communities than it has with the media/political example they hold up. They offer a model of a different, more purposeful and democratic relationship between TV

---

3. *Bad Aboriginal Art*, p112.

and communities of all kinds - particularly those that feel undernourished by the dominance of centralised and increasingly global television systems.

During the writing of this piece I tried to find the Dukakis film. It turned out to have been released but seems to have sunk without trace. BBC1 screened it last June, and it was released on video for a while: but it has since - in the jargon of the video trade - been 'deleted'. I've managed to see it only because a colleague in the BBC found me a copy.

Simon's tape will be back on the shelves at EVTV - a contemporary *tjukurrpa* alongside the Seven Sisters and all the other dreamings. Maybe he puts it on occasionally, interrupting AUSSAT's transmission of ABC or the commercial station from Alice, so the community can re-live the joke of the enormous bonfire.

A SPRING OFFER TO SOUNDINGS READERS
Travel & urban geography titles from Lawrence & Wishart

Each title is individually reduced or get ALL THREE for just £25.00 POSTFREE

Rising in the East: The Regeneration of East London
Tim Butler and Michael Rustin (eds)

Every modern global city needs its urban hinterland, and London has its ever expanding East End. This area now attracts huge volumes of public and private investment, in what has become the largest urban development zone in the United Kingdom. The East End now takes in a large part of Essex, on some definitions stretching as far as Southend; its population is one of the most ethnically diverse in Britain; it is becoming significantly more middle class; and its industrial base is shifting. This fascinating book of essays explores the meanings of these changes.

'An excellent series of essays' *Labour Euro News*

'Challenging and insightful' *IMA Agenda*

Special offer price £12.00 POSTFREE
Normal price £14.99pb (224pp)

Staying Close to the River: Reflections on Travel and Politics
Ken Worpole

Ken Worpole weaves a rich literary tapestry as he reflects on memories of friends and places he has known and loved. Through a unique series of letters, *Staying Close to the River* charts a route through four generations of family life, the political progress of the left, the cities of the world, and human fallibility. Both moving and funny, Ken's style is a testimony to the art of detailed evocation and meticulous observation, whether at home in the East End, sweating on the road to Tuscany, or discussing the arrival of 'Dallas' on Russian TV. This book is a rare gem.

'It's strange to discover something fresh in an age stale with literary invention, but Worpole pioneers a type of freewheeling epistolary travelogue'
Elizabeth Wilson, *The Guardian*

'It is a rough, idiosyncratic, touching diary.' *New Statesman*

Special offer price £8.00 POSTFREE
Normal price £9.99pb (192pp)

The Green London Way
Bob Gilbert

The first urban long-distance walk - a 92 mile route through the green spaces and commons of London, combining insights into the history of London's people with an in-depth knowledge of its land and wildlife.

'The Green London Way is admirably written, with stirring tales of how the citizenry banded together to save their priceless open spaces from the clutches of heartless developers.' Michael Leapman, *New Statesman*

'Bob Gilbert's philosophy is that city wildlife is just as exciting as the countryside, the book has a large fan following.' **Nicola Baird, BBC Wildlife**

'a refreshingly outspoken, well researched and opinionated critique.' *Time Out*

Special offer price £8.00 POSTFREE
Normal price £9.99pb (216pp)

LAWRENCE & WISHART

Lawrence & Wishart is an independent radical publisher, with titles ranging over cultural studies, education, gender and politics. Committed to the generation of new thinking, L&W has a reputation for producing quality books of intellectual distinction, which engage with contemporary critical concerns.

Recent titles include:

The Body Language: The Meaning of Modern Sport
Andrew Blake £12.99pb

The Urbanization of Injustice
Andy Merrifield & Erik Swyngedouw (eds) £14.99pb

The Blair Agenda
Mark Perryman (ed) £12.99pb

Male Order: Unwrapping Masculinity, new edition
Jonathan Rutherford & Rowena Chapman (eds) £12.99pb

Reclaiming Truth: Contribution to a Critique of Cultural Relativism
Christopher Norris £12.99pb

We also publish a range of classic political theory titles, including The Collected Works of Marx and Engels in 50 volumes; Marx's Capital - A Student Edition; and selections from Gramsci's prison notebooks.

Journals published by Lawrence & Wishart include, *Soundings*; *Rising East* a journal of East London studies; *Renewal* a journal of Labour politics, and *new formations* an interdisciplinary journal of cultural debate, history and theory.

For the full range of L&W titles send for a **FREE 1997 L&W CATALOGUE** with inspection copy details and journal subscription information.

Send to: Catalogue requests, L&W
99a Wallis Road, London E9 5LN.
Tel 0181-533 2506 Fax 0181- 533 7369
E-mail: catalogues@l-w-bks.demon.co.uk

What lies between mechatronics and medicine? the critical mass of media studies

Tim O'Sullivan

Media Studies: What's the fuss about?

One of the defining characteristics of modern social and cultural life has involved living and learning to live in a culture of mediation. From the late nineteenth century onwards, western and other cultures have become increasingly reliant upon and saturated with forms of mass communicated information and entertainment. The rise of the popular press and publishing industries, the expansion of film, radio, advertising, and television have transformed and extended the experience of everyday life and redefined relations between public and private. In the process, our senses of identity - who we think we are - and of immediate situation - where we think we are - have become powerfully linked with forms of culture which are mediated from beyond the geographical and temporal confines of the everyday and the personal. As Arjun Appadurai has argued, the *'mediascapes'* of modern life have become increasingly global in their operation and character.[1]

The mass media have not only expanded and developed as a prerequisite for modernity, they have also gained a problematic reputation and been defined as problems for modern times. These debates have centred on three levels of concern: first, the power of the media as *public* institutions charged with the responsibilities of making sense of the world for their audiences, readers and viewers; second, the assumed or claimed impact of forms of media consumption on the *private* sphere; third, a particular focus on the media's role in the production of *popular* culture. From their early days, modern media have been regarded with suspicion and have themselves become the central figures in a series of cyclical moral panics about their perceived increasingly pervasive and intrusive presence.

The structure of much modern popular debate about the media was established in the early part of the twentieth century when the media seemed perfectly to encapsulate aspects of the mass society which was perceived to be emerging as the condition of modern times. On the one hand, the new media seemed capable of mass manipulation, capable of exercising new sorts of control over vulnerable, atomised populations, uprooted and estranged from their traditional communities and ways of life. On the other, the appearance and the success of new, twentieth-century, mass mediated cultural forms was also perceived to indicate a profound challenge to the good, the civilised and the cultured. At the heart of these concerns lies a view of the modern media as powerful institutions which have become increasingly technologised and which are capable of direct effects on their audiences and users. Isolated and general levels of violence, criminality and many other negative social developments have recurrently been attributed to the media. The tendency to isolate the media from their social and commercial contexts and to cast them as causal agencies has underpinned the modern debate about the media.

If the media have been defined as problematic they have also endured a problematic relationship with formal education. How, why and whether to include the media as objects within educational curricula has resulted in a number of educational responses. These have oscillated between arguments about making available certain kinds of critical awareness of the media, and an emphasis upon teaching and learning about participation and practice in

---

1. 'Disjuncture and Difference in the Global Cultural Economy', *Theory, Culture and Society*, 7, 1990.

the production of media output. The first of these positions stresses the necessity for an informed and critical media literacy, in touch with (post)modern times and enabling full and critical participation in contemporary media culture. Given this state of affairs, the subjects provide 'what you need to know' in order to live in the contemporary world. The second response has advanced a different case which has foregrounded forms of media education for practice; for practical involvement, vocational preparation and creative relevance. In recent years however, the expansion of educational provision in Media Studies and related subjects including Cultural and Communication Studies, has itself become an object of media attention.

Along with leaking waterpipes, mad cows, alcopops and pay rises to the demobbed captains of industry, Media Studies has become one of the scandals of the 1990s, a convenient target for a range of indignant and self-justifying attacks. These have been articulated (is there a paradox here?) in the press with recurrent coverage in both broadsheet and tabloid titles, and to a lesser extent the agenda set here has been picked up in various broadcast forms. The relatively benign comedy of George Webber, Posy Simmons' caricature of the Social Sciences lecturer in 1970s polytechnics, may well have given way to the more knowing humour of the Biff cartoon or of Professor Lapping in the department of Media Studies at the University of Poppleton in the 1990s, but Media Studies has developed a more controversial reputation.[2] The knives, it would appear, are out.

Associated particularly with developments across undergraduate provision in the old polytechnics - now the newest universities - in the early 1980s, Media Studies, together with cognate fields of enquiry such as Communication and Cultural Studies, is a multi-disciplinary subject area which has attracted a somewhat shrill and mounting chorus of invective. If the concept of representation has been jolted in recent years from the heartland of Media Studies, the subject's own media misrepresentation has formed an interesting if painful reminder of the state of things, part of the 'uncomfortable times' referred to in the editorial of the first issue of *Soundings*. Much of this has simply and depressingly replayed older elitist or profoundly anti-intellectual anxieties about the value of the study of popular

---

2. Lapping and his Department form the basis for a weekly column in *The Times Higher Education Supplement*, written by Laurie Taylor.

forms. However, much of the recent wave of this criticism has undoubtedly been reignited by the rapid growth in the numbers of students applying for and graduating from such courses.

Skillset, the industry training body for broadcasting, film and video, has recently estimated that there are 32,000 places on courses with media components in Further and Higher Education, compared to about 6000 in 1990.[3] The British Film Institute's *Media Courses UK* comprises some 220 pages of densely packed information. Applications to universities and colleges appear to have peaked last year, with a downward dip of about 9 per cent, although these figures for 1996 need to be set against the patterns of previous years which saw surges in applications of between 30 per cent and 55 per cent each year.[4]

At one point, Media, Film and Television, together with Communication Studies, were reported to be second only to Medicine and Accountancy in the number of applicants for each place.[5] Such growth in numbers of applications and courses at the Further and Higher educational levels is often viewed horizontally - as if they existed as isolated layers across education. This is clearly not the case, as the period from the mid-1980s onwards has seen growth in the subject from primary, through secondary to postgraduate levels of course provision. Developments at GCSE, GNVQ, BTEC and 'A' level (in excess of 7000 candidates for the 1995 examination) have been extensive.

As more than one commentator has remarked in the light of this rapid growth in numbers, Media Studies has become the 'fashionable' subject of the mid-1990s, and many have been quick to extend this idea. For Jeremy Paxman:

> As a whole, the subject is to the Nineties what sociology was to the Seventies. Which is to say fashionable and incoherent.[6]

Growth attracts publicity. This has come from a number of positions and quarters. The first has been manifest in the concern regarding standards. The increased volume of students is equated with falling standards and lack of academic rigour. For example, the *Sunday Telegraph* in its discussion of the

---

3. Skillset Consultancy Paper, London 1996.
4. See J. Langham, 'Higher Education in Flux', *20:20*, 3, Autumn 1995 for more detailed data.
5. *Independent*, 22 April 1992.
6. *Evening Standard*, 3 November 1990.

1996 85 per cent 'A' level pass rate - contrasted with the 70 per cent pass rate achieved in 1951 when the 'A' level system began - claimed that part of the rise in entries and attainment had been 'boosted by the introduction of such subjects as sports and media studies'.[7] From the early days of Media Studies, the press have tended to be fixated with the idea that Media Studies involves the study of television soap operas.[8] For Leo McKinstry, writing in the 'Watchdog' column in the *Sun*, 'Universities should be about gaining knowledge, not swallowing propaganda'. In a discussion which takes in a government research grant awarded to study the effects of Sylvester Stallone's movie *Judge Dredd*, Popular Music Studies, Peace Studies, Race and Ethnic Studies, Leisure and Food Studies, Gender and Women's Studies, and the pressure on universities to fill places, McKinstry confides to his readers that 'what worries me most are some of the courses they're teaching'. And he was not just talking about 'trendy media studies where

'Along with leaking waterpipes, mad cows, alcopops and pay rises to the captains of industry, Media Studies has become one of the scandals of the 1990s'

lecturers and students are given grants to watch ("analyse" in their jargon) their favourite films and soaps ("contemporary cultural interfaces")'. Should any of the *Sun*'s readers be in any doubt he asserts that 'large sums are squandered on a bizarre cocktail of irrelevant, jargon-ridden, PC nonsense, dressed up as academic teaching.'[9]

McKinstry represents one voice in a recurrent, populist critique which has continued in the 1990s - one of the reasons for Media Studies current 'scandalous' reputation. Tax-payers' money, useful 'employability' and our old friends, the left-wingers in local government, are blended with a definition of the subject as profane, dealing with the everyday and mundane, 'what everybody knows' on the one hand, and at the same time on the other, too esoteric - just 'jargon-ridden', ideologically suspect and theoretical.

7. 18 August 1996.
8. See for instance: 'School for Soaps', *Observer*, 21 January 1996 and 'Several thousand fresh-faced undergraduates will gather in lecture theatres and seminar rooms over the next few weeks to dissect Eastenders', *Observer*, 1 September 1996.
9. 1 September 1995.

If the position taken by the *Sun* is in many senses predictably populist and anti-intellectual, less easy to comprehend is the position which has recently been taken by the *Independent*. In late October 1996, the release of a report from Brunel University prepared for the Council for Industry in Higher Education was used by the *Independent* for a full scale attack on the subject. 'Media Students face low job prospects' was the headline. The revelation in the article, that 15.2 per cent of Media Studies students are still unemployed after six months of completing their degree (*not* that 84.8 per cent are successful in finding employment), was used as a springboard for a sustained attack in the education supplement and on the leader page.[10] 'The Trendy Travesty' was how Lucy Hodges developed what she defined as the key issues: 'It (Media Studies) is very political with a clapped-out Marxist agenda and offering nothing except to destroy someone's prospects of honest employment'. The spectre of 'hundreds of unemployed people schooled in the semiotics of *Neighbours*, together with the suggestion that the payment of tuition fees might concentrate students' minds on other subjects, concludes the article. In addition the leader offered the following advice:

> How not to be a journalist. Media studies is a trivial, minor field of research, spuriously created for jargon-spinners and academic make-weights. Students learn nothing of value because the subject doesn't know its own purpose, is unimportant, and because most people teaching it don't know what they're talking about. Yet it is the fastest-growing subject in higher education. Careers counsellors might wonder why they have failed to stop students applying to waste their time and tax-payers' money. Perhaps we can help: this paper regards a degree in media studies as a disqualification for the career of journalism. That might put a few of them off.

Not surprisingly, this example of independent journalism ('it is ... are you?') provoked a number of responses.[11]

Added to these issues have been other criticisms from within the educational and academic sphere, but voiced from other disciplines and subject areas. Educational priority in a time of shrinking budgets is one worry. 'Dons despair as

---

10. 31 October 1996.
11. See letters from Paul Rickard, Peter Golding, David Morley, Angharad Thoms, 7 November 1996; and James Curran, David Morley and Angela Phillips, 'The view from here', 14 November 1996.

students spurn science in favour of media studies', or 'Oxford? Sorry Prof, I'm into media studies' are two typical headlines.[12] They also encompass those who argue for more essential categories and definitions of education which foreground the production of suitably refined, or useful knowledge, which stands in a functional relationship to the economy.[13] Predictably, Media Studies is found wanting on both counts. Its assumed objects and methods of study guarantee it a status of barbaric vulgarity and of useless knowledge.

A key part of the critique emphasises that the knowledge Media Studies produces does not translate into recognisable and economically useful skills for students - although this is often asserted without any convincing or credible comparative evidence concerning the performance of other subjects. But Media Studies has recently been accused of a greater crime - one of deception and dishonesty.

The issue of vocationalism and unrealistic student aspiration has seen industry voices join the fray. These have come largely from television where, according to Alexander Garrett,

> If a career in the media is seen as sexy, television is its most erogenous zone ...
> a generation of wannabes is having its hopes unjustly raised to fill university
> places.[14]

The suggestion here is that Media Studies courses lead their students to believe - unrealistically - that they will readily gain access to jobs in media production and that this promise has been used unscrupulously to recruit students to university departments mindful of the importance of filling their quotas of student numbers. As Ed Boyce, Head of Training at Meridian Television has reportedly put it:

> too many courses lead people to believe they will walk into the industry, and
> they won't. The courses are not vocational; the people teaching them don't
> know what the media needs. It is a mess, frankly. Young people are being
> cheated'.[15]

---

12. *Independent on Sunday*, 25 June 1995; *Independent*, 1 January 1996.
13. See for instance Max Beloff who identifies 'a rash of "media studies" and "gender studies" and the rest, whose only contribution to the economy is keeping young people off the labour market', *THES*, 9 August 1996.
14. *Observer*, 1 October 1996.
15. Cited by Maggie Brown, 'So you want to be in the media ...' *Daily Telegraph*, 25 September 1996.

The traditionalist critique has resurfaced (a variant of the 'Harry Hardnose' School of Journalism and hard knocks) which stresses the ineffective, inaccurate, unrealistic training or preparation for training provided by Media Studies courses. Viewed from this perspective, the subject is something to be avoided; it is deemed too theoretical, and too far removed from the realities of work culture. Steven Peak and Paul Fisher argue that:

> Course content tends to the theoretical and earns the contempt of practitioners, most of whom did what they regard as more rigorous liberal arts degrees in the 1970s and 1980s.[16]

For Andrew Popplewell, writing about his experience of recruiting for BBC World Service radio:

> It is my experience that many of those who achieve degrees in these voguish subjects haven't learned much of any use ... why have I been faced by queues of young people, fresh from their degree ceremonies, who can't even tell me what a microphone does?...Media Studies may teach some big issues, but they are a waste of time for anyone who wants to make a career in radio.[17]

Some disgruntled industry voices have blamed Media Studies for the increasingly heavy and problematic demands on media organisations - in terms of the scale and quality of applications, requests for voluntary work experience or observation, or for other kinds of educational involvement. The *Observer*, for example, cites the case of Bob Nelson, Head of Organisational Development at the BBC, who 'receives 80,000 inquiries about broadcasting careers each year - yet last year it took on only 2,100 people at all levels'.[18]

This call, for a more effective 'gatekeeping' role on the part of media educators, has recently been linked to a key issue concerning media employment. This involves the number of media graduates seeking to break through the catch twenty-two which requires of them work experience, and has meant that many will work, in the short term at least, for nothing. Who you know, and your media contacts, continue to exercise a strong influence over appointments. In the context of changes within the organisation of employment within broadcast

16. *The 1996 Guardian Media Guide*, p234.
17. *Independent*, 24 October 1995.
18. 1 October 1996.

and other media sectors in Britain, this has added another dimension to debates over casualisation, exploitation, 'downsizing', 'freelancing' and so on.

These attacks on the subject area have drawn varied responses and awakened old divisions within Media Studies. Principal among these are the tensions between critique on the one hand and useful, applied or practical knowledge on the other. Our response is to insist that the subject is a perfectly legitimate academic, research based focus, more concerned with a specialised branch of sociology, political science or psychology. The popular critique is thus deflected, because it is held fundamentally to misunderstand the subject, by expecting a direct and pragmatic outcome in terms which it has not been developed to deliver. Harder versions assert the right of courses of study to exist without direct and necessary vocational relevance as the sole criteria for existence. Both emphasise the diversity of Media Studies and the fact that many students enrol with only vague vocational motivations.

Against this, another form of response has been to assert the vocational relevance and success of students graduating from Media Studies courses and the importance and vitality of links with changing professional and practitioner communities. A significant issue here concerns the question of access to costly and changing generations of state-of-the-art technologies and the constraints on internal educational budgets for human as well as technical resources. In between these polar responses lie a number of 'middle ways'. These coexist within the largely modular structures of contemporary course organisation which permit diversity and student choice. This argument advances a qualified case for the coexistence of theory with practice within frameworks which seek to reconcile the demands of critical analysis with those of a vocational pragmatism - though this will rarely measure up to Harry Hardnose practitioner standards. It makes little sense that the two should be divorced. Critical studies of media output should, and do, have a bearing on media practice; and media production is seldom enacted - or indeed effectively taught - in a hermetically sealed vacuum.

Two recent responses are worthy of note, both sponsored by the Standing Conference for Cultural, Communication and Media Studies in Higher Education, in an attempt to counter recent media coverage and treatment. The first consists of a survey undertaken to study the destinations of graduates from Media Studies and related courses between 1992 and 1994. On the basis of a limited preliminary sample, such graduates appear to have a slightly *better* chance of employment when compared to the national average for graduate employment. The largest single areas of employment appear to be those associated with the media and cultural industries: journalism, broadcasting, publishing and advertising are the biggest areas of employment, and jobs in marketing, public relations and press and promotions are also popular first destinations. Significantly fewer Culture, Communication and Media Studies graduates appear to opt for further study than the national average, but those that do choose mainly vocational training courses.[19]

The second initiative consists of a pamphlet prepared by the Standing Conference for students applying for degree courses in Media and related studies. It has been circulated to all sixth forms and further education colleges in the country, and is designed specifically to *caution* prospective undergraduate students against the view that such degrees will automatically lead to jobs in media production:

> Many people are excited by the possibilities of learning the skills that might get them jobs in, say, television or film. But the truth is that *very few* degrees in our field would even claim to be doing this. Even the few that do, will tell you that such jobs are very hard to come by.[20]

A number of issues confront Media Studies at the end of the twentieth century. These include the problems and possibilities involved in achieving a productive relationship between the critical research orientated traditions and those which have developed more applied and vocationally driven emphases. For both of these wings, which need to keep in touch, perhaps one of the key challenges is keeping pace with fundamental changes in the media and cultural industries themselves, and to respond effectively to developments such as the internet, digital technologies and forms, and the much vaunted information superhighways which threaten to make old understandings of the mass media obsolete. Such analysis and strategy need to continue to engage with the relevant, and in the face of the current popularity of undergraduate courses, work needs to be devoted to the development of both intellectual and vocational forms of legitimacy and advocacy.

In the face of the criticism which fuels the current controversy, it is important to restate certain key tenets which have underpinned media education initiatives

19. *First Report on Survey into First Destination of Cultural, Communication and Media Studies Graduates*, SCCCMSHE, 1996.
20. SCCCMSHE, 1996

from their inception. This is essentially a liberal, emancipatory and participatory project. Media Studies represents an important educational response to changing times, to changing regimes of information and entertainment, a response to changing conditions of citizenship, an attempt to safeguard and to foster what Paddy Scannell has called the 'communicative rights' of modern citizens.[21] Media Studies courses in Britain are diverse in their content and approach, their vitality and academic standards are high, and the field is highly regarded internationally. Most students understand before enrolment that degrees in the field will not cut a great deal of ice with the older generations of industry gatekeepers and do not approach their studies with unrealistic vocational aspirations. They are not 'hoodwinked' in their applications by false promises. However, Media Studies courses can and do produce 'useful graduates'; multi-skilled, analytically engaged, research competent, versatile, resourceful and bright. For some, these courses do provide useful vocational preparation, not always for the massively oversubscribed, glamorous jobs in broadcasting or journalism. Not all graduates have these stars in their eyes. Many have their sights set on more attainable and realistic targets, for an expanding number of occupations which will require or involve aspects of media or communications management, media and cultural literacy, and an understanding of the social, political and commercial forces which shape the communications and information industries. Others are simply interested in studying the forms and processes which occupy modern populations for increasing amounts of time each day. And what is wrong with that?

---

21. 'Public Service Broadcasting and Modern Public Life', *Media, Culture and Society*, 11, 1989.

Lawrence & Wishart invite you to join The LW Club. Launched to mark our 60th anniversary, the LW Club offers more than a conventional book club. As well as all new L&W paperback titles, LW Club members receive special discounts to a wide range of conferences and events, and discounts on all L&W backlist titles.

You can become a member of the LW Club for just £15.00 quarterly. As an LW Club member you will receive absolutely free all new paperback books on publication* (approximately 10 - 15 pa. - *at cover price this would average £160.00pa*). Upon joining you will receive a free book chosen by you (see below) **.

LW CLUB MEMBERSHIP INCLUDES

All New Lawrence & Wishart Paperbacks FREE*

as they are published, a constant source of rewarding and intellectually stimulating reading.

Free tickets for conferences/ events

sponsored by Lawrence & Wishart, including the popular Signs of the Times annual conference, various book launches, and all New Times events.

Discounts on conferences

including the annual Unions conference organised by Democratic Left, and the Signs of the Times seminar series.

Exclusive discounts on all L&W titles

the chance to purchase any L&W paperback or hardback title published prior to your membership at a 35% discount.

Free catalogue and bookmarks

plus a quarterly newsletter with details of forthcoming publications; details of journals, New Times books, website offers; letters and a special feature.

And we hope you will join us at our Christmas events.

Early applications for membership will receive a free t-shirt featuring the popular route map from *The Green London Way* (While stocks last).

For a further details, membership application form & FREE catalogue write to:

L&W, 99a Wallis Road, London E9 5LN.
Tel: 0181-533 2506 Fax: 0181-533 7369 E-mail: l-w-bks.demon.co.uk

*This excludes journals
** Free book list includes: *You Tarzan: Masculinity Movies and Men*, Janet Thumim & Pat Kirkham (eds); *Activating Theory: Lesbian, Gay, Bisexual Politics*, Joseph Bristow & Angelia Wilson (eds); *Black Tribunes: Black Political Participation in Britain*, Terri Sewell.

The 1997 Summer **Post-Election Conference Saturday 21 June**

City University, Northampton Square, London EC1

Between now and May a General Election will take place likely to determine the fate of politics into the early twenty-first century. A new Labour victory offers the opportunity for a rebirth of radical hopes and visions, a successful Tory revival could set the seal on any remaining alternatives to one-party rule.

This summer's *Signs of the Times* conference offers a unique opportunity for academics, politicians, journalists, researchers, activists and students to review, study and debate not only the short-term subjects that come to dominate the election but also the long-term waves that are reshaping society and culture well beyond the narrow conception of party politics.

CONFERENCE THEMES

- **How New is the New?** A deeper shade of modernisation; politics and language in the age of the spin-doctor; new Labour and alternative forms of political organisation.

- **A World of Difference** Race, nation and the making of a young country; new Labour in a new Europe; the globalisation debate.

- **Models of Democracy** Citizenship, stakeholding and political settlement; a radical democratic agenda for the twenty-first century; family, psychoanalysis and the new moralism.

- **Generation Why?** Facts and fiction in the new black writing; tradition and rupture in Asian dance music; new unions for a new generation; the challenge of eco-protest.

For further information: Signs of the Times, PO Box 10684, London N15 6XA. Tel 0181-809 7336

Soundings

Soundings is a journal of politics and culture. It is a forum for ideas which aims to explore the problems of the present and the possibilities for a future politics and society. Its intent is to encourage innovation and dialogue in progressive thought. Half of each future issue will be devoted to debating a particular theme: topics in the pipeline include: 'Young Britain', Active Welfare in Britain, America, Africa, and The European Left.

Why not subscribe?
Make sure of your copy

Subscription rates, 1997 (3 issues)

INDIVIDUAL SUBSCRIPTIONS:	UK - £35.00	*Rest of the World - £45.0*
INSTITUTIONAL SUBSCRIPTIONS	UK - £70.00	*Rest of the World - £80.00*

Please send me one year's subscription starting with Issue Number _____

I enclose payment of £ _____

I wish to become a supporting subscriber and enclose a donation of £ _____

I enclose total payment of £ _____

Name _____

Address _____

_____

_____ Postcode _____

Please return this form with cheque or money order payable to Soundings and send to:

Soundings, c/o Lawrence & Wishart, 99A Wallis Road, London E9 5LN